WILD
swimming

wild-swimming (n.):

1. Swimming in natural waters such as rivers, lakes and waterfalls. Often associated with picnics and summer holidays.

2. Dipping or plunging in secret or hidden places, sometimes in wilderness areas. Associated with skinny-dipping or naked swimming, often with romantic connotations.

3. Action of swimming wildly such as jumping or diving from a height, using swings and slides, or riding the current of a river.

Second Edition

Daniel Start

WILD
swimming

Contents

Swims by Region

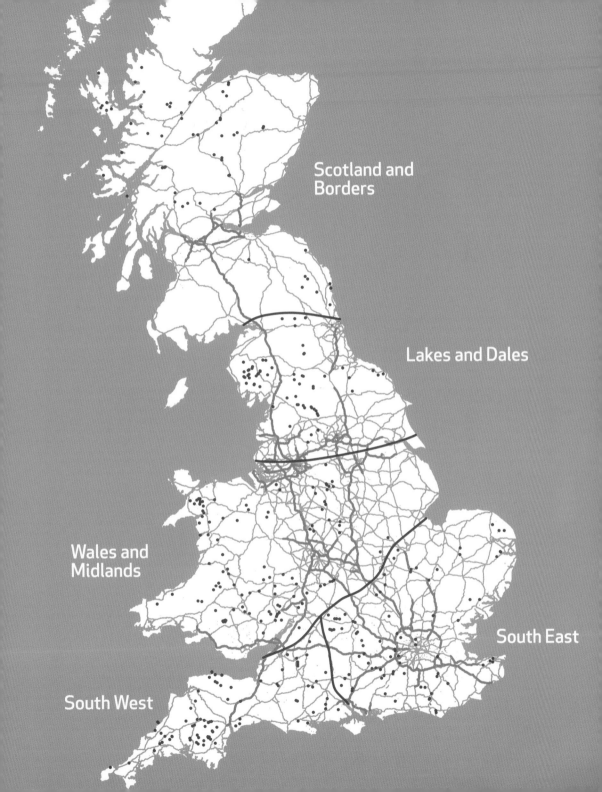

Scotland and
Borders

Lakes and Dales

Wales and
Midlands

South East

South West

Foreword

A lot has changed in the five years since we first published *Wild Swimming*. Popularity and recognition have exploded and there has been a huge increase in the number of outdoor swimming events and local groups, inspired by the Outdoor Swimming Society and the River and Lake Swimming Association, amongst others.

Attitudes of some of the biggest land managers and advisors have softened. The National Trust now recommend wild swimming as an essential experience in a healthy childhood. The Environment Agency, which has a statutory responsibility 'to promote recreation on rivers where appropriate' is becoming less prohibitive of swimming. The Royal Society for the Prevention of Accidents has admitted that swimming in rivers and lakes isn't actually that dangerous. Even David Cameron and Nick Clegg have said they like a wild dip.

But a huge amount remains to be done, to improve access to our natural waters and inland beaches, and to continue to improve water quality. Sadly, most water companies and local authorities, guardians of some of our safest and most beautiful national lakes, still refuse to officially sanction swimming, for fear of litigation or additional costs. While there are a few rivers with a clearly enshrined legal right to swim, for the rest we rely on traditional usage rights and 17th century Statute law.

So when you go out swimming this summer, please be discreet and respectful, particularly to fishermen (who have been a great ally in campaigning to clean up our rivers and lakes over the last 20 years). But do not be disheartened if you are told you have no right to swim. *No Swimming* signs are more often than not a protection against liability, and in other cases are legally or morally unenforceable. We need to respect land owners and other water users, but realise that bathing in natural waters is good for our society, for our health and for the environment. So join the movement for wild swimming and dive into a joyful world of watery adventure.

Daniel Start, March 2013

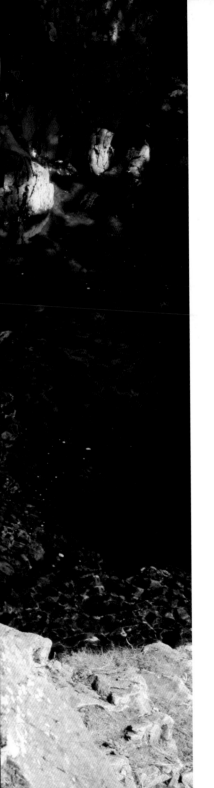

Introduction

One branch of evolutionary theory, expounded by Sir Alister Hardy in the 1950s, suggests that being by and in water is more than just a pleasure, it is at the core of our human condition. During the ten million years of the Pliocene world droughts, while our species was busy evolving into uprightness, we did not, suggests Hardy, choose the arid deserts of Africa as our home, as mainstream evolutionists believe, but the more tempting turquoise shallows of the nearby Indian Ocean. There we became semi-aquatic coastal waders. Our subsequent life on dry land is a relatively recent and bereft affair.

Could this explain some of our more peculiar habits and features? Apart from the proboscis monkey, we are the only primate that regularly plays in water for the sheer joy of it, and whose offspring take naturally to water from birth. We are also alone in having subcutaneous fat, like a whale's blubber, for buoyancy and warmth. We are almost hairless, like the dolphin, and what little hair remains is arranged to make us streamlined for swimming.

Perhaps this is why Greek art and mythology abounds in stories of water nymphs, naiads and sirens as magical, sexual, mischievous creatures, inhabiting their wild 'nymphaea': natural pools, rivers and swimming holes, so beautiful they lure unwitting mortals to their watery ends.

As the nineteenth century dawned, a new era of contemporary European artists was rediscovering the appeal of the swimming hole. The waterfall, surrounded by trees and mountains, was now regarded as the quintessence of beauty. Wordsworth, Coleridge and De Quincy spent much time bathing in the mountain pools of the Lake District. The study and search for the 'picturesque' and 'sublime' – an almost scientific measure of loveliness and proportion in the landscape – had reached epidemic proportions. The fashionable tours of Provence or Tuscany were replaced by trips to the valleys of Wales, and the dales of Cumbria and Yorkshire, as Turner and Constable painted a prodigious flow of falls, tarns and ponds.

As the Romantic era took hold, the water held its place in the artists' gaze. Ruskin and others moved south to paint the river pools of Cornwall and Devon. Meanwhile, Charles Kingsley was dreaming of water babies on the Devon Dart and Henry Scott Tuke was opening his floating studio in Falmouth, painting scenes of children swimming in the river. Soon Francis Meadow Sutcliffe gained notoriety for his Water Rats photograph of naked boys, while across the Atlantic Thomas Eakins was creating a stir with his homoerotic painting of the *Swimming Hole*. Water and nudity were pushing at the boundaries of rigid Victorian society and creating space for new ideas, freedoms and creativity.

Pools and springs have long been revered by our Celtic and pagan ancestors. Even the Romans built shrines to water goddesses, and several accompany the bathhouses along Hadrian's Wall. Fresh water was seen as a sort of interface with the spirit world, a place where miracles – or curses – could manifest. 'Mermaid Pools' dot our Pennine mountain tops and ancient holy wells and springs are found across the Welsh and Cornish hills. No wonder, then, when Christianity came the Britons were quick to embrace river baptism as a doorway to a new god.

From a secular perspective the health and psychological benefits of dipping in natural waters were also long known. George Bernard Shaw, Benjamin Britten, Charles Darwin and Florence Nightingale were all advocates of regular cold baths to strengthen the mental constitution and physical state. Cold immersion soothes muscle aches, relieves depression and boosts the immune system. All wild-dippers know the natural endorphin high that raises mood, elates the senses and creates an addictive urge to dive back in. However the world seemed before a swim, it looks fantastic afterwards.

The long-term impacts are also well researched: NASA studies have shown that, over a 12-week period, repeated cold swimming leads to substantial bodily changes known as 'cold adaptation'. These bring down blood pressure and cholesterol, reduce fat disposition, inhibit blood clotting and increase fertility and libido in both men and women. Far from quelling passion, a cold shower will boost vitality and desire.

By the 1870s, river- and lake-based recreation was entering mainstream culture. London was expanding at a rate of knots and the middle- and working-class population woke up to the potential of the Thames, with its villages, boats and watering holes lying only a cheap rail fare away. 'We would have the river almost to ourselves,' recalled Jerome K. Jerome, 'and sometimes would fix up a trip of three or four days or a week, doing the thing in style and camping out.' In 1889 he wrote the best-selling *Three Men in a Boat*, which was a manifesto

With worries about climate change, obesity and urban youth crime, we need, more than ever, new and exciting ways for our children to engage with the natural world and to explore it in safe and responsible ways. Swimming is the favourite sporting activity for girls and is second only to football for boys. Perhaps opening up our rivers, lakes and waterfalls again can provide new opportunities to satisfy an appetite for adventure while attaching new meaning to the environment and the wild.

for a simple way of living: close to nature, with river swimming before breakfast. Ratty declared in *The Wind in the Willows* that there 'was nothing, simply nothing, more worthwhile than messing about in boats' and by 1909 Rupert Brooke was writing poems about bathing in Grantchester.

It was an idyllic period. Europe had been relatively peaceful for a hundred years. It was an age of relaxed elegance, of 25-mile-a-day walking tours, sleeping under canvas and bathing in the river. Brooke spent his days studying literature, swimming, living off fruit and honey and commuting to Cambridge by canoe. His passion for the outdoor life was shared by writers Virginia Woolf and E. M. Forster, philosophers Russell and Wittgenstein, economist Keynes and artist Augustus John. As they swam naked at Byron's Pool in moonlight and practised their 'belly-floppers' in picnic diving practice along the Cam this nucleus formed the emerging Bloomsbury Group and whom Woolf later dubbed the 'Neo-Pagans'.

Grantchester Meadows became the site of one of the first formal bathing clubs in the country, with an elegant pavilion, separate changing areas and stone steps down into the warm waters of the River Cam. Similar clubs, 'Parson's'Pleasure' and later 'Dame's Delight', quickly followed at the Cherwell in Oxford. Soon every major public school was following suit with its own special riverside swimming facilities. By 1923 over 600 informal river swimming clubs were in existence around the country with regular inter-county river swimming competitions and galas. Henry Williamson was swimming with *Tarka the Otter*, and Arthur Ransome immortalised the Lake District in *Swallows and Amazons*. Wild-swimming had reached its heyday.

The post-war years brought a great thrust of industry and development and rivers bore the brunt of the pollution. By the 1960s pesticides had driven the West Country population of otters to near extinction. It was not until new legislation was introduced in the 1970s and 1980s that the trend began to turn. Thirty years on, over 70 per cent of our rivers are in good or excellent condition again. They are hidden havens for wildlife once more, secret corridors into forgotten corners of our countryside.

For many of us this kind of communion with our ecology is moving. It's a place to seek inspiration, intuition and peace and also to be humbled by the immensity and wonder of nature. These are places where children see their first kingfisher or find their first otter track. Here we learn to play Pooh Sticks and build dams before falling asleep in the grass. Use this book to open up a fresh world of adventures, romantic escapades and family days out. The water's fresh, so pick up, strip off and jump in!

'I can go right up to a frog in the water and it will show more curiosity than fear. The damselflies and dragonflies that crowd the surface of the moat pointedly ignore me, just taking off for a moment to allow me to go by them, then landing again on my wake. In the water you are hidden and submerged, enveloped in the silkiness of a liquid that is the medium of all life on earth.'

Roger Deakin, author of *Waterlog*, naturalist and forefather of wild-swimming, describing swimming in his moat in Suffolk.

Getting Started

10 ways to be wild and safe

1 Never swim in canals, urban rivers, stagnant lakes or reedy shallows

2 Never swim in flood water and be cautious of water quality during droughts

3 Keep cuts and wounds covered with waterproof plasters if you are concerned

4 Avoid contact with blue–green algae

5 Never swim alone and keep a constant watch on weak swimmers

6 Never jump into water you have not thoroughly checked for depth and obstructions

7 Always make sure you know how you will get out before you get in

8 Don't get too cold – warm up with exercise and warm clothes before and after a swim

9 Wear footwear if you can

10 Watch out for boats on any navigable river. Wear a coloured swim hat so you can be seen

See pp 264-266 for more detailed information.

Staying safe: There's nothing inherently dangerous about wild swimming, but cold water does reduce your swimming ability, at least until you get used to it. So stay close to the shore and increase your range slowly.

Staying warm: The water will be cold, so arrive hot, so hot that you can't wait to strip off and plunge in. Plan a good hearty walk to get you there, and put on lots of warm clothes before you arrive. Once you're in the water it takes a few minutes before the cold feeling goes away, so persevere and you'll feel great. In general, the more you swim in cold water the less you will feel the cold and the greater the health benefits. This called 'cold adaptation'. Don't stay in so long that you start to shiver, though, and definitely get out and warm up after 20 minutes. Wetsuits can be a great help and allow you to stay immersed indefinitely. Put on warm clothes immediately after a swim and combine this with something active like walking up a hill or star jumps.

Equipment: You'll have more confidence, and be better able to explore, if you have footwear (e.g. old trainers, jelly beans etc) and goggles. Make sure you bring towels, a picnic rug, midge repellent, suntan lotion (P20 is great), sunhats and a plastic bag for all your wet kit. Inflatables are popular but make sure people won't drift away on them, especially non-swimmers. A buoyancy aid is safer, and fun too.

Access and the law: You will find plenty of places where there are *No Swimming* signs and notices, yet people regular swim and always have. The signs are to limit land owners' liability, in case someone has an accident and tries to sue. Places like this, with uncertain access, are marked with a ❓ through the book. See p267.

Water quality: Water quality constantly varies, reducing during droughts or after flooding. All swims in this book are in good (B) or excellent (A) quality waters, as rated by the Envionment Agency. A few, marked with **C**, are average water quality and you may want to avoid swimming front crawl. See p266 for more detailed information.

Skinny-dipping: If you come across a magical pool on a walk it's quite possible to swim even without any kit. Wear your undies or go naked if it is secluded. If you have no towel wipe most of the water off with your hands then sacrifice one item of clothing to dry yourself or travel with a small, light cotton sarong.

Finding the swimming holes in this book

Co-ordinates: Each of the locations is provided with a latitude and longitude in decimal degrees (WGS84 standard). These are universally accepted by all online and mobile mapping services. We still provide postcodes (though in the countryside the nearest post code may not be very close to the actual swim location) and Ordnance Survey National Grid references (for use with paper maps) but you'll need to look these up at the back of the book. Here you can also find a conversion formula if you need minutes and seconds, though these days most devices accept decimal if you choose the right settings.

Online maps: Ordnance Survey Landranger maps at 1:50,000 (Purple Cover) and Explorer maps at 1:25,000 (Orange Cover) are still the best maps for exploring the countryside. You can access these online at *bing.com, streetmap.co.uk* or *getamap. ordnancesurveyleisure.co.uk*. Google Maps is fine for driving and cycling directions, and for satellite images, but does not provide footpath information. Make sure you print out good maps before you leave home, or why not load one of many apps which turn your phone into a GPS (e.g. ViewRanger, MemoryMap or EveryTrail). You can also buy this book as an app with links to all these resources built in.

Using the directions: You can use the written directions, but you will need a road atlas to get you to the overall area first and you should bring a map or GPS / phone with you too (note GPS does not work well in very hilly areas or deep valleys). The abbreviations given relate to points of the compass: N, NE, E, SE, S, SW, W and NW. Left (L) and right (R), when used in relation to a river's bank, are always in the direction of the river flow, facing downstream. Swims are clustered into groups, by river or area. Where swims in the same column are not in the same area we have used white dividers.

Best for Paddling

Mainly shallow and popular with families

Best for Literary Swims

Where famous poets, writers or artists once swam

Best for Skinny-dipping

Remote and secluded, perfect for a natural dip

Best for Picnics

Beautiful places, not far from parking with good picnic areas or grassy banks

Best for Train Access

Within walking distance of a train station

Best for Cycling

On dedicated cycle trails or routes

Best for Canoes & Boats

Good, legal access with your canoe (or possibility to hire a boat *)

Best for Pubs

A cosy, warming pub just a splash away

Best for Camping

Fantastic river or lakeside camping. Good for a moonlight swim perhaps?

Best for Jumping

Mainly shallow and popular with families

Best for Tubing & Chutes

Great for playing in surf or current, or using a rubber ring

Best for Waterfalls

Magically situated under waterfalls, big and small

Buscot Weir

South East

The journey starts with Great father Thames who flows through Oxfordshire and Berkshire and is filled with literary association. In the east the alluvial soils provide warmer swims along Grantchester Meadows, the Great Ouse, the Suffolk Stour and the Norfolk Broads. The Surrey and Sussex hills are surprisingly rich in secret wood lakes and the ancient downlands of Hampshire create the world renowned shallow, clear chalk streams of the Wylye, Test and Itchen.

Highlights
South East England

Our favourites include:

4 Cheese Wharf, a deep bend in the young River Thames, great for swimming and once the location for barges loaded with Gloucestershire cheese

3 A beautiful weir pool, lined by willow trees and rope swings with grassy National Trust lawns for sunbathing

6 Minster Lovell - Bait crayfish by the ruins of an old hall in the clear waters of the Cotswolds Windrush

11 In the centre of Oxford, not far from the station, the riverside at Port Meadow inspired Lewis Carroll in the opening of Alice in Wonderland

14 Beautiful stretches of the River Thames that provided the setting for Three Men in a Boat and Wind in the Willows

18 Grantchester - The famous Grantchester Meadows were a popular river bathing location of Lord Byron, Rupert Brooke, Virginia Woolf and members of the Bloomsbury Group

33-35 Buxton to St Benet's Abbey - a beautiful Norfolk rivers which flow on to form the ancient Broads

38 Dedham Vale - Dedham Vale, an English landscape lost in time, where Constable painted The Hay Wain and you can still swim in the famous River Stour

43 One of Britain's oldest and most famous bathing ponds, these pools were constructed 400 years ago to provide London with drinking water through hollowed-out elm tree pipes

62 Hire rowboats from the Anchor Inn and swim along two miles of Sussex's most remote and rural river

71 A popular inland beach, set in ancient Surrey heathland, built by the Bishop of Winchester in the sixteenth century

82-84 White shingle beach and dancing water buttercups line the crystal-clear chalk streams that drain Hampshire's Watership Down

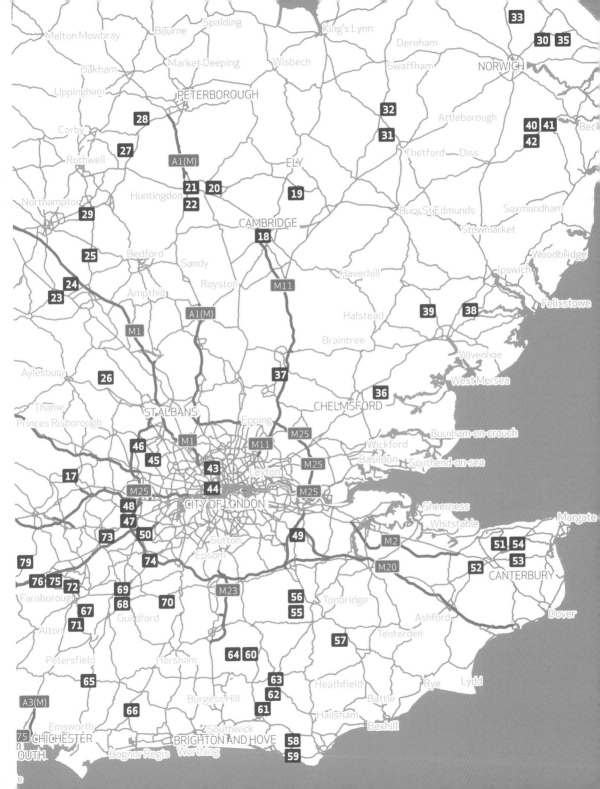

Cotswolds and the young Thames

The young Thames is a quiet river, rising in the Cotswolds and flowing peacefully through the Oxfordshire plains. Distant church spires peek over billowing wheat fields and wild flowers wave in the hedgerows.

Three hundred years ago things were a little busier on the upper reaches of the Thames. Lechlade was a bustling port, loading Cotswold stone and Gloucester cheese, and the new Thames and Severn Canal had just opened where the Round House now stands. But with the decline of the canals more recreational pursuits took over: Lechlade became renowned for its water carnivals and swimming galas. The ha'penny bridge, built famously high to accommodate eighteenth-century sailing barges, was popular for diving competitions. Though the organised activities have now gone, boys still jump from the bridge and the area is still a designated Waterside Park providing swimming and boating for hundreds on hot summer weekends.

The open fields of the Waterside Park are a pleasant and convenient place to swim but downstream, around Buscot and Kelmscot, the real beauty and charm of the Upper Thames begins. At the Cheese Wharf in Buscot, once a loading bay for twenty tonnes of cheese a day, there is a rope swing and deep pool for swimming and diving.

A mile or so on, past the graceful riverside gardens of the Old Parsonage and church, the old weir at Buscot has scooped

8

10

6

out a deep and clear natural pool, lined with weeping willow. Swimmers splash about among the tendrils, appearing through the leaves that brush the water. The older children climb the low boughs and use them as platforms to jump in from while the younger ones play among the deep roots and use them as handrails to pull themselves out. This is a justifiably popular place for swimming. The National Trust lawns that border it are dotted with inflatable boats and deckchairs and the lock keeper is tolerant as long as you stay away from the weir itself. Further downstream is the honey-stone village of Kelmscot, once home of William Morris, the founder of the Arts and Crafts movement.

By Chimney Meadows bulrushes tower overhead like wheat in a children's cornfield and the wild flowers of Chimney Meadows, populated by wild grasses since Saxon times, break through; meadow barley, buttercup, crested dog's tail, lady's bedstraw and bird's-foot trefoil.

As you approach Oxford the Windrush joins the flow, the idyllic Cotswold stream. In Bourton-on-the-Water there are ducks and high street riverways. In Little Barrington there are perfect riverside pubs and in Minster Lovell it flows past the remains of a fifteenth-century manor. Here, alongside the great old arches and ruined walls, you can bathe in the blue-tinged waters and catch crayfish big enough for supper.

The Evenlode is another beautiful river which runs parallel a little way to the north. It was at Stonesfield, famous for its honey-coloured stone quarries, that the first ever dinosaur remains were found in 1824. The Jurassic limestone dates back 160 million years to the time of the Megalosaurus, or the 'Great Lizard of Stonesfield', whose discovery changed the face of history. Dinosaur bones had, in fact, been found prior to the 1800s, but were thought to be the fossilised remains of some giant human, now extinct, or the bones of elephants brought to Britain by the Romans. The river here is only shallow but the vale through which it runs is beautiful, with sunny steep banks, a footbridge, pool and the remains of a Roman villa too. If you're lucky and search the riverbed you may even find your own dinosaur bones.

1 LECHLADE PARK, R THAMES

A popular stretch of fields and river upstream from town with good access and a nice pool below footbridge. Watch kids jump from the Ha'penny Bridge.

→ Large car park is on the S of town (Swindon road). Continue upstream ¾ mile for pool above the footbridge, near the Round House.

15 mins, 51.6885, -1.7042 🏊🚣🍴

2 CHIMNEY MEADOWS, R THAMES

Meadows and nature reserve bordering a remote stretch of the Thames.

→ Walk 2 miles downstream from Trout Inn at Tadpole Bridge (SN7 8RF, 01367 870382). You might also like to seek out the secret shallow glade pool at Duxford (51.6990, -1.4660).

40 mins, 51.6945, -1.4900 🏊⛰️

3 BUSCOT WEIR, R THAMES

A large deep weir pool with trees, rope swings and lawns in pretty NT hamlet.

→ 2 miles E of Lechlade (A417), turn by mirror, signed 'visitor parking'.

3 mins, 51.6809, -1.6683 🚣🏊

4 CHEESE WHARF, R THAMES

Deep, with a good swing.

→ Just upstream from Buscot, on A417. Signed with some parking among trees.

1 min, 51.6839, -1.6765 🏊🍴

5 KELMSCOTT, R THAMES

Wild open stretch of Thames.

→ Start at this lovely village with good pub (Plough Inn GL7 3HG, 01367 253 543). Follow the river 2 miles downstream through endless open fields and pools all the way to Grafton Lock and on to Radcot Bridge.

30 mins, 51.6857, -1.6303 🏊🏊⛰️

6 MINSTER LOVELL, R WINDRUSH

A small, clear, pretty Cotswold river running through romantic grounds of the ruins. Just deep enough to swim with deeper sections downstream at footbridge.

→ Follow the signs for the church to find Minster ruins down a path behind.

10 mins, 51.7991, -1.5295 🚣🚶

7 ASTHALL, R WINDRUSH

More fields and swimming / paddling. Also a lovely pub.

→ Downstream of bridge, just beyond pub.

5 mins, 51.8021, -1.5790 🚣🍺

8 BURFORD, R WINDRUSH

Water meadows and pool by old willow.

→ A mile downstream from Burford on route to the ruined church at Widford.

20 mins, 51.8008, -1.6175 🚣

9 SHERBORNE PARK, R WINDRUSH

Secluded, secret river pools in woods.

→ Lane S of Clapton on the Hill.

40 mins, 51.8409, -1.7283 ⛰️

10 STONESFIELD, R EVENLODE

Pretty footbridge and paddling. Grassy banks below gentle Cotswold escarpment. Site of the first ever dinosaur fossil find. Roman villa.

→ Follow Church Street, and then Brook Lane (track) from the cemetery down to the stream (500m).

15 mins, 51.8453, -1.4304 🚣🚶

Pangbourne, River Thames

Oxford and the Lower Thames

The Thames, from Oxford downstream, has inspired generations of charming tales from *Alice in Wonderland* to *The Wind in the Willows*. Meandering through rolling countryside and stone villages, these are some of the most civilised swims in England and in many places the river is as unspoilt as it was 100 years ago, and a whole lot cleaner.

The Thames enters Oxford along Port Meadow, England's largest and oldest continuous meadow; recorded in the Doomsday Book of 1086. It has never been ploughed, and is older than any building in Oxford.

At the northern end near Wolvercote there is swimming under the bridge and beneath the weir with grand views of the dreaming spires. This is the setting and inspiration for the opening lines of Alice in Wonderland who was 'beginning to get very tired of sitting with her sister on the bank…' and the closing lines where Alice sees 'an ancient city and a quiet river winding near it along the plain'. At the southern end of the Meadows, closer to the train station, the river has cut out little shallow beaches along its course, popular with families. In early summer it is awash with daisies and by evening you'll see flocks of lapwing and plover rising into the sky.

Oxford has long been a wild-swimming university and the dons established a naked bathing site on the Cherwell in 1852. Christened 'Parson's Pleasure' one story tells how a number of dons were sunbathing on the banks when a group of students floated by in a punt. The startled dons covered their modesty, all except one who placed a flannel over his head explaining: 'My students know me by my face'. A site just downstream

13

14

15

for female dons – 'Dame's Delight' – followed in 1934 but both were eventually closed in 1991. All that now remains of Parson's Pleasure is a beer named in its honour.

Towards the end of the nineteenth century the river downstream of Oxford had already become a playground for London society. Clifton Hampden, six miles south, was a favourite with Jerome K. Jerome for boating trips. 'Sometimes we would fix up a trip of three or four days or a week, doing the thing in style and camping out.' In 1888 he wrote Three Men in a Boat, which became a manifesto for a simpler way of living with nature – river swimming before breakfast, kippers after and a snooze before lunch. Today the long grass and river banks are set against billowing hay fields and the area is a wonderful piece of bucolic tranquillity close to London.

Below Reading the river is still clean enough for swimming. The stretch between Hurley and Marlow is the inspiration for much of Kenneth Grahame's The Wind in the Willows. This is where Ratty spent so much time swimming with the ducks, and Mole so much time trying not to fall in. Kenneth Grahame's own childhood was spent with his grandparents being rowed out to little islands and other riverside haunts near Cookham Dean – Toad's dungeon is based on the Ice House in Bisham Woods and Badger's Wildwoods is based on the Quarry Woods nearby.

Grahame moved to live by the Thames after his retirement from the City in 1908. He was probably the most unlikely – and most unhappy – moneyman ever appointed to the post of Secretary of the Bank of England. But within months of his early retirement he had written The Wind in the Willows. 'As a contribution to natural history, the work is negligible,' The Times wrote stiffly. But Grahame's fable has become one of the best-loved works in literature.

'…we all talked as if we were going to have a long swim every morning. George said it was so pleasant to wake up in the boat in the fresh morning, and plunge into the limpid river. Harris said there was nothing like a swim before breakfast to give you an appetite…'

Three Men in a Boat, 1906

11

11 PORT MEADOW, R THAMES

2 miles of river with beaches and grassy meadow on both banks. Shelving to up to 2m deep. Beware of boats and cattle!

→ Two approaches. From A40 take Wolvercote exit from Woodstock Road (A4144) roundabout. Park on L near the popular Trout Inn (OX2 8PN, 01865 302071). There's a popular pool and ropeswing under the bridge. Or approach from Oxford train station at S end. Turn R onto main road and after 300m drop down to Thames footpath on R. Follow for ¾ mile upstream. First footbridge leads to W bank (open meadow), next leads to E with path and access to The Perch inn (OX2 0NG, 01865 728891).

15 mins, 51.7698, -1.2881

12 PARSON'S PLEASURE, R CHERWELL

Historic university river bathing pool, though water quality can be variable.

→ Take cycle path at lights on corner of St Cross Rd and South Parks Rd and continue behind Linacre College 200m down to the punt rollers, or anywhere upstream.

10 mins, 51.7606, -1.2458

13 APPLEFORD, R THAMES

Quiet beach a short walk from station.

→ Follow footpath behind church 200m, or continue on to Little Wittenham. Also Sutton Pools upstream (51.6466, -1.2739).

10 mins, 51.6411, -1.2327

14 CLIFTON HAMPDEN, R THAMES

A pretty bridge and pub. Sandy bays shelving to deeper water bordered by flower-filled meadows. Beware of boats.

→ Off A415 between Abingdon and Wallingford. Cross bridge and park opposite Barley Mow pub (OX14 3EH, 01865 407847) and campsite. Walk to bridge, turn R and continue downstream for up to 2 miles towards Dorchester.

15 mins, 51.6567, -1.2049

15 CHOLSEY, R THAMES

Very quiet, secluded stretch of river.

→ From A329 S of Wallingford, turn down Ferry Lane (dead end), opp the South Moreton turning. and continue to boatclub at end. Explore downstream. Beware fast moving rowing eights.

10 mins, 51.5649, -1.1336

16 PANGBOURNE, R THAMES

Undeveloped and picturesque stretch of river along the edge of the Chiltern Hills. Clear with chalk beaches.

→ Walk from Pangbourne to Goring on the NE bank (and return by train). About half way is a pretty wooded section. Or access from opp bank at Lower Basildon (signed off A329 N of Pangbourne). Downstream of Pangbourne the meadows stretch for over 2 miles (e.g. 51.4902, -1.0708).

40 mins, 51.5080, -1.1109

17 HURLEY ISLAND, THAMES

A historic village with wooded river islands, camping and a 1,000-year-old pub. Several places to swim.

→ From A/M404 take A4130 dir Henley. After a mile turn R to 'Hurley village only' and turn R down Mill Lane, signed 'boatyard' and find riverside car park on R. Cross bridge to island to find a beach and shallows on far side. Or explore upstream above lock (also parking in village centre near The Olde Bell, SL6 5LX, 01628 825881). Camping 01628 824334.

10 mins, 51.5522, -0.8061

Grantchester Meadows

Cambridgeshire and Great Ouse

Take tea at Grantchester and enjoy a stretch of river and meadows that is little changed since Edwardian times.

Grantchester was already a fashionable location for Cambridge students when the boyish, charismatic, 22-year-old graduate Rupert Brooke became a resident in 1909, commuting to and from Cambridge in his canoe and often 'sitting in the midst of admiring females with nothing on but an embroidered sweater'. In Cambridge it was an age of relaxed elegance: long walking tours, sleeping under canvas, picnicking on the grass and naked bathing. Many brilliant young minds gathered around Brooke and his outdoor lifestyle.

Today it seems little has changed along Grantchester Meadows. On a hot summer day the languid mile-long stretch of river is dotted with leisurely picnic parties. Punts and canoes glide by, some heading downstream towards Cambridge's famous Backs, others heading upstream to the tea gardens in Grantchester village. At intervals you hear another splash as either a punter or picnicker decides to cool off.

Paradise Pool is a narrow wooded area on the edge of town at the top end of the Meadows. There's a curly tree ideal for diving but anywhere along the Meadows is good for swimming, particularly on the outside of the bends where the river deepens, often to over six feet. Be warned though: while the river is clear, clean and warm, the banks and bed are muddy and squelchy.

18

25

20

Many of East Anglia's rivers suffer from siltation and high quantities of fertiliser run-off, a side effect of the alluvial soils and intensive agriculture in the region. The Cam is actually one of the cleanest rivers in the area, though you should never swim in the actual city or along the Backs where the sewers can harbour rats and Weil's disease.

Grantchester village is a good place to end your explorations. The Orchards has served tea from its meandering gardens for well over a hundred years. A great lounging sweep of meadow reaches down to the water's edge and the deckchairs and low wicker tables are a wonderful place to refuel after a long punt or swim.

It was here that Brooke and the young Bloomsbury Group spent long summers camping and river bathing. Virginia Woolf, who once went naked night-swimming with Brooke near here, christened her Grantchester friends the 'Neo-Pagans'. Their philosophy was for a simpler, gentler lifestyle, closer and more in tune with nature with strong values of reciprocity and friendship.

These idyllic times in Cambridge were to be short-lived. Rupert Brooke died tragically just a few years later in the First World War, aged 28. He was widely recognised posthumously for his poetry, including 'The Soldier' and became a symbol of the innocence of youth and the appreciation of simple pleasures and pastimes. When his contemporary Bertrand Russell returned to Grantchester after the war he said of Brooke's death: 'I am feeling the weight of the war much more since I came back here…with all the usual Grantchester life stopped. There will be other generations – yet I keep fearing that something of civilisation will be lost for good…' Visit Grantchester, punt and swim, and ensure Brooke's legacy lives on.

'In Grantchester their skins are white; They bathe by day, they bathe by night;'

From *The Old Vicarage, Grantchester* Rupert Brooke, 1912

21

18 GRANTCHESTER MEADOWS, R CAM

Over 2 miles of meadows and swimming from Sheep's Green down to the Orchard Tea Gardens in Grantchester. Deep banks make this good for diving, but it can be muddy! Some weeds but clean.

→ From A603 / Barton Rd take Grantchester St by lights and find footpath at bottom, L, heading to river and fallen tree 200m (Paradise Pool). Continue on and park at bottom of Grantchester Meadows. There's a good pool within 150m on a bend, or continue down to The Orchard Tea Gardens (CB3 9ND, 01223 845788).
5 mins, 52.1907, 0.1046 🏊🏊🍴

19 WICKEN FEN, UPWARE

Filtered and purified by the reed beds of the famous nature reserve, Wicken Lode is clear, clean and beautiful. Be silent.

→ Head for the Five Mile inn in Upware near Wicken A1123 (CB7 5ZR, 01353 721654) with pleasant gardens along the River Cam. Turn R and after 200m take the footpath L by sluice / bridge leading to footbridge after 300m and bear L.
15 mins, 52.3033, 0.2613 ⛴️🍴❓

20 HOUGHTON MILL, R GREAT OUSE

Wide meadows and calm deep water for a long swim. Fun millstreams for paddling too. NT mill and café to visit.

→ Mill is signed from A1123 between Huntingdon and St Ives. Park and walk down the path, beyond the caravan site, bearing R across the wooded mill streams to reach open riverbank. The opposite bank is accessible from Hemingford Abbots. Or walk the river path, an hour from Huntingdon train station.
10 mins, 52.3282, -0.1171 🚂🍴🏊

21 BRAMPTON, R GREAT OUSE

Wide, secluded stretch of bucolic river bank with a few beaches.

→ Turn down River Lane by Frosts, as approaching from S on B1514. At bottom head R, upstream.
2 mins, 52.3142, -0.2116 🏊

22 GRAFHAM WATER

A secluded pebble beach. Be discrete.

→ Follow footpath from behind church in Grafham village. Blue-green algae risk.
10 mins, 52.3060, -0.3048 🏖️❓

23 PASSENHAM, R GREAT OUSE

Pretty riverside picnic area / parking with slipway. W side of Milton Keynes.

→ Via Old Stratford (A5) to S Passenham
2 mins, 52.0497, -0.8527 🏊🏊

24 HAVERSHAM, R GREAT OUSE

A ruined riverside church in an area of lakes on the N edge of Milton Keynes.

→ Turn L off Wolverton Rd at the bridge / pet store, a mile E of Wolverton station, or walk / cycle from the station (2 miles).
3 mins, 52.0776, -0.7831 🚴🚉

25 OLNEY, R GREAT OUSE

Easy access with steps at the recreation ground or much wilder behind the church.

→ Park in East Street cul de sac, walk down Timpsons Row and cross playing fields.
5 mins, 52.1551, -0.6925 🚂

26 TRING BLUE LAGOON, FOLLY FARM

Chiltern chalk pit with clear water.

→ By roundabout of B488 / Northfield Rd. Nice walk from Tring via Pitstone Hill.
10 mins, 51.8182, -0.6336 ✅

River Bure

Suffolk, Essex and Norfolk

Two hundred years after Constable painted it, Willy Lott's cottage still sits pretty by the banks of the pastoral Stour, the spire of Dedham church rising above the meadows as ever and the wide majestic sky is filled with purple-tinged clouds.

The horse-drawn hay wain may no longer trundle across the river's millstream at Flatford, but there is still something of antiquity and calm in this little vale. As a boy, John Constable spent his childhood fishing, swimming and exploring, the soft light and wide skies inspiring him to become a painter. 'I may yet make some impression,' he wrote, 'with my "light", my "dews", my "breezes" – my bloom and my freshness – no one of which qualities has yet been perfected on the canvas of any painter in the world.' From Dedham village it's a mile's meander down to Flatford Mill via Fen Bridge. I was to meet a friend, Rosy, and her little girl. They have swum in the pool beneath the bridge all their lives.

Further downstream, on our way to find chocolate cake and tea at Flatford Mill, we swam again. The distinctive bank-side willows, planted and pollarded over a hundred years ago, have grown into fat great sinewy bundles. The water is dark with

35

36

38

occasional strands of weeds floating up from the bottom, but the river is warm, clear and clean.

There also used to be barges on the river and, though the locks and wharfs have disappeared, the public still retain the right to navigate from Sudbury to the sea. The Stour is now a popular canoeing and boating river and you'll find many clinker rowing boats filling its reaches in summer.

As the Stour forms Suffolk's border with Essex, so the Waveney forms its border with Norfolk, while also being the southernmost of the Norfolk Broads. The Waveney was also the local river of the late Roger Deakin, modern father of wild-swimming, whose beautiful book, Waterlog, detailed his journey swimming through Britain by river, lake and sea. Outney Common is one of the best places to swim in the Waveney with excellent riverside access for more than a mile. Deakin paddled his canoe, *Cigarette*, along here as part of a Radio 4 documentary exploring the natural history of the river.

The nearby landscape of the Norfolk Broads, a unique low-lying patchwork of interlocking rivers and lakes, was originally believed to have been formed as the result of natural processes. It was not until the 1950s that Joyce Lambert proved otherwise. She showed that the sides of the deep lakes should be gently sloping if naturally formed, but instead they were steep. She also analysed the high demand for peat as fuel in the middle ages, suggesting the lakes were in fact flooded peat quarries abandoned in the fourteenth century as the sea levels began to rise and inundate them.

Once perfectly clean and clear, the Broads have suffered from pollution over the last thirty years with increasing algae concentration from the intensification of Norfolk farming. Now several projects are working to remove nutrients using reed bales. However, the upstream reaches are still mainly clean and the Bure, north of Buxton and Lamas, provides one of the prettiest river swimming stretches.

'I associate my careless boyhood with all that lies on the banks of the Stour. Those scenes made me a painter, and I am grateful...' John Constable to a friend, 1814

41

27 WADENHOE, R NENE

Interesting riverside church, nice pub and good access to river along footpath.

➜ Park at the pub (Kings Head, PE8 5ST, 01832 720024)) and follow the river path towards the church and then upstream.

5 mins, 52.4390, -0.5156

28 FOTHERINGHAY, R NENE

S facing grassy banks lead down from the castle earthworks to the river

➜ Follow footpath to the 'castle site' which gives access to the water.

10 mins, 52.5243, -0.4369

29 SUMMER LEYS, WELLINGBOROUGH

Explore this network of wild gravel lakes along the R Nene, or take a dip in the river itself.

➜ Find 'dead end' road a mile W of Wollaston, off the Hartwater Rd. Lakes on L or continue up to Nene river bridge and walk L 200m to lake shore and river banks. Lovely fishing lakes all along lane at Castle Ashby too (52.2318, -0.7324).

5 mins, 52.2677, -0.7007

30 SALHOUSE BROAD, WOODBASTWICK

The only Broads lake you can easily swim in, with beachy area and canoe hire.

➜ Pretty walk from carpark and WC. E of Salhouse or a mile W of Woodbastwick (Fur and Feathers, NR13 6HQ, 01603 720003).

15 mins, 52.6893, 1.4288

31 SANTON DOWNHAM, LITTLE OUSE

Pretty chalk stream running through deep forest. Chalky riverbed, up to 2m deep.

➜ Signed Santon Down from Brandon (A1065). Swim below bridge / village hall and downstream on path, or turn R (signed St Helen's Forest) and continue ¾ mile to parking and footbridge. Or a 2½ mile riverside walk from Brandon station.

2 mins, 52.4530, 0.6863

32 LYNFORD, WISSEY

Enchanting shallow woodland pool with lakes downstream.

➜ Turn R off A1065 at Ickburgh, a mile N of Mundford, and continue 1½ miles to bridge. Or turn R off before, to explore the vast lakes of Lynford Water.

2 mins, 52.5225, 0.6979

33 BUXTON MILL POOL, R BURE

A huge mill pool with a strong race, right by the road. More secluded upstream.

➜ Look for a large white mill building just outside Buxton on the road to Lamas. Upstream footpath is on the river's R, accessed via front of mill. Also on the Bure Valley Railway from Wroxham.

2 mins, 52.7566, 1.3144

34 COLTISHALL / HORSTEAD, R BURE

Upstream of all the pleasure boats, this is an idyllic stretch of the Bure. Look out for the ruins of the little lost church.

➜ Start at the river bridge in Coltishall and explore upstream, up to 2 miles to the bridge at Little Hautbois. Or large mill pond and grassy area 200m downstream of Coltishall bridge (Horstead Mill).

5 mins, 52.7313, 1.3478

35 ST BENET'S ABBEY, R BURE

Impressive riverside ruin on classic Broads stretch. Mind the boats!

➜ Turn off A1062 at Dog Inn / Ludham Bridge, turn R after ¾ mile, to road end.

5 mins, 52.6863, 1.5251

38

36 ULTING, R CHELMER

A pretty little church on the banks of the river Chelmer. Wide, deep section used by pleasure crafts. Slightly brown but the water is some of the cleanest in the county. 2m deep. Please swim from the bank opposite the church.

→ Signed Nounsley / Ulting off B1019 at S end of Hatfield Peverel (A12). Turn L then first R direction Maldon. Continue 2 miles to find Church Rd on R, but please continue ½ mile and walk upstream on the opposite bank from Ulting lock / weir (best views of church too). Also explore river meadow path downstream from Ulting lock, or downstream from Boreham Bridge (51.7485, 0.5596).

5 mins, 51.7485, 0.6081

37 SAWBRIDGEWORTH, R STORT

A pretty rural stretch for up a mile down to Feakes Lock. Water quality is average - high in nitrates / phosphates - so don't drink it!

→ Follow the Stort Walkway from Sheering Mill Lane, or via Pishiobury Park.

15 mins, 51.8094, 0.1566

38 DEDHAM VALE, R STOUR

A beautiful, open and historic vale, site of Flatford Mill, where people row boats and occasionally swim. Fen Bridge is a quiet spot with 2m deep river pools and shelving access. Some weeds to watch for. Grade C due to fertiliser content (nitrates) but safe enough to swim.

→ Exit A12 at Stratford St Mary. Park at Dedham bridge, opposite the Boathouse (food and rowing boat hire, CO7 6DH, 01206 323153). Follow footpath downstream ¾ mile (L bank) to Fen Bridge. 45mins walk from Manningtree Station via Flatford Mill.

15 mins, 51.9623, 1.0079

39 RUSHBANKS FARM, R STOUR

Simple riverside campsite with jetty and open canoe hire.

→ 2 miles W of Nayland near Wissington. (CO6 4NA, riverstourboating.org.uk, 01206 262350). Turn off A134 at Nags Corner and follow Wiston Rd then Bures Rd. Or follow from Wissington downto the river and footbridge, direction Little Horkesley.

10 mins, 51.9644, 0.8373

40 OUTNEY COMMON, R WAVENEY

Open common. Good water quality. Popular for canoeing and swimming.

→ Turn off A143 at the roundabout signed Ditchingham and find footpath / track immediately on L (parking at Duke of York, NR35 2JL). Follow path, through woods, then over bridge (500m). Bear R along river bank to large pool with willow. Or keep exploring upstream. Canoe hire from the caravan site (NR35 1HG, 01986 892338).

10 mins, 52.4660, 1.4325

41 BUNGAY, R WAVENEY

Lovely riverbanks in a little alternative town with independent cafes and shops.

→ Head down pretty Bridge Street, then first R after bridge (Falcon Lane). Also try the riverside music pub downstream at Geldeston (NR34 0HS, 01508 518414).

10 mins, 52.4572, 1.4413

42 HOMERSFIELD, R WAVENEY

Secluded river dip with swing.

→ 2 miles N of Mendham on quiet cycling lanes. Take footpath opposite Valley Farm.

2 mins, 52.4129, 1.3605

London and Suburbs

Within London's great concrete sprawl there are a surprising number of hidden green oases, and efforts by local authorities to prohibit swimming have catalysed a number of campaigns to reclaim wild-swimming rights.

The three Hampstead Heath swimming ponds are probably the best known of central London's wild swims. The Mixed Pond is the closest to the tube and always rings with a holiday air. Groups loll about on the lawn, picnics are consumed, friends breast-stroke down the avenue of trees catching up on old news and gossip. The Men's Pond is bigger and Ladies' Ponds wilder, but both are a little more difficult to reach if you don't have a bike.

The ponds date back to the end of the seventeenth century when the Hampstead Water Company dammed two brooks that drain the Heath, piping the water down to the city in hollowed out elm trees. When the 'New River' from Hertfordshire to Islington superseded the ponds they became important for recreation, and a painting by Constable depicts people bathing at Hampstead as early as 1829.

Given this long tradition it's not surprising that the Hampstead Heath Winter Swimming Club was up in arms when health and safety officials told them they could no longer swim there in the winter months. The club, which includes several prominent public figures, won their case to swim, in a landmark ruling in

43

49

50

2005. The judge spoke out in favour of 'individual freedom' and against the imposition of 'a grey and dull safety regime'. This 2005 ruling has inspired other swimmers to reclaim their London ponds too.

Bury Lake at the Aquadrome near Rickmansworth tube is one such example, long used by recreational swimmers, who happily co-habit with dinghy sailors, ducks, toy boaters and fishermen. Local campaigner Molly Fletcher shows 1960s photographs of the lake teeming with hundreds of people swimming and playing. 'There were no more or less sailing boats, swimmers of fishermen then,' she explains. 'No more or less blue–green algae.' An ardent campaign is seeking to have the 'no swimming' notices removed on this peaceful and enticing lake. The growing cult of health and safety, compensation claims and the nanny state means many local authorities are unsure what to do with their many traditional swimming lakes. During the 1990s many decided to put up 'no swimming' signs, fearing expensive lawsuits. The spring-fed mere at Black Park Country Park near Uxbridge was closed, as was the sandy lake at Ruislip Lido. All the same, many hundreds of families do still swim and paddle here through the summer.

Gravel pits offer further opportunities for swimming near London. The Colne valley, along the M25 western corridor, provided much of the gravel for London's building boom in the twentieth century. These pits quickly filled with spring water and returned to nature, becoming beautiful wildlife reserves close to the heart of the city. The six-mile bike path from Rickmansworth to the Denham Country Park passes more than twenty gravel lakes and close to Staines there are even more. My favourites are around Wraysbury and Hythe, a four-mile mosaic of wooded island archipelagos, open water, grassland and scrub. These sites, now SSSIs, provide nationally important wetland habitats for wintering wildfowl, rare marigold, horned pondweed, tufted duck, gadwall and goosander. The banks are fringed with alder and crack willow and the water shelves deeply into the chalky green depths, as pure and clean as you could want. If it wasn't for the drone of the M25, and the Heathrow flight path, this could be the West London Lake District.

43 HAMPSTEAD PONDS, THE HEATH

Three beautiful woodland swimming lakes set in the rolling hills of the heath. Deep and green. Changing areas and lifeguards. Close to train and tube.

→ From Hampstead tube turn R down High St, then L after 500m down Downshire Hill. Cross onto Heath, 200m, bear L, to pass first then second ponds (non-swimming). Drop down to causeway, cross pond and turn L to find entrance. Ladies' and Men's ponds are ½ mile away, on opposite side of Heath or via Millfield Lane off Highgate West Hill (N6 6JB). Ladies' pond is beautiful and enclosed by trees.

15 mins, 51.5608, -0.1655 🖼🖼

44 SERPENTINE LAKE, HYDE PARK

40 acre lake in the central London fed by underground springs.

→ On S side of lake, to E of bridge, with changing rooms. Between Lancaster Gate and Knightsbridge tube stations (SW7 1LR). Waterside café (020 7706 8114).

10 mins, 51.5050, -0.1692 🍴🖼

45 RUISLIP LIDO LAKE

Sandy beach. Traditional swimming pond.

→ Reservoir Rd, signed off Ruislip main road. Large car park (HA4 7TT). Or by tube to Northwood Hills (Metropolitan Line).

10 mins, 51.5886, -0.4302 🚲🅿❓🖼

46 RICKMANSWORTH LAKES

These days Bury Lake is for watersports only, but to the W are three wild lakes: Stockers, Springwell and Inns.

→ Turn L off Uxbridge Rd (A412) on Springwell Lane and find small car park on R after 300m. Lakes on either side of road or continue another 300m to find path on L up Colne stream (not canal) to shores of Stocker's Lake. Be discrete. Rickmansworth tube ½ mile via Bury lake.

10 mins, 51.6288, -0.4964 ❓🖼

47 HYTHE END LAKE, STAINES

Steep wooded banks. Near the Thames.

→ From M25 / J13 head for Wraysbury Rd / B376 . Entrance is opposite Bell Weir Garage (TW19 6HE). The Runnymede banks of the Thames are close by too.

5 mins, 51.4445, -0.5369 🖼

48 WRAYSBURY LAKES

Vast area of wild gravel lakes a short walk from Wraysbury train station.

→ Turn L out of station (W) and turn R down Douglas Lane (TW19 5NF) after ½ mile. Lake shore on L or continue on 200m, across railway line to find Kingsmead Lake to L. Great sunsets.

30 min, 51.4652, -0.5475 🖼🖼❓🖼

49 EYNSFORD, R DARENT

Clear, clean, shallow ford and stream with pub and ruined castle. Great fun for kids.

→ From M25 J3 follow 'Farningham A225' then Eynsford. The stream is by The Plough (DA4 0AE, 01322 862281), signed St Botolph's Churchfrom the shop.

3 mins, 51.3680, 0.2092 🚲🖼

50 CHERTSEY BRIDGE, R THAMES

Large area of open park and river bank with several beaches, downstream of bridge. Dumsey Meadow - a large area of undeveloped meadow - is opposite.

→ Find small car park 300m E of bridge on R, along Chertsey Bridge Rd.

5 mins, 51.3879, -0.4810 🖼C

Sussex Downs and Kent

The Sussex Downs – between the Ouse and the Cuckmere rivers – were the rural heartland of the Bloomsbury Group. Now, as then, the rivers provide beautiful wild-swimming, from the reaches of the upper Ouse to the warm lake-land meanders of the Cuckmere Vale.

The great winding paths of the river Cuckmere became separated from their stream in the nineteenth century when a bypass 'cut' was built to stop the vale-land meadows flooding. The abandoned curves are now warm, safe lagoons, ideal for paddling, rafting and swimming. With panoramic views of the Seven Sisters cliffs and the sea, this is a stunning location to combine some saltwater and freshwater swimming. How long the meanders will survive is now in doubt as there are plans to let the sea flood these flatlands again and return them to their original ecology.

Above the Vale and over the Downs is Charleston Farmhouse, where Vanessa Bell lived after her separation from her husband. From here she could walk to visit her sister, Virginia Woolf, at Rodmell, on the Ouse. The houses, and area, became the rural retreat of one of the most influential literary and artistic groups of the twentieth century, known for their love of nature and wild-swimming.

E. M. Forster, schooled and brought up in nearby Tonbridge, visited more than once. Himself known to wild swim with Rupert Brooke in Grantchester, one of Forster's more famous

56

64

59

literary scenes is of Freddy, George and Mr Beebe rebelliously dipping in the Surrey 'Sacred Lake' in *A Room with a View*. Mocking the world of Edwardian manners and social codes, it symbolised the great liberation of thought and feeling that Forster and his contemporaries believed natural bathing provided. Forster grew up swimming in the Medway, fed by the dark waters of the Ashdown Forest – home of Winnie the Pooh – between Kent and Sussex. You can still swim in the Medway, near Penshurst Place, to this day. The banks of the river slope steeply into rich, clean and weed-free water. The peaty smell and brownish hue are flavoured by the Wealds of Kent. To swim here is to be infused with an elixir of leaf litter and pine cones.

If you do visit Virginia Woolf's Rodmell, the Ouse there is no great place to swim. The straight, tidal channel has swampy edges and a slick current as it runs under a bleak, open sky and its lack of charm is not helped by being the site were, just a few hundred yards from her home, the writer chose to kill herself. Woolf had suffered from periods of manic depression throughout her creative and brilliant life. She felt she was going mad again and after months of suffering she did not believe she would ever recover.

Just north of Rodmell and Charleston, upstream on the Ouse, the open fields of Barcombe Mills are a perfect place for cricket, leapfrog and other riverside games. The Ouse here is deep with pretty grassy banks, ideal for cooling down after cartwheels or diving in for a long swim among the rushes.

The well-known Anchor Inn is nearby, just a mile upstream, at the bottom of a dead-end lane. You can hire one of its fleet of blue rowing boats or swim for over two miles through remote countryside, the spire of Isfield church the only building in sight for the entire journey.

'The three gentlemen rotated in the pool breast high, after the fashion of the nymphs in Gotterdammerung. For some reason or other a change came over them. They began to play. Mr Beebe and Freddy splashed each other. A little deferentially, they splashed George…Then all the forces of youth burst out.'

E. M. Forster, *A Room with a View*

61

51 FORDWICH, R GREAT STOUR

Flowing through England's smallest town the river is first open and sunny, then becomes wooded and secretive, leading to a wild lake. Good canoeing.

→ Off A23, 2 miles NE of Canterbury (Sturry train station). Follow the river's L bank from the bridge to an easy entry point after ½ mile or continue another ½ mile to find a wooded glade on R. Westbere Marshes lake is accessible to L, though best reached on N shore from Westbere (turn down Walnut Tree Lane after Ye Old Yew Tree Inn, CT2 0HH, 01227 710501, over railway line then continue along lake shore to 51.3047, 1.1462). Cycle route 1.

40 mins, 51.3001, 1.1513 🏕🚲🚶🛶⛵

52 CHARTHAM, R GREAT STOUR

Popular, with rope swing and lakes too.

→ From train station, or 3 miles SW of Canterbury on A28. Park at the village hall and follow the path 300m down along the stream to find small weir, deep pool beneath and rope swing. Continue on 300m to find lake on L. Cycle route 18.

5 mins, 51.2562, 1.0215 🚶🚲⛵

53 WICKHAMBREAUX, R LITTLE STOUR

Pretty stream and shallow pool near chocolate box pretty village.

→ 4 miles E of Canterbury, off A257. Turn at the Rose Inn (CT3 1RQ, 01227 721763) then first R after school down Seaton Lane. After 300m find footpath on L. Cross field to find stream after 500m.

10 mins, 51.2860, 1.1961 🚶🚻

54 UPSTREET, R GREAT STOUR

Clean and silky after 4 miles meandering through the Stodmarsh nature reserve.

→ Opposite Grove Ferry Inn (CT3 4BZ, 01227 860302) signed off A28, find NNR / Stodmarsh gate and river path.

5 mins, 51.3226, 1.2029 🏕🛶⛵

55 POUNDSBRIDGE, R MEDWAY

In remote fields, a bridge and deep pools under red earth banks. Watch out for leaping kids.

→ Take footpath upstream (cross once) for 1½ mile. Opposite Enterprise Centre sign, near Penshurst Bridge.

30 mins, 51.1580, 0.1914 🌳🚶

56 ENSFIELD BRIDGE, R MEDWAY

Open, sunny stretch of river by road bridge with river paths in both directions. Steep banks but good for a longer swim.

→ W of Tonbridge. A mile S of Leigh station on lanes. Also on Cycle route 12 to beautiful Penshurst Place. Busy road, so park respectfully and keep off road.

2 mins, 51.1857, 0.2133 🚶🛶⛵🚲

57 BEWL WATER

South east England's largest water body, surrounded by orchards and no end of secret beaches to dip from discreetly.

→ Footpath access around the entire perimeter and a 12 mile mountain bike route. From the main visitor centre head W along the N shore to Bramble Bay. Or try Rosemary Lane off the A21 (51.06300, 0.42055) at the E end. Swimming is prohibited but many do. Bike hire 01323 870059. Camp at Cedar Stables off A21, Flimwell (TN5 7QA, 01892 890566). The footpath behind leads down to a sunset facing wooded cove (20 mins, 51.0675, 0.4097). Scotney Castle is also close by.

20 mins, 51.0759, 0.3805, 🚶🏕🚣⛵❓

River Ouse

63

58 LITLINGTON, R CUCKMERE
Wide grassland vale beneath white horse. Tidal and muddy but fun at high tide.

→ Approaching from A259 E of Seaford, footpath to river is on L as you enter village, 200m before the excellent Plough and Harrow (BN26 5RE, 01323 870 632). Head downstream to footbridge.
10 mins, 50.7920, 0.1505 ▨▮

59 CUCKMERE MEANDERS
Wide, shallow, warm oxbow lakes cut off from the main river. Stunning setting with option of sea swimming too.

→ On A259 W of Seaford. Park at the visitor centre at Exceat. Follow the path down on the L side of the valley ½ mile.
10 mins, 50.7707, 0.1544 ▨ ▣

60 HORSTED KEYNES
Large area of hammer ponds in beautiful woodland setting. Avoid fishermen.

→ Signed off A275, 2 miles N of Sheffield Park. Park at the church then continue down road 300m to main lake on R. Smaller grassy ponds for picnics further along.
10 mins, 51.0447, -0.0269 ▨

61 BARCOMBE MILLS, R OUSE
Popular stretch of grassy river bank and meadows. Steep banks and deep water.

→ Off A26, 2 miles N of Lewes. Park on L after a mile and head upstream past sluices to meadow. Another mile leads to the Anchor Inn.
5 mins, 50.9151, 0.0411 ▨▨▣

62 ANCHOR INN, R OUSE
Remote riverside pub. Bucolic swimming and boating for further 2 miles upstream as far as Isfield.

→ Continue to Barcombe village, turn R then R again (3 miles) or walk upstream 1 mile. (BN8 5BS, 01273 400414)
5 mins, 50.9264, 0.0513 ▨▮▨

63 LAKE WOOD, UCKFIELD
Lovely lake with rocky crags and extraordinary cave grotto complex.

→ From Isfield continue N towards Uckfield 3 miles. Cross the A22 to find West Park nature reserve on L.
5 mins, 50.9762, 0.0820 ▨▨

64 ARDINGLY LAKE, BALCOMBE
A beautiful two-pronged reservoir near Balcombe train station. Good path along N shore. No Swimming, but people do.

→ From Balcombe follow Mill Lane (signed Ardingly) from mini roundabout / postbox. Pick up footpath from parking layby at bottom, beyond bridge. From Ardingly follow Balcombe Lane. Park after a mile in layby R, at top of lane. Take first footpath on L, along E shore to bench (300m).
15 mins, 51.0489, -0.0991 ▨▨▨

65 MIDHURST, R ROTHER
Sandy Bay is the traditional place for a paddle, in front of the Cowdray ruins.

→ 150m upstream from the castle's old bridge. Or take the path by the hospital, (Haslemere road) to secret wooded river.
10 mins, 50.9890, -0.7330 ▨▨

66 BURY, R ARUN
Remote grassy riverbank on tidal Arun.

→ N of Arundel, off A29 at Squire & Horses. Take footpath downstream 300m. Or upstream from Amberley station.
5 mins, 50.9055, -0.5562 ▨▨▨

© Friday Street

Surrey Hills and the River Wey

I first glimpsed Frensham Great Pond on a fuggy summer afternoon with the smell of reeds and heath in the air and the crunch of dry heather underfoot. Placid and fat, dark columns of cumulus clouds were rising high above it and two clinker dinghies were moving languidly near a far bank.

You'd be forgiven for not being too excited about the prospect of natural swimming in Surrey, but it does have its wilder pockets. Strangely it's the most wooded county in England, which means less nitrates from farmers and less watershed pollution. Much of its downland is protected within an Area of Outstanding Natural Beauty and the ancient chalk ridgeway of the North Downs runs across its hills.

The clouds above me were on the turn, stacking up against the hills, the heathland pines deep green against the grey of a pre-storm sky as I slipped gingerly into the mauve waters of Frensham Great Pond. A cheery moorhen paddled happily some distance from me before she took up a frantic taxi across the waters, her feet dangling as she struggled to become airborne and the first rain began to fall. A kaleidoscope of concentric circles rippled across the glassy surface as I glided on through the cooling waters, the humidity purged from the day.

This shallow, warmish lake has two bays with natural sandy beaches marked out for swimming. Built as a fish pond by

67

71

69

the Bishop of Winchester when he took up a prolonged stay at his nearby castle at Farnham in 1246 it was drained every five years to cleanse it and grow barley. The last time it was emptied, however, was in 1942, during the Second World War, as it had become a great moonlit landmark for the German bombers.

Frensham Little Pond is on the other side of the A287 and both ponds feed into the Wey which flows down into Tilford. This is a truly English scene with a cricket green and pub, river paddling above a ford and a bridge built by medieval monks. It's a perfect place to while away a summer afternoon with lunch and a paddle or swim – there is a rope swing below the weir and some deeper sections above the bridge.

Moving east there are several more wooded lakes. Bolder Mere on Ockham Common near the M25 is a rare remnant of the heathland ponds that used to cover much of Surrey. It's an important site for dragonflies and damselflies, and also for the rare hobby – one of the few birds that can actually catch a dragonfly. Wildlife here is definitely the main priority – when two common tern chicks were found by the side of the lake people were asked to refrain from swimming too close to them. This is Site of Special Scientific Interest (SSSI) run by Surrey Wildlife Trust, so it's best to slip into the water silently and carefully, with a view to blending in.

Just outside Guildford, the Silent Pool, in a hollow beneath the escarpment of the Downs, is springfed from the chalk aquifers. Like other chalk streams it is very cold and very clear. Surrounded with vegetation and overhung by huge silver birches it was greatly admired by the poet Tennyson for the clarity of its water. I once tried to swim there during a very hot summer but it had completely dried up. More recently it was used as the film set for the skinny-dipping scene in *Hippie Hippie Shake* with Sienna Miller. Legend has it that a local woodcutter's daughter was bathing naked in the lake when she heard a horse and rider. With no time to cover her body she made for the deeper water, despite not being able to swim. She drowned and her ghost can be seen at midnight, wading through the waters.

68

67 TILFORD COMMON, R WEY

Paddling and pools just downstream of the bridge. Village green, cricket and pub.

→ 3 miles SE of Farnham off B3001. Parking opposite Barley Mow pub (GU10 2BU, 01252 792205)

10 mins, 51.1820, -0.7499 🖼️ 🚻

68 GODALMING, R WEY

Meadow, ancient oaks and deep water.

→ From Manor Hill / Beefeater pub garden (A3100, Guildford Rd, GU7 3BX, 01483 427134) follow river path downstream to open fields and meadow (300m).

10 min, 51.1984, -0.5862 🚻 🖼️

69 ST CATHERINE'S HILL, R WEY

Sandy beach, ruined chapel and bridge for jumping on the old Pilgrims' Way.

→ Walk down Ferry Lane from the Ye Olde Ship Inn (GU2 4EB, 01483 575731) or walk 20 mins from Shalford station (follow cycle path opposite water fountain, across railway, then L down to river, crossing over at St Catherine's lock).

20 mins, 51.2243, -0.5772 🖼️ 🚻 🚻 🚻

70 FRIDAY STREET, LEITH HILL

Mill pool and inn lost among wooded hills, traditionally used for swimming and fishing. OWNERS NO LONGER ALLOW SWIMMING. NO SWIMMING SIGNS.

→ Along lane at RH5 6JR. Locals swim discreetly from E wooded edge. Stephan Langton Inn just up lane (Tel 01306 730775). Etherley Farm camping with local produce at RH5 5PA, 01306 621423.

3 mins, 51.1999, -0.3865 🚻 ⛺ ❓

71 FRENSHAM GREAT POND, FARNHAM

Sandy lake with beaches and buoyed-off swimming area. Set among forest and open heathland. Parking, café and small museum. Popular with young families.

→ 5 miles S of Farnham (A287) signed Frensham Pond Hotel on R, then first L after ½ mile. Frensham Little Pond is signed on L 4½ miles S of Farnham. This is more beautiful but 'no swimming' signs. Nearby Mellow Farm camping (GU10 4HH, 01428 717815) is excellent with a small river for playing (51.1427, -0.8260)

5 mins, 51.1575, -0.7919 🍴 ⛺ 🖼️

72 BOURLEY BOTTOM, ALDERSHOT

Series of old reservoir lakes in pine forest on MOD training land. Popular in summer.

→ Bourley Rd runs between Fleet and Aldershot. Half way along there is a large gravel car park. Opposite a gated track leads 300m up to first lake, more beyond.

15 mins, 51.2488, -0.8117 🖼️

73 CHOBHAM COMMON, SUNNINGDALE

Medieval fishpond hidden amongst shrub land sometimes used for fishing.

→ About 1½ miles S of Sunningdale Station / Broomhall on B383 find car park on L. Lake is opposite the Victoria Memorial, on other side of road.

10 mins, 51.3824, -0.6198 🖼️ ❓

74 BOLDER MERE, OCKHAM COMMON

Just off the M25 near RHS Wisley, a nature reserve but a popular spot for a discreet dip.

→ A3 south, 600m after M25 / A3 junction. Also the stepping stones on the River Mole at Boxhill Country Park (TQ 173513).

5 mins, 51.31352, -0.45701 ❓

Houghton, River Test

Hampshire Chalk Streams

The wide braids of the River Test run through some of the least developed parts of the South East. Wily and fast, the stream picks its way through the most tranquil parts of Hampshire as it heads for the sea.

Watership Down, that chalk downland immortalised by Richard Adams, is the headwater for the river Test. These were the hills down which Pipkin and Hazel fled, first from the bulldozers, then from Efrafan rabbit soldiers, before jumping onto a punt moored on the river at Laverstoke. Like the Salisbury chalk streams, public access to the bankside is rare, with fishing rights charging out at up to £1,000 per day. But at Chilbolton Cow Common, near Cherwell Priory, there has been public access since ancient times.

The little footbridges here are a magnet for families paddling and playing Pooh Sticks on a hot summer day, but as I arrived at seven o'clock on an early evening in June the last picnickers were leaving. The clear waters of the chalk stream are the home for many unique plants and as I dipped in the shallow waters it was like bathing in an underwater flower meadow. The long fronds of yellow starwort rippled in the current like buttercups and the white water's crowfoot waved like daisies. The downland mineral water teemed through my hair and made rivulets about my fingers.

80

84

78

The chalk shingles of these streams were laid down long ago. Coral reefs and sea plankton collected during the landscape's time as part of an equatorial archipelago thousands of millions of years ago. Then the water would have been a balmy 30 Celcius but the temperature now is far from tropical – a chilly 15 Celcius. Rising from aquifers deep beneath the hills, the temperature remains remarkably constant throughout the year so that even on frosty winter mornings the Test is relatively warm, and it is famous for its steaming river mists. Then, a bath here feels almost balmy.

At Houghton, another favourite paddling location five miles away, a white shingle bay opens out onto a large shallow pool under a bridge where you can swim against the current. The old trackway crosses water meadows to John of Gaunt's deer park and the ancient yews at King's Somborne. The river course has changed much in the last three hundred years. In John's time new channels were being cut for the creation of 'floating' water meadows. A system of sluices encouraged the river to flood the fields, nourishing the grass and protecting it from frost to make possible earlier lambing and increased sheep stocking. It's now difficult to know which is the original river course and which an old irrigation path.

Running through nearby Winchester, the Itchen is another chalk stream that has been much altered by man. It was deepened for barge navigation in the eighteenth century but most of it has returned to shallows though there is still a deep pool under the little waterfall at Twyford. Just upstream the river is about one metre deep and good for a longer swim, if you don't mind occasionally scraping your knees.

A path follows the Itchen all the way to Winchester making a pleasant two-mile walk, despite the noisy motorway which passes overhead. The Twyford Downs, site of the road protests of the 1990s, are up on your right and you might like to take a dip in Tumbling Bay. Eventually you'll reach the water meadows of St Cross where there are also some deeper pools by the medieval hospital.

75 TUNDRY POND, DOGMERSFIELD

Remote parkland lake with picnic tables.

→ Off Basingstocke Canal, W of church.
10 mins, 51.2656, -0.8900

76 ODIHAM CASTLE, HOOK

Spring-fed crystal clear canal with ethereal hues by pretty Odiham castle.

→ Descend to canal and old tunnel from Greywell (S of M3, J5) and continue ½ mile.
15 mins, 51.2609, -0.9623

77 WOOLHAMPTON, R KENNET

Secluded river downstream, secret lakes upstream. Pub, station & cycle path.

→ Head upstream 300m from Rowbarge Inn (RG7 5SH, 01189 712213), turn L at footbridge, to find lakes on R.
10 mins, 51.3934, -1.1844

78 SULHAMSTEAD, R KENNET

Beautiful open meadows and good access up and downstream of lock. Cycle path 4.

→ Turn off A4 at Spring Inn, 6 miles W of Reading, and find parking at second bridge.
10 mins, 51.4186, -1.0999

79 SHERFIELD ON LODDON

Mill pool in meadows behind pub.

→ Accessible from Longbridge Inn RG27 0DL, 01256 883483) or road bridge.
5 mins, 51.3189, -1.0199

80 ST CROSS WINCHESTER, R ITCHEN

Water meadows and pools behind the great ancient almshouse.

→ Heading into Winchester from S, turn down by the Bell Inn (SO23 9RE, 01962 865284). Also riverside Bush Inn with riverside walks at Ovington (SO24 0RE, 01962 732764) NE of Winchester.
5 mins, 51.0477, -1.3197

81 TWYFORD, R ITCHEN

Deep pool (remains of old lock) above footbridge and below hatch, partly lined with concrete. Clear and cold!

→ ½ mile walk from Shawford station. Or M3 / J11 to Twyford, turn R into Berry Lane and continue from church over footbridge, 500m along fence boundary to pool. Tumbling Bay sluices ½ mile upstream.
10 mins, 51.0272, -1.3221

82 LONGPARISH WALK, R TEST

Exquisite stretch of the young Test.

→ From the Cricketers Inn (SP11 6PZ, 01264 720335) turn R and R again across water meadow to arrive at millhouse (10 mins, small pool) then bear R on lane to find ½ mile of grassy banks for paddling only.
30 mins, 51.2005, -1.3710

83 CHILBOLTON COW COMMON, R TEST

Ancient rural common with paddling in crystal clear pools by footbridge.

→ Turn off the A305 at the pretty riverside Mayfly (SO20 6AZ, 01264 860283) and after a mile turn L down Joy's Lane. Park at end and head to footbridge (200m). Also similar at Stockbridge Common.
20 mins, 51.1591, -1.4442

84 HOUGHTON, TEST

A wide, white chalk bay at the end of bridleway in beautiful countryside. Crowsfoot and water buttercup in spring.

→ Entering Houghton from Stockbridge find footpath at end of village on L (Clarendon Way) and follow it to bridge.
2 mins, 51.0843, -1.5119

Piles Copse

South West

The high moors of Bodmin, Dartmoor and Exmoor dominate this region providing the headwaters for fantastic swimming in the Fowey, Dart and Barle and the Tarka region of the Torridge and Taw. Heading east into the gentle landscape of Somerset, Dorset and the New Forest Avon you'll find riverside churches, chutes and weir-pools, river swimming clubs and the prettiest of chalk streams.

Highlights
South West England

Our favourites include:

93 Farleigh Hungerford - Picnic by the river and exchange favourite wild-swimming locations at Britain's longest established river swimming club

96 Claverton Weir - Swim and play at one of the longest river weirs in the UK

104-106 Swim along the famous Dorset Stour in Sturminster Newton where Thomas Hardy spent the happiest years of his life

111 Tarr Steps - Paddle, swim and eat a pub lunch at this popular and ancient 'Clapper Bridge' made of great obelisk-sized stones

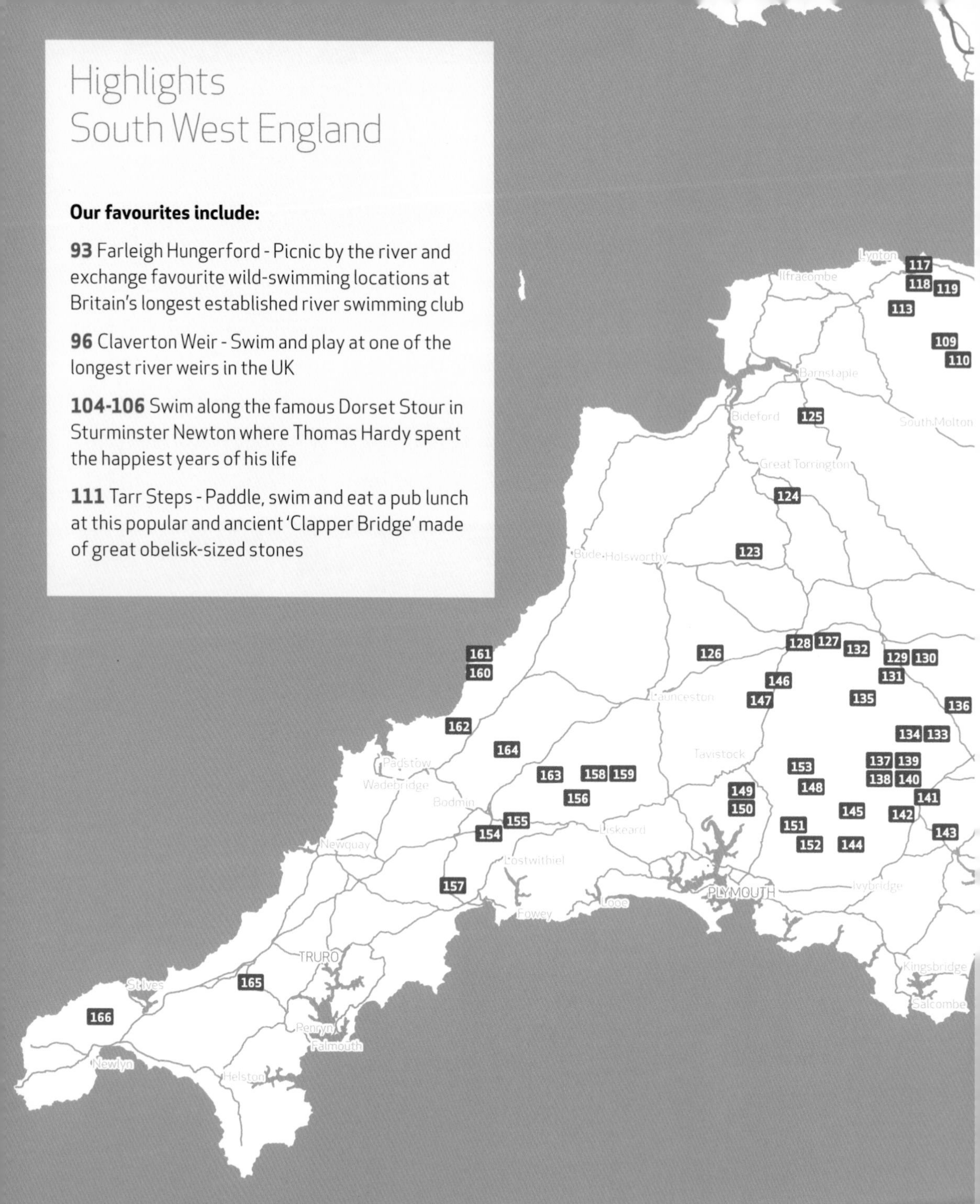

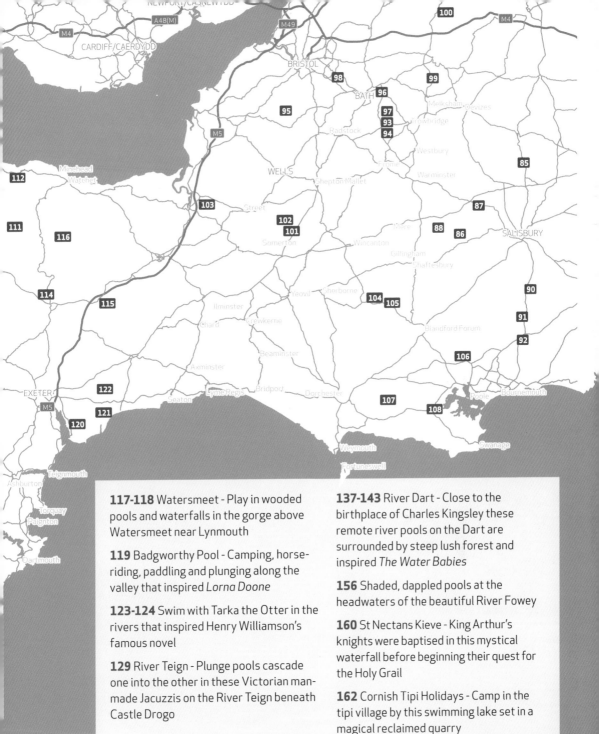

117-118 Watersmeet - Play in wooded pools and waterfalls in the gorge above Watersmeet near Lynmouth

119 Badgworthy Pool - Camping, horse-riding, paddling and plunging along the valley that inspired *Lorna Doone*

123-124 Swim with Tarka the Otter in the rivers that inspired Henry Williamson's famous novel

129 River Teign - Plunge pools cascade one into the other in these Victorian man-made Jacuzzis on the River Teign beneath Castle Drogo

137-143 River Dart - Close to the birthplace of Charles Kingsley these remote river pools on the Dart are surrounded by steep lush forest and inspired *The Water Babies*

156 Shaded, dappled pools at the headwaters of the beautiful River Fowey

160 St Nectans Kieve - King Arthur's knights were baptised in this mystical waterfall before beginning their quest for the Holy Grail

162 Cornish Tipi Holidays - Camp in the tipi village by this swimming lake set in a magical reclaimed quarry

Castle Hill, River Avon

Wiltshire Chalk Streams and New Forest

Salisbury Plain is the headwater for three chalk streams – the Nadder, Wylye and Hampshire Avon – that all descend on Salisbury and continue along the edge of the New Forest to Christchurch. Percolating from the hills, they are fabulously clean, clear and cold!

I arrived at the Avon in Figheldean, just south of Stonehenge, to find bikinis hung on a Morris Minor, a picnic hamper spread out under a willow tree and a mother and her three children paddling and shrieking in cold glee. This is a beautiful pool above a footbridge at the end of a little lane by the church. The water is exceptionally clean and clear and roars in over a simple sluice-type affair, first into a deep hole, and then over white pebble shallows and flint sand banks with views out over hay fields.

Two young men in shorts and wellies had also just arrived from across the fields and were racing each other to be first to dive into the deep pool beneath the small waterfall weir. Elizabeth, an elderly resident of the village, was spectating from a deckchair, calling out comments and clapping at all the action. In the old days, she said, the pool was always packed in the summer, particularly with servicemen from the airbases. During the war there were Land Army girls here too. Some said their naked bathing was distracting the village from the

89

85

87

war effort and the local policeman, who also ran the village swimming lessons, ordered that bathers should be suitably clothed for decorous bathing.

The Nadder, some miles away, is a much quieter, smaller stream splashing down through the uplands of the Cranborne Chase. I was quickly lost among the narrow lanes searching for a public footpath that might give bankside access. There, on a hill brow, with a sign pointing down through a billowing wheat field to a little bridge, I finally found a tiny map-marked public right of way.

The riverside is neatly mown and cordoned off, clearly prepared for some very well organised fishing. I dare say fishermen would not welcome wild swimmers so I followed the footpath gingerly, not wishing to disturb the peace, but I saw no one, save a dipper and a wagtail, and I arrived alone, hot but delighted, as the river widened into a clear shelving pool behind shrubs. A chute of the purest spring water poured in over an old hatch. Making a neat pile of clothes on a fishing bench, I climbed down the soft grass bank, tiptoed along the deepening riverbed and swam breaststroke into the pool. Pebbles of whites, greys and reds formed a wobbling mosaic on the cool rive rpool floor.

The third chalk stream – the Wylye – runs in between the Nadder and Avon. I had initially been attracted to Steeple Langford by a series of lakes I spied from the main road late one evening. What were once gravel pits are now a nature reserve and just as I was preparing to head home disappointed that a silent dip wasn't allowed I spied a tiny lawn with a bench, opposite the nature reserve entrance, and a small sign: 'Entry to the pool is prohibited to those unable to swim.' With these magic words a small but beautiful pool appeared, turning a silver green hue in the fading evening light! A mother swan was collecting some final weedy titbits before tucking up her cygnets for the evening and the church warden was cycling by on her bike, making home for supper. I tiptoed excitedly over the white shingle and waded into the pool. Here, floating like Ophelia, I lay in a perfect stillness, starring up at an indigo sky and the first stars of the evening.

91

85 FIGHELDEAN, R AVON

Chalk shingle shallows with deep pool beneath a small weir - deep enough to jump. REPORTED FENCED OFF & CLOSED so explore upstream Avon instead.

→ From SP4 8JJ Figheldean dead end lane opp cottages leads to footbridge and pool above. Alternatives include road bridge at Netheravon 51.2358, -1.7867 (SP4 9RX - shallow pool below or footpath upstream on L bank) or explore L bank river path between Coombe and Fittleton - all MOD access land with MOD bridge (51.2505, -1.7906).

2 mins, 51.2262, -1.7846 🏊 🍴 🚐

86 TEFFONT EVIAS, R NADDER

Small, secret pool under hatches. Public right of way, but don't swim if fishermen.

→ From B3089 (W of Salisbury) turn L after Dinton (signed Chicksgrove). After a mile find footpath sign L by tree. Follow down to stream, across bridge and along river 400m. (Public right of way actually marked as near bank on maps, but now seems to have been diverted to far bank.)

10 mins, 51.0704, -2.0192 ❓ ⛺

STEEPLE LANGFORD, R WYLYE

Pretty village pool with shelving access, grassy banks and bench. White chalk shingle riverbed.

→ 8 miles W of Salisbury turn off A36 signed 'The Langfords'. Turn L down Duck Street. Nature Reserve is 500m on L, just over bridge. Pool opposite, R through gate. Also Heytesbury pool (51.1794, -2.1002).

2 mins, 51.1328, -1.9485 🏊

87 FONTHILL BISHOP LAKE

Majestic landscaped lake. Look out for the strange grotto cave on hillside above.

→ Heading W from Fonthill Bishop turn immediately R through archway (signed Fonthill Gifford) and find layby parking and entrance to wooded lakeshore path after ¾ mile.

5 mins, 51.0843, -2.0957 ⛵ ❓

88 BALMERLAWN, BROCKENHURST

Very popular for picnics and paddling.

→ ½ mile N of Brockenhurst (A337 Lymington). Deeper pools near bridge.

2 mins, 50.8265, -1.5692 🏊

89 CASTLE HILL, R AVON

A very steep wooded descent leads to rope swings and deep swimming.

→ Heading S out of Woodgreen, turn R signed Castle Hill. Continue ½ mile, past main car park, to find layby on L. Descend to river. Or dip at the bridge N of Woodgreen (50.9672, -1.7491) or at Sandy Balls camping (SP6 2JZ, 0845 2702248).

5 mins, 50.9468, -1.7624 🏊 🚶 ⛺ ❓

90 IBSLEY BRIDGE, R AVON

The weir pool is fenced but continue down stream to find meaders in pretty meadow.

→ 3 miles N of Ringwood A338, turn L signed Harbridge. Find path on L by bridge.

5 mins, 50.8858, -1.7930 ⛵ 📷 ❓

91 RINGWOOD, R AVON

Wide meaders in empty water meadows.

→ From A31 follow B3347 a mile S. Turn R (dead end) just after L turn signed Burley. Continue a mile down Hampshire Hatches Lane until parking at end and follow path N over footbrige 300m. Try also Watton's Ford (50.8156, -1.8064).

5 mins, 50.8352, -1.7913 🏊 ⛵ ❓

North Somerset's Frome and Avon

The Somerset Frome near Bath is the home of one of the country's last surviving river-swimming clubs, with stories of camping galas and wild swimming parties.

The Farleigh and District Swimming Club occupies a great sweep of south-facing meadow by an old diving frame and gravel-bedded weir pool on the Frome. With over 2,000 members, people come here from far and wide to experience real swimming and to sunbathe on the grassy banks.

The club was founded in 1933 during the great boom in British river swimming. The village was already popular with the people of Trowbridge a few miles away who would walk over to Farleigh at the weekend to swim, visit the castle and have a drink at the Hungerford Arms. The four Greenhill brothers owned the farm on the opposite side of the bank and also loved to swim. One day they invited some of these regular bathers to form a swimming club and for the next 20 years the club flourished. Summers saw a regular group who would camp out on the banks, rise at six for an early-morning dip and then go off haymaking for the day. There were Wednesday evening swimming galas, great bonfires and general summer antics, all with the enthusiastic support of the Greenhills.

In more recent years the club has swapped banks. The new landlords are just as enthusiastic and they run a campsite

99

98

94

and tea shop a mile upstream. This river is a beautiful setting for a summer afternoon with children swimming among the moorhens and alder roots and the spray from the weir catching the floating dandelion seeds. There are no galas or bonfires here anymore but the bighearted welcome still exists.

Two miles upstream at Tellisford the landowners have also been modernising with a sensitive eye for wild swimmers. A beautiful weir pool is located a little way up from a medieval packhorse bridge among wide fields and an odd Second World War bunker – apparently this was a position on the 'Somerset Stop Line Green' where the British planned to defend the country against an attack coming from the south coast. This weir, like the one at Farleigh, was constructed in the early nineteenth century to power the village mill. Although it stopped working many generations ago, the weir pool has been saved by a local project to generate 60kW from the renovated mill chase – enough to power the whole village. This is an exciting green initiative which has preserved the weir pool, provides a more stable supply of electricity than wind and is less unsightly than a turbine.

Weir power is fairly common in this area. Claverton (Warleigh) Weir, five miles downstream and on the outskirts of Bath, forms a long, meandering waterfall across the River Avon. It looks a little like a miniature Victoria Falls stretching into the distance. At over one hundred yards long it was built in 1810 to power a pump that would lift water from the river to the nearby Kennet and Avon Canal. It has created a huge pool in the Avon, and a spectacularly wide waterfall. Children play under the dam and in the shallows. Adults can take a long swim above the weir and up the Avon, for the best part of a mile.

'The water fell as rain around 10,000 years ago and then sank to a depth of about 2km. Here it is heated by high temperature rocks before rising back up through one of the three hot springs in the centre of the City, the Cross Spring, Hetling or King's Spring, which supplies the Roman Baths. The actual source of the waters remains a mystery. It was believed that the source was in the Mendip Hills 30 miles to the south of Bath but more recent findings suggest that the rainwater enters through the carboniferous limestone closer to the City and the Avon Valley..' www.thermaebathspa.com

96

93 FARLEIGH HUNGERFORD, R FROME

Deep, narrow, pleasant stretch of the Frome, above a weir with lawns. Ruined castle and good campsite just upstream.

→ Descend into the village from A36 (signed Trowbridge), over two bridges then enter field immediately on R.

2 mins, 51.3179, -2.2810 ⬛⬛🏕🍴

94 TELLISFORD, R FROME

Large weir pool with medieval packhorse bridge and pillbox ruin.

→ Continue on from Farleigh 1 mile and turn R (B3109 Rode). After 1½ miles turn R (Tellisford Bridge), park at end and continue down hill to river and bear L.

10 mins, 51.2975, -2.2807 ⬛

95 BLAGDON & CHEW LAKES

Fabulous locations but No Swimming!

→ Meadows at Blagdon are good at high water, nice for picnics. From dam follow path N for ½ mile then bear R. For Chew, good beach at Sutton Wick if no fishermen (51.3294, -2.6140). Follow 'dead end' road off the A368, BS39 5XR. No parking!

2 mins, 51.2567, -2.5524 ⬛⬜❓

96 CLAVERTON WEIR, AVON

Long curving weir by meadows. Old ferryman's steps below and a long deep stretch above. On the cycle path from Bath, or from Dundas aqueduct.

→ 3 miles E of Bath on A36, turn L at Claverton, down Ferry Lane, just before sign for The American Museum on R.

10 mins, 51.3772, -2.3003 🚲⬛🔽

97 AVONCLIFF, BRADFORD-ON-AVON

Large, fun river-pool above weir, with rope swing. Long deep stretch upstream all the way to Tithe Barn in Bradford.

→ Avoncliff station, cross aqueduct (Cross Guns riverside pub, 01225 862335) and continue 200m along canal to find a path on L that drops down through woods to the weir. Or a 20-min walk downstream from Bradford on Avon, (canoes or cycles hire at TT Cycles, BA15 1LE, 01225 867187).

5 mins, 51.3391, -2.2797 🏠🍴⬛🚲🔽

98 AVON VALLEY PARK, SALTFORD

Grassy picnic riverside area, by old railway bridge. There's a wooden landing stage and it's fun to jump in.

→ In fields next to the cycle route, where the bridge crosses the river. 1 mile N of Saltford or 1 mile S of Bristol edge on A4. The Jolly Sailor in Saltford is also a popular swimming spot with a good rope swing on the opposite bank, above the weir. Don't play on the weir.

20 mins, 51.4171, -2.4600 🏃🏠⬛🔽🍴

99 LACOCK ABBEY, AVON

River beach below abbey and tree jump 300m upstream into deep pool.

→ From main NT car park turn R and continue 500m on lane to find footpath L between two bridges.

10 mins, 51.4146, -2.1150 🍴⬜

100 LITTLE SOMERFORD, AVON

Idyllic deep pools in orchard and meadow upstream of mill.

→ 3 miles E of Malmesbury. Take Mill Lane by railway bridge. Park in layby on L and continue on footpath ½ mile, around side of Kingsmead Mill, over bridge and into woods. Also downstream in Great Somerford (Volunteer Inn, 01249 720316).

15 mins, 51.5597, -2.0686 🏕🏠

Wimborne Minster

Dorset Stour and Somerset Brue

The meandering rivers of Thomas Hardy's Wessex twist and turn through lush pastures and cider-growing levels. Blossoms line the Somerset Brue in spring and yellow water lilies fill the Dorset Stour in summer.

Camping in fields close to the River Stour I awoke to a glorious morning mist, dew-clad spider webs hanging in the dried husks of cow parsley and tall brown bull rushes lining the banks. After sipping at a hot mug of tea, I walked up to Colber Bridge on the common beneath Sturminster Newton. With little sign of life from the village above, I slid down the muddy bank and into the cool water. The shadow of gudgeon darted through the murk and the odd weed tickled me as I swam under the bridge and down towards Bather's Island, the site of the old river swimming club.

Sturminster Newton is situated at an historic fording point of the Stour as it runs down through the Blackmore Vale, classic Dorset dairy country. It was at Colber Bridge that Thomas Hardy and his wife Emma spent their happiest years walking and swimming by the river. Their friend, English poet William Barnes, also lived nearby for many years and wrote about the 'cloty Stour' – filled with its yellow water lilies and arrowhead much as it is today – in his *Poems of Rural Life in the Dorset Dialect*, written in the thick, wonderful, old Dorset tongue.

Another popular Dorset Stour swimming hole is ten miles downstream at Pamphill towards Wimborne Minster. Here an old Roman ford, footbridge and weir create a large space for swimmers to paddle and play. Upstream the waters are wider and deeper.

Like many other southern English rivers, the Stour's wildlife suffered a great decline with the intensification of dairy farming in the 1970s. Lapwing, snipe and redshank all became

103

104

101

rare. The river today is much recovered, but a new project – organised by the rural heritage charity, Common Ground – is keeping the issue of river ecology in people's minds with a project to make music inspired by the river.

If river music is your thing then St Peter's Church, set alongside the River Brue at Lydford, is noted for its choral tradition. Dorothy, an energetic, silver-haired woman in her 60s, has swum here since she was a child. 'I loved listening to the choir practise as we glided past the blossoms in spring. It was like a natural baptism.'

The smell of ozone from the tumbling water and the swooping manoeuvres of the damselflies are sure signs of how clean the river is today. Directly below the old weir is a small pool where children paddle and play. On warm weekends in summer you might find the neat lawns of the churchyard laid out with deckchairs and towels and a mixture of swimmers and spectators, of all ages, jumping in from the bridge or swimming breaststroke back and forth along the blossomed reach, pulling themselves out between the two cherry trees, then sipping Earl Grey tea on the grass.

Somerset literally means 'land of the summer people', because the area could not be populated in the winter due to the great sea floods that inundated the levels. Lydford stands on the edge of this flood plain. From here it's only a couple of miles to Baltonsborough Flights, another swimming hole, where the river drops down a weir via a large pool before beginning its journey to the sea, through the heady blossoms of cider groves, willow and teasel.

'An' zwallows skim
the water, bright
Wi' whirlèn froth,
in western light;
Wi' whirlèn stwone,
an' streamèn flour,
Did goo the mill
by cloty Stour.'
William Barnes, 1862

101

101 WEST LYDFORD, R BRUE

A pretty stretch of river running by the church lawns, with rope swing.

➔ West Lydford is just off the A37, near the B3153 junction (Lydford-on-Fosse). Footpath runs through churchyard to weir and then footbridge. Better views and a rope swing via track on opposite bank. Please help keep churchyard litter free.

2 mins, 51.0846, -2.6236 🏊🚶‍♂️🚻

102 BALTONSBOROUGH, R BRUE

Large, stepped weir cascade on River Brue with pool beneath.

➔ Follow river footpath downstream from West Lydford 2 miles or find footpath S of Baltonsborough, on R.

5 mins, 51.1019, -2.6473 🏊📓

103 PARCHEY BRIDGE, CHEDZOY

King's Sedgemoor 'drain' is actually a very clean and wild river, albeit a bit straight.

➔ From M5 J23 follow A39 Glastonbury, then R at lights, A39 Bridgewater. Turn L signed Chedzoy. Turn L in Chedzoy at the T-juction (Front Street). Cycle Route 3.

5 mins, 51.1353, -2.9278 🏊🚶‍♂️🚲🏕️

104 STURMINSTER NEWTON, R STOUR

An open stretch of the Stour with grassy banks by Colber Bridge. Water is a little weedy and slow, but clean and deep.

➔ Walk down The Row by the library and village hall. At end of the cul-de-sac (100m) pass through iron gate and follow footpath down the hill and straight over (150m). Long swims in either direction.

5 mins, 50.9280, -2.3105 🏊🚻

105 FIDDLEFORD MANOR, R STOUR

Mill pool and sluices by old manor.

➔ Signed Fiddleford Manor on L, a mile E of Sturminster Newton (A357). Free car park and free entry to the lovely 14th-century 'solar' with extraordinary ancient roof.

5 mins, 50.9215, -2.2855 🏛️🏊

106 WIMBORNE MINSTER, R STOUR

A wide, popular river pool with a riverside beach, footbridge and a small weir. Good walks or swims. Kingston Lacy NT, beech avenue and Babury Rings nearby.

➔ Heading W out of Wimborne on the B3082 Blandford road, turn L down Cowgrove Rd, signed for the football club.

Continue ¾ mile to find small parking area and river on L.

2 mins, 50.8000, -2.0076 🏊🚻

107 MORETON FORD, R FROME

A wide, gravel ford and shallow pool, lined with willows and tree swings. Popular with families – the long footbridge is good for Pooh Sticks. Next to the church where Lawrence of Arabia was buried.

➔ Signed on L off the B3390, S of Tolpuddle. Turn L at Moreton Tea Rooms (well worth a visit – a regular winner of Dorset tea room of the year DT2 8RH, 01929 463647).

2 mins, 50.7047, -2.2763 🍴🚻

108 WAREHAM BRIDGE, R FROME

A popular spot for swimming, picnics and boating on a hot summer day.

➔ Wareham old bridge is in the centre of the town, off the A351. The downstream side is best for putting boats in the water but you can also walk and swim upstream to find a bit more tranquillity.

2 mins, 50.6839, -2.1095 🏊🚣🚻

© Landacre Bridge

Somerset Exmoor and River Barle

Heather-topped hills, bracken-covered combes, tumbling waterfalls and wooded river valleys prompted the Victorians to name the magnificent scenery and quiet charm of Exmoor the 'Little Switzerland of England'.

Straddling north Devon and Somerset, this ancient landscape of iron-age barrows, hut circles and high flat hills was popular with the first humans to colonise Britain after the ice age. Exmoor is now Britain's least-visited National Park but contains several small and delightful swimming rivers.

An old friend Hue – and his dog Felix – had offered to take me to one of their swimming holes near Cow Castle, a pre-historic hill fort on a remote part of the River Barle. We met at Simonsbath, an auspicious-sounding place for the job at hand, and dropped down through Birchcleave woods to the river. The Barle runs in a narrow vale lined with bright orange asphodels for much of the two miles to Cow Castle. It is a shallow stream that twists and turns between avenues of birch and the ruins of old mine workings. As it reaches the conical hill of the fort it deepens and slows into a pool.

Swimming against the current of this small buffeting stream was harder than we had anticipated and soon we had a competition going to see who could beat the river and make it upstream. We then tried to out-swim the dog. Once we were

113

110

111

all thoroughly exhausted we ran up to the top of the castle knoll and collapsed on the grass, the wet dog panting and the evening sun glowing low.

From here the course of the Barle winds its way another two miles before it reaches Sherdon Hutch and Landacre Bridge. These have long been popular Exmoor bathing and picnicking spots with shallows by the bridge and a deeper hole at the confluence of the Sherdon brook upstream. According to Hue, locals believe there is a hot spring somewhere along its course near here that makes the water especially warm. Perhaps the hot spring was broken the next day because the water was pretty invigorating at Landacre. Despite this, several families had taken up positions along the bank. At Withypool, a few miles further on, barbeques and picnics were in full swing and a small flotilla of inflatable boats was in operation.

At Tarr Steps there were even more people. The clapper bridge here is truly impressive. Constructed from megalithic flat stones laid end to end and propped up on boulders, it is one of the best-known monuments on Exmoor and several theories claim it dates from the Bronze Age, although others date it to around 1400ad. One myth has it that the Devil built it to win a bet and swore he would kill anyone who tried to cross it. To test his curse the villagers sent a cat across. That was promptly vaporised so the terrified locals sent the parson across next. Although the Devil swore and intimidated him, the parson swore back and finally the Devil succumbed and allowed people to pass, except when he wanted to sunbathe.

Between, above and below the flagstones, children were chasing minnows, skimming stones and getting thoroughly wet. I decided to find some peace and headed upstream a couple of miles through the beautiful National Nature Reserve. The woods here are internationally renowned for their mosses, liverworts and lichens, including a type of moss found in burrows, which appears to glow in the dark. They are also home to the rare barbastelle bat, which breeds in the cracks of old trees. Feeling wonderfully relaxed away from everyone I found a perfect pool, not too deep, some way down from a footbridge. Here I swam, disturbed by no one, not even the Devil.

109

109 COW CASTLE, R BARLE
Remote, small pool in the babbling River Barle at foot of the impressive Cow Castle hill fort, halfway between Simonsbath and Landacre Bridge.
→ From Simonsbath (good pub Hunter's Inn, 01643 831506) take footpath opposite and follow river's L bank 2 miles. 40 mins, 51.1237, -3.7254 ▲ ▣

110 LANDACRE BRIDGE, R BARLE
Stone bridge, grassy river banks and popular Exmoor spot for paddling.
→ Signed Landacre/S Molton off B3223 near Exford, just N of turning for Withypool (also a popular place for paddling and minnowing 51.0919, -3.6351). For deeper pools continue up moor road and take track on R after 500m and follow down to river 500m (Sherdon Hutch, at confluence with a smaller stream 51.1119, -3.7078). 2 mins, 51.1121, -3.6922 ▦ ▨

111 TARR STEPS, R BARLE
Ancient stone clapper bridge, in deep wood at end of lane. Very popular with children for paddling. Deeper pool with open grassy banks about ½ mile (15 mins) upstream through woods on L bank, on corner below footbridge.
→ Signed off B3223 (Liscombe). Very good food and accommodation at Inn by waterside. Tarr Farm Inn, Dulverton, TA22 9PY, 01643 851507
15 mins, 51.0820, -3.6291 ▦ ▮ ▨

112 POOL BRIDGE, HORNER WOOD
Remote woodland campsite with stream and paddling. Deeper downstream.
→ Turn L in Porlock by museum, signed Doverhay. Take second (hard) R after a mile. Continue 2 miles to the hairpin bend/ stream. (TA24 8JS, 01643 86252).
15 mins, 51.1906, -3.6142 ▦ ▲

113 PINKERY POND, CHALLACOMBE
Old reservoir on high, lonely moor.
→ Between Challacombe and Simonsbath (B3358) find gate and tarmac track off road at bridge (Pinkery ENPA) and follow for a mile. The Long Stone megalith can be found on moor, a 1½ mile boggy trudge to the NW.
20 mins, 51.1658, -3.8275 ▨ ▲ ▢

114 WASHFIELD WEIR, R EXE
Weir and pools in secluded fields, though reported gated 2016.
→ 1½ N of Tiverton on A396, turn L shortly after water works. Follow lane, then rough track, to weir. Shallow below, deep above.
5 mins, 50.9337, -3.5042 ▦ ▨

115 RIVER CULM, CULMSTOCK
Riverside woodland and meadow with places to paddle and dip.
→ Take the footpath by the bridge, opposite the Culm Valley Inn (01884 840354, EX15 3JJ) and follow the river downstream for up to a mile.
15 mins, 50.9157, -3.2845 ▨ ▮

116 WIMBLEBALL LAKE, UPTON
Large lake on the fringes of Exmoor.
→ The W edge has a campsite, visitor area and easily accessible shore. The E shore is secluded, shallower and more gently shelving. Cycle path around shore. No swimming but some people do, discreetly.
20 mins, 51.0617, -3.4473 ▣ ▨ ▢ ▢

118 Long Pool, East Lyn River

Devon Exmoor and the Lyn

Lynmouth was the site of one of the most devastating floods in British history. The upper reaches of the River Lyn sweep through the peaceful Doone Valley, the setting for the famous novel *Lorna Doone*. There are good pools and waterfalls along its entire course.

The River Lyn took on ferocious force on the night of 15th August 1952. An intense tropical storm rolled in from the Atlantic and dropped nine inches of rain on the already waterlogged moors. None of the rivers could cope and banks burst all over Exmoor. At Hawkridge the massive Tarr Steps were washed a hundred yards downstream, and in another village a row of ten cottages were completely swept away. But the worst devastation was on the Lyn at Lynmouth where an avalanche of churning trees and boulders destroyed over 100 buildings and 29 bridges. 38 cars were washed out to sea and in total 34 people died. New evidence now suggests that the extreme weather events of August 1952 may have been a result of top secret cloud-seeding experiments taking place at the time off the Devon coast.

As you stand at Watersmeet, a Victorian fishing lodge, now a quaint National Trust-run tea shop, it's sobering to think of

121

120

119

the force of this water and debris piling down the hillside. Yet, ironically, the Lyn has a long history of water power. In 1890 it was one of the first places in the world to install a hydroelectric generator which provided lighting and powered an ice-maker for the local fishing crews.

The main attractions at Watersmeet now are the simple waterfalls and woodland walks. The closest falls are impressive and popular so if you're not shy why not take a dip right there? If you'd prefer to be a little more discreet then follow the river path a couple of miles upstream to the little-known Long Pool, a deep narrow gorge which can be found in the woods beneath the path. Further on the path continues to Rockford and before you get there you'll find several more pools with small cliffs to jump from. As I was exploring I met two families kitted out with wetsuits and rubber dinghies. They had spent much of the afternoon playing in these shady pools and said it was more fun than being on the nearby beach.

In Rockford you'll find the well-known brewery and real ales of the Rockford Inn. Follow the river further upstream to Malmsmead to discover the notorious setting of *Lorna Doone: an Exmoor Romance* by R. D. Blackmore, one of the bestselling books of all time. The church at nearby Oare is where the novel's famous conclusion was set.

This land of murder and outlaws has tumbling streams and dense woods. Wildlife abounds throughout the area. Red deer, ponies and sheep graze freely, watched over by falcons, buzzards and even the rare merlin. Cloud Farm is a great place to stay, with pony trekking, a campsite and river paddling in the Badgworthy, a tributary of the Lyn. But on a hot summer day Deer Park Pool is the place to be, a mile further up the stream. As you come out of the woods and into an open grassland clearing you'll find a circular plunge pool flowing under a large ash tree. Although small, it's deep enough for a good splash, as my friend, Hue, and his dog, Felix, demonstrated. The path continues on and up to more Doone country on Brendon Moor, or you may prefer to return to the farm shop for one of their famous *après*-swim cream teas.

118

117 WATERSMEET, LYNMOUTH
A fine series of pools and falls. The NT tearoom has been serving teas in the old fishing lodge since 1901: try the Exmoor speciality, whortleberry jam. A good location to watch salmon leaping; see otters, red deer and buzzards, too. Bluebells in May.

→ 300m upstream there is a series of rocky pools down beneath the path on R. Another ½ mile, before Ash Bridge, find several beachy areas and deep corner pools. Lots of paddling for kids. Another 1½ miles upstream leads to Long Pool.

5 mins, 51.2262, -3.7908 🔒 ⛱

118 LONG POOL, ROCKFORD
Deep, long secluded pool in a small, verdant ravine beneath a waterfall.

→ From Watersmeet, or descend from excellent Rockford Inn (EX35 6PT, 01598 741214, turn onto B3223 from A39, just N of Lynton, then immediately L up steep narrow lane). Or for a real adventure do the whole route to Watersmeet in wetsuits, but beware the various waterfalls and drops.

15 mins, 51.2203, -3.7873 🔒 ⛱ ⛱

119 BADGWORTHY POOL, MALMSMEAD
Charming but small plunge pool underneath shallow waterfall and big tree in popular Doone Valley woodland walk.

→ Malmsmead is a tiny village off A39 Lynmouth–Minehead road and is at the heart of Doone country (tea rooms). Park here or drive ½ mile up to Cloud Farm campsite to use their shop or campsite (EX35 6NU, 01598 741278). From here cross footbridge, follow path 1 mile upstream until woods clear and path bears R up onto moor. On L, under a lip of bank, find small pool by large tree.

20 mins, 51.1951, -3.7285 ⛱

120 SQUABMOOR LAKE, BUDLEIGH
Lily pond and reservoir high on East Budleigh Common.

→ Head N on B3179 from Budleigh Salterton. About 1½ miles from roundabout (with B3178) turn R at brown sign for 'reservoir' (opposite farm shop sign). Pass pretty Bystock lily pond on L to find parking on R. Continue on track through trees down to reservoir.

5 mins, 50.6486, -3.3592 ❓

121 COLATON RALEIGH, R OTTER
Lovely little beach and deep corner pool beneath red cliffs with ivy and ferns.

→ Turn down Church Rd off B3178, opposite Woods Village Shop. Pass church and follow footpath from botton of road (near farm) to river and downstream for 5 mins. You could also try the beaches 1 mile N at the bend 50.6862,-3.2957 (footpath off Church Rd).

10 mins, 50.6745, -3.2925 ⛱ ⛱

122 FLUXTON WEIR, R OTTER
Good pool above the weir in pastures S of Ottery St Mary. Interesting old mill house on way.

→ Follow signs for Tipton St John from A3052/Sidmouth, pass Red Lion pub and bridge and up Tipton Vale to find parking behind bus stop (½ mile) and footpath beyond on R. Weir is just under a mile, 5 mins beyond Fluxton Mill. Continue 1 mile (20 mins) up river to a deep corner pool on the inside of a deep hairpin bend/oxbow (50.7397, -3.2827).

20 mins, 50.7267, -3.2891 ⛱

Roadford Lake

North Devon Tarka Trails

Tarka the Otter, one of Britain's best-loved nature stories, was set along the north Devon rivers of the Torridge and Taw. I followed the rivers, from highland pools to wooded river valleys, swimming in Tarka's paw-steps.

Henry Williamson was a disillusioned young man when he arrived on his racing motorcycle from London to live in a tiny cobb cottage on the north Devon coast. He had just returned from the horrors of the First World War, weary and nerve-wracked, at odds with his family and desperate to be a writer. He lived alone, hermit-fashion, tramping about the countryside, swimming in brooks and often sleeping out. The doors and windows of his new cottage were never closed, and his strange family of dogs, cats, gulls, buzzards and magpies were free to come and go as they pleased. This was to become the sanctuary for the real-life Tarka: an orphaned otter cub which took up refuge with Williamson.

High on north Dartmoor, the headwaters of the Torridge and the Taw provide an excellent vantage point to survey Williamson's famous 'Tarka Country'. Here on the East Okement, an important tributary of the Torridge, the army blew out a small but beautiful pool at Cullever Steps, just below Scarey Tor, as somewhere for servicemen to cool off during hot summers. It can still be reached via the decaying network of moorland military roads. As you bathe here, among the grazing wild ponies, Devonshire's rolling countryside unfolds like a soft counterpane below, with the steep wooded river valleys of

123

127

125

the Torridge and the broader, gentler reaches of the Taw just discernible to the north.

At Halsdon Nature Reserve, ten miles away on the Torridge, the otter population is almost back to its pre-1950 levels. Historically Devon has been an international stronghold for otters, but in the 1950s and '60s their numbers crashed as industry and farming intensified. Watercourses became contaminated with chemicals and farm runoff. By the late 1960s the local otters were almost extinct. A massive clean-up over the last thirty years has had a major impact on the health of all British rivers. Now at Halsdon you'll see white-legged damselflies, kingfishers, sand martins, herons, dippers and grey wagtails. There are even freshwater pearl mussels.

Halsdon won't welcome you to swim as it disturbs the wildlife, but downstream, near Little Torrington, you can wade across the river at the old ford near Undercleave. This is a remote spot and the river here runs wide, fast and shallow under a tunnel of tall trees. Great Torrington Common, below Great Torrington town, is an accessible stretch of fast-flowing, shady river with some deeper holes. It was here that Tarka learned to swim, to play and to hunt and also first encountered the poachers with their trap lights like 'little moons which he could touch and bite'.

Seven miles to the east the Taw is a very different kind of river and runs through flatter, more open countryside. Behind the remote Chapelton Station on the Barnstaple line you'll find a meadow and footbridge with good access to the river from open fields. The river is wide, flowing across smooth gravels with a perfect current against which you can swim.

Bathing in the rivers and streams of this area was one of Henry Williamson's greatest pleasures. He brought up his children at Shallowford, six miles to the east, and spent much of his time in the river Bray fishing or swimming. He describes in his memoirs lying still in the golden gravels of the ford, watching the clear, cold water foaming over his body. It took him a long time to get over his experiences of the war and feel at peace with his world but it was at moments like this, he said, that he could finally feel 'a part of the great stream of life'.

123

123 SHEEPWASH, R TORRIDGE

Superb section of the young Torridge.
There is a large, deep swimming hole
just below the bridge. A little upstream
there are many more sandy beaches and
deep pools in open meadow (Sheepwash
Woodland). Charming village with square
and fine pub (Half Moon Inn, EX21 5NE,
01409 231376). A good place to pick up
the Tarka cycle trail.

→ Sheepwash is signed off A3072. Find
path from bridge on downstream, L bank.
For meadows continue 300m up lane
towards village and find entrance on L. For
best pools and beaches bear L.
5 mins, 50.8314, -4.1498 🏊🚩🚴

124 BEAFORD BRIDGE, R TORRIDGE

Remote wooded stretch with ladder steps
down to deeper water above old weir.

→ Between Merton (A386) and Beaford
(A3124). Climb lane 300m from Beaford
Bridge (dir Beaford) and follow footpath on
R for 10 mins down through woods. Also a
good place for canoe launch.
10 mins, 50.9083, -4.0699 🏔️❓

125 CHAPELTON STATION, TAW

Open meadowland by footbridge behind
small halt on Barnstaple branch line.
Wide, fast-flowing, but mainly shallow.
Good for swimming against the current.
Popular with fishermen.

→ 5 miles S of Barnstaple on A377 (dir
Exeter) find station on L, after the chapel.
Walk through gate to L of station building,
over railway line and across field to
footbridge.
5 mins, 51.0173, -4.0228 🏊❓

126 ROADFORD LAKE

Pastoral reservoir lake surrounded by
meadows. Some dip discretely in its
warm waters from the E shore. There
is camping on western shore near the
sailing club.

→ Follow the approach road from A30 but
turn R before the dam, onto a lane signed
'Clovelly Inn'. There's a car park picnic area
on the L after ½ mile, or continue, bearing
L, to find another after a mile (50.7026,
-4.2126). Do not disturb the fishermen!
10 mins, 50.6932, -4.2270 🏔️❓📷

127 CULLEVER STEPS, EAST OKEMENT

Small plunge pool in a pretty, rocky valley
below Scarey Tor. Grass for picnics and
large rocks for sunbathing.

→ From Okehampton town centre follow
red army signs S to 'Camp'. After 1½ miles
arrive at T-junction on moor (army camp
on R) and turn L on old army 'ring road' with
many potholes. After 1 mile, up and over a
hill, 50m before the bridge/ford, find rough
track off to L. Park and follow track down
to another ford, 800m. Follow stream L
another 300m down to pool.
15 mins, 50.7148, -3.9769 🏊🏊🏔️

128 MELDON QUARRY LAKE

Superb quarry pool with rope swing and
steep rock cliffs. On cycle path.

→ Travel SW from Okehampton on the
B3260 (A30 direction). Meldon Quarry is
signed on L (opposite garage) and leads
over the A30 to a car park and information
board. Walk ½ mile down across stream to
lake. Continue up the stream 300m to find
a small waterfall pool, or head up to the
reservoir (500m) for a big swim!
10 mins, 50.7109, -4.0350 🚴🛶🏊🔺

East Dartmoor and the Teign

The most spectacular pools on the Dartmoor Teign are the Victorian 'Salmon Leaps' in woods beneath Castle Drogo. Three rectangular square pools cascade, one into the other, like stacked glasses of champagne.

Castle Drogo was the last castle built in England. Constructed in the 1920s by merchant millionaire Julius Drewe – self-styled as Baron Drogo de Teign – it stands high over the wooded gorge of the Teign. As part of his landscaping project the 'Baron' installed several weirs to create river pools to help stock the river with salmon. The first pool is a long, peaceful stretch of river which runs beneath an elegant suspension bridge. Drewe had a problem because the dam that creates the pool also stopped the upward migration of spawning salmon so to solve this he built an impressive series of salmon 'leaps'.

While the peaceful pool above is popular with the local girls, the salmon leaps are popular with the lads. Each pool is about four feet deep, with a flat concrete bottom. The turbulence literally lifts you off your feet but you soon get the knack of bobbing about in these mountain jacuzzis. The water bubbles wildly as it tumbles from one pool to the other, massaging and pummelling all the muscles in your body.

135

133

129

This river stretch has plenty of Dartmoor legend. A pile of stones up above in the woods is called the Pixie Parlour, after a struggle between a farmhand and a creature from the underworld. There is also a rocking 'logan' stone in the riverbed downstream of the leaps thought to belong to the Druids.

Another mile or so downstream you'll find a second weir and river pool before arriving at Fingle Bridge and its pub. This narrow, medieval packhorse bridge was built to service the gorge's once busy industries: corn milling, charcoal burning and bark ripping. It has long been a local beauty, paddling and picnicking spot and even in 1894 the unknown author of *A Gentleman's Walking Tour of Dartmoor* suggests it is a 'great place for Pic-Nics. We were there in July and found two Pic-Nics going on at once to the tune of a hideous German band'.

Little has changed and if you want more peace and quiet the weir behind Chagford is charming. Or why not visit the town-run swimming pool? It's fed by the river, which comes straight off the moor, though the health-and-safety people still insist that chlorine is added. It was dug in 1947 as a co-operative effort by the village and some of the original old boys still come down to make tea. These days it has solar heaters and an indoor cafe, in case it rains.

An important source of the Teign is Blackaton Brook, which rises by the windswept stone circle of Little Hound Tor, back up on the moor. From here it gathers momentum through Raybarrow Hill and Throwleigh Common before arriving at the tiny and rather secret Shilley Pool. In this sheltered and sunny glen bathers and nymphs have built up a low dam to create a perfect bath.

The water flows in across wide stone slabs, perfect for sunbathing, and the depth reaches about three feet. Lying in the stream, the current scooping eddies along one's length, in the warmth of the afternoon sun, you feel a very small part of some much larger, more wonderful thing. Dartmoor has many secret bathing spots, often difficult to find, and this is one of its most special. Bathe here and you drink in an elixir of all of Dartmoor's magic brew.

129

129 SALMON LEAPS, R TEIGN

Long river pool above weir in woods
beneath Castle Drogo. Three large,
square, smooth-lined plunge pools
cascade down into each other. Great for a
pummelling massage!

→ 150m S of Sandy Park Inn (Chagford,
TQ13 8JW, 01647 433267, W of Castle
Drogo/Drewsteignton) find footpath and
follow the river downstream into woods,
½ mile.
10 mins, 50.6926, -3.8097

130 FINGLE BRIDGE, R TEIGN

A deep, thickly-wooded gorge, 1 mile
downstream from the Salmon Leaps.

→ Walk upstream 5 mins (200m) from the
bridge and pub (Fingle Bridge Inn, EX6 6PW,
01647 281287) to find a deep pool above
a small weir. 1 mile E of Castle Drogo/
Drewsteignton.
5 mins, 50.6955, -3.7811

131 CHAGFORD LIDO

River-fed swimming pool, open May- Sept
→ Chagford, 01647 432929, TQ13 8DA
2 mins, 50.6808, -3.8326

132 SHILLEY POOL, THROWLEIGH

Small plunge pool, falls and stream on the
edge of the moor. Paddling for children
and a great place for picnics.

→ 1 mile NW of Throwleigh, park and
find rough track on L, 100m before
cattle grid and stream bridge, just after
Clannonborough Cottage. Follow Blackaton
Brook up onto moor ½ mile.
10 mins, 50.7050, -3.9093

133 HAYTOR QUARRY

Sheltered, south-facing, sun-trap under
popular Haytor Rocks. There are two
pools big enough for a short swim. Both
have clean, waist-high water and smooth,
rounded stones on the bottom. Look for
the granite tramway that runs from here
to Yarner Wood.

→ Park at Lower Haytor by the Vistor
Centre, (B3387, 3 miles from Bovey
Tracey). There's a visitor centre at this car
park and usually an ice-cream van. Cross
the road and walk 500m to the piles of
broken rocks below the tor.
10 mins, 50.5835, -3.7529

134 BECKA BROOK LAKES

Two tiny secret lakes in beautiful ancient
woodland beneath Hound Tor.

→ Hound Tor car park is on lanes between
Widecombe and Manaton. Walk 300m E of
Greator rocks, to find lakes in the wooded
valley below.
30 mins, 50.5931, -3.7655

135 FERNWORTHY LAKE, CHAGFORD

Remote forested reservoir. Shores may
be sandy or muddy, depending on water
level. Look for bilberries in forest.

→ 5 miles SW of Chagford. Continue right
around the lake until you come to a large
wooden hangar. Park and head down past
the bird hide to the R.
5 mins, 50.6387,- 3.8930

136 KENNICK AND TRENCHFORD

Secluded reservoir lakes deep in conifer
woods. Shallow, clear and warm water
with shelving beach access.

→ Second R off A382, 2m N of Bovey
Tracy. No Swimming signs and occasional
fishermen, but people do dip discreetly.
5 mins, 50.6333, -3.6829

Staverton Weir

South Dartmoor and the Dart

River pools and sandy bays, oak gorges and towering tors. The River Dart is the setting for Charles Kingsley's The *Water Babies* and one of the most beautiful wild-swimming rivers in the UK.

In a deep gorge far upstream of Newbridge, lying on the flat hot rocks by a gurgling river, I am miles from anywhere. Dense woodland tumbles down the side of the moor, a light spray lifts off the water and the forest twitters with birdsong.

Somewhere along here the hero of *The Water Babies*, Tom the chimney sweep, was lulled into the water by the fairies. Wrongly accused of theft he escaped across Lewthwaite moor before falling into a deep, exhausted sleep by the river. In his new life under water he goes in search of the other water babies and meets many river creatures on the way: the foolish trout, the wise old salmon, the crafty otter and the trumpeting, happy gnats. He learns many things from them before eventually finding the girl he truly loves.

In the pub in the village of Holne, birthplace of Charles Kingsley, you get the sense they're a little bored with the story but they know the good swimming holes if you ask nicely. Holne Pool is ten minutes' walk down through the fields. You'll find a large rock by a small waterfall, partly in sunshine, partly in shade, a place made for lazy picnics and sunny afternoons.

Exploring further downstream brings you first to Horseshoe Falls and then Salters Pool and within twenty minutes you'll arrive at the car park of Newbridge where a narrow medieval bridge crosses the river. There's a National Park visitors' hut and an easy walk downstream to the green lawns of Spitchwick Common. With its easy access, gentle pools and

139

140

145

good swimming it's popular among families and can be busy on a summer day.

Head back up the other side of the river for a good half an hour and you'll arrive at Wellsfoot Island. On the far side of this romantic piece of woodland there's a red sandy beach in a bend of the river under Holne cliff. This is a fabulous deep pool by a coppice of spindly birch. Feel the fine-grain sand running with the current between your toes.

But the best pools are also the most remote, miles upstream of Newbridge, in the forest halfway to Dartmeet, below Mel Tor. These legendary swimming holes are surrounded by large flat rocks with chutes between them for floating down on rubber rings. Whether you walk up the river from Holne, down from Dartmeet, or you scramble over the steep slopes from Mel Tor, it's quite a trek. You should be able to find your own pool – there are plenty to choose from.

While I mused I suddenly saw three wet-suited swimmers on rings riding the river current who must have come from Dartmeet, at least two miles upstream. 'Is there anywhere good to swim up there?' I called out, ever searching for the perfect pool. 'Everywhere's good to swim!' they replied. Apparently the Dartmeet-to-Newbridge run is popular with the most daring local swimmers but not generally recommended unless water levels are very low and you know where the waterfalls are. The sport of 'hydrosurfing' is catching on in France, where they gear you up with helmets and padded suits. One local told me that the best swimmers here do it without anything at all, just in their trunks, and have learnt to curl their bodies like eels to pass in between the rocks and slip unharmed over the waterfalls. They can feel the micro-currents with their skin and move through the water like otters. If you're looking for the Dartmoor waterbabies, all grown up, I think these might be them.

'Tom…was so hot and thirsty, and longed so to be clean for once, that he tumbled himself as quick as he could into the clear cool stream. And he had not been in it two minutes before he fell fast asleep, into the quietest, sunniest, cosiest sleep that ever he had in his life…' from *The Water Babies*, 1863

138

137 SHARRAH POOL, R DART

Sharrah is the largest and best pool on this wild and wonderful river stretch in the forested Dart Valley nature reserve.

→ Descend to river from Holne and bear L along a good path for 40 mins to find this long narrow pool. 500m upstream are the Mel Pools (50.5346, -3.8447), a range of smaller pools, including a few good chutes if you have an inner tube.

40 mins, 50.5301, -3.8396 🏊 ⛺

138 BELLPOOL ISLAND, R DART

Pretty wooded island and deep secret pool with old iron ladder scaling the cliff.

→ As for Sharrah Pool, but 300m downstream on L bank branch.

30 mins, 50.5272, -3.8363 🏊 🔵

139 HORSESHOE FALLS, HOLNE

Small, easily accessible, waterfall and natural jacuzzi. Large rock for sunbathing.

→ On footpath down through fields from Holne (Church House Inn, TQ13 7SJ, 01364 631208 with ancient oak for drinks after).

15 mins, 50.5195, -3.8200 🅿 🏊

140 WELLSFOOT ISLAND, NEW BRIDGE

Wonderful wooded island with secluded red-sand beach shelving into deep pool.

→ Follow the river upstream from Newbridge car park side (river's L bank) just under 1 mile, to reach island with bridge.

20 mins, 50.5170, -3.8274 🔵 🏊 ❓

141 SPITCHWICK COMMON

The most popular and accessible Dart swimming location, especially in summer, when litter can be a problem (take some away). Flat, grassy areas.

→ From Ashburton A38 follow signs to River Dart Country Park. Park at New Bridge, cross road and head downstream 300m. Swim 1 mile down to Lovers Leap.

5 mins, 50.5261, -3.8141 🏊 🔵 🍴

142 HEMBURY WOODS, R DART

Ancient oak woodland leads down to a deep, secret stretch of the river Dart.

→ From A38 Buckfastleigh, cross Dart bridge, turn immediately R, signed Buckfast, then R fork, signed Hembury Woods. After bridge, park on L.

15 mins, 50.5026, -3.7912 🏊 🔵

143 STAVERTON WEIR, R DART

Deep and straight above the weir, more secluded with a tree jump downstream.

→ Park at steam-train station and continue downstream, beyond weir. Return loop via Sea Trout Inn (TQ9 6PA, 01803 762274).

10 mins, 50.4613, -3.7051 🏊 🔵 🅿

144 PILES COPSE, CORNWOOD, ERME

Remnant of ancient oak woodland with exquisite stream and waterfall.

→ Quickest access is from road end NE of hamlet of Tor (via Ivybridge then Cornwood, 50.4337, -3.9377). Follow track up around waterworks and around hillside, 1 mile, dropping down to the stream. Continue on to Red Lake, 4 miles.

20 mins, 50.4417, -3.9113 🏊 ⛺

145 RED LAKE, HUNTINGDON WARREN

Possibly the most remote swim on Dartmoor. Two large lakes with hillock.

→ 6-mile route, possible on a bicycle, along the old mineral tramway (Two Moors Way) from Harford, via Leftlake Mires lake.

60 mins, 50.4863, -3.9107 🚶 ⛺ 🏊 🔲

Tucker's Pool, Lydford Viaduct

West Dartmoor and the Lyd

The romantics of the early nineteenth century loved waterfalls and Lydford was a famous stop on the Grand Tour, particularly when Europe was closed for business during the Napoleonic Wars. Prior to that, it was famous as a hide-out of a large family of outlaws – the Gubbins – who terrorised the neighbourhood and stole sheep from the farms of Dartmoor.

I dreamt of verdant waterfalls as I camped by the swollen river Dart that night. A persistent drizzle had started, pattering gently on the tent and raising the river to a roar. By morning it had abated but a warm, sloth-like mist had descended. I met up with a local friend and after a hot pot of tea we decided to head for the relative shelter of Lydford Gorge, a series of rounded pots and thundering waterfalls carved deep into ancient rocks on the west of the moor.

We took our dip in a discreet pool a safe distance above the waterfalls. Under the road bridge and upstream, where the footpath ends at a shallow ford, there's a small plunge pool called Tucker's Pool that shelves into the deep entrance of a narrow ravine. We swam up it a little way, large droplets of water falling on us from the vegetation and forest above. It was only a few feet wide in places and the rock walls were smooth and sheer with few hand grips.

The main part of the gorge is hugely impressive but certainly no place to get into the water, even if you were allowed. A

150

153

151

narrow chasm cuts its way deep into the grey Devonshire slate where grinding gyrations of river stones churn out huge, smooth cavities. The National Trust has repaired a Victorian viewing gangway that takes you right into the heart of one of the pots and you can stand over and stare down into the almighty whirlpools of the great Devil's Cauldron. Further downstream there are paddling places and the impressive White Lady Falls which tips a thirty metre plume on sightseers below, its great white globules as hard as hail.

During a warming and thoroughly waterproofing late fry-up at the hotel in Lydford - coats and maps hung out to dry on radiators all around - the waitress explained the route to some nice pools she knew further upstream on the moor beneath the stone-built landmark of Widgery Cross. This 1887 commemoration of Queen Victoria's golden jubilee proved elusive to find in the muggy mist but we were feeling rather diehard. We followed the small river for several hundred yards. Startled sheep loomed out of the bracken. Finally, beneath a craggy outcrop and a memorial to a lost soldier, we came to the most beautiful of mountain pools. As the rain thickened the surface broke out in a melody of concentric rings and we leapt about among the rocks, splashing and squealing in the stream.

By midday the skies were clearing and we made for Crazywell Pool high on the moor above the prison at Princetown. This is a tin-mining area dating back almost a thousand years. Tin was so important to the Dartmoor economy that three independent 'stannary' parliaments were established in the sixteenth century with a dedicated stannary prison at Lydford. Crazy Well is a quarry that was probably dug about the same time. Now it's one of the few 'natural' lakes on Dartmoor. As such it has collected more than its fair share of legends. Its level is said to change with the tides at Plymouth and, of course, it is said to be bottomless (ten sets of weighted bell ropes from Walkhampton Church were tied end-to-end and still no bottom was found). To us though, on a blustery August afternoon, clouds racing across a blue sky, it was simply a wonderful moor-top lake, sheltered and wide and finally sunny, with views out over the world.

150

145 WIDGERY CROSS, R LYD

Small plunge pools in moorland valley beneath Brat Tor/Widgery Cross. Tumbling stream, gorse and heather.

→ Turn off A386 by Dartmoor Inn (EX20 4AY), opposite turning for Lydford. Follow lane to car park and walk up onto the moor. After 800m meet stream and follow its R bank 400m to find pool under bench and plaque on R up under tall rocky outcrop.

20 mins, 50.6500, -4.0772 🏔 🥾

146 TUCKER'S POOL, LYDFORD

Lesser known pool in jungly terrain, just upstream of the famous NT gorge.

→ Take dead-end lane opp war memorial to 50.6456, -4.1031. Follow footpath to old viaduct then downstream on perilous path through gorge 200m to pool. (Cross stream for a small path into NT Lydford Gorge).

5 mins, 50.6416, -4.1107 🧗

147 CRAZY WELL POOL

A spring-fed, mystical, moor-top lake excavated by medieval tin miners.

→ Ascend from head of Burrator reservoir.

35 mins, 50.5167, -4.0011 🏊 🏔

148 DOUBLE WATERS, R WALKHAM

Enchanting oak woodland with spring flowers. Good pool 200m upstream or head downstream 300m of confluence with Tavy.

→ Turn R off the A386 2 miles S of Tavistock at Grenofen, opposite the Halfway House. Take first L. cross river at Grenofen Bridge and park (50.5189, -4.1312). It's 1½ miles to the confluence and you can return S on the other bank via Buckator and Sticklepath wood.

30 mins, 50.5090, -4.1511 🥾 🏔

149 DENHAM BRIDGE & WEIR, R TAVY

Deep-section pool below Denham Bridge - 40 feet deep, according to the old sign.

→ Bridge is on narrow lane between Buckland Monachorum and Bere Alston. Swim here or follow the river 300m downstream through the woods to a wide, open, pebble beach. Explore upstream to find a lovely, quiet stretch of river and old weir (50.4944, -4.1539). Follow lane up hill towards Buckland for 300m, then follow driveway down to L along river 10 mins.

2 mins, 50.4899, -4.1481 🥾

150 CADOVER BRIDGE, R PLYM

Open moorland stream with shallow pools and grassy banks. Attracts crowds on holidays. Great pool downstream.

→ Well-signed from Plympton (6 miles) via Shaugh Prior. Follow the path a mile downstream from the bridge, keeping on the near side of the river, to reach waterfall and deep pool (50.4557, -4.0589).

20 mins, 50.4644, -4.0370 🥾 🍴

151 BIG POND, CADOVER BRIDGE

A large, clear, warm lake in open moorland with pebble beach. Usually deserted. REPORTED 'NO SWIMMING'.

→ Turn R on road track, just before Cadover Bridge. Continue a mile to parking.

5 mins, 50.4503, -4.0090 🏊 🏞

152 FOGGINTOR QUARRY

Impressive flooded quarry with cliffs and ruins. Granite used for London Bridge.

→ 2½ miles W of Two Bridges on B3357 find a farm track and parking on L (Yellowmeade Farm). Follow track 1 mile. Or cycle track from Burrator.

20 mins, 50.5444, -4.0245 🏊 🧗 🏔 📷 🥾

Goldiggins Quarry

South Cornwall and Bodmin

The River Fowey drops in cascades down through dense, sessile oak woodland on the edge of Bodmin Moor. There are humid aromatic glens and the trees are draped with rare ferns, mosses and ivy. This area, known as Golitha Falls, is home to otters, which live among the river roots, and bats, which sleep in the old mine workings.

In 1995 a big cat skull was found in the woods and claimed as the final proof of the 'Beast of Bodmin', thought to be a species of small wild cat similar to a puma. The skull in question turned out to be that of a leopard taken from an exotic Leopard-skin rug and planted by a hoaxer.

Where the main path ends, at the beginning of a series of shallow falls, pick your way further down one of the narrow trails. Wagtails criss-cross the stream and a small, gladed pool opens up a few hundred yards below, out of sight of any crowds. When I was there the yellow sand of the stream threw up a golden light on the rocks around as I eased myself into the pool. It was hot and I was tired but the babbling moorland water soon cut through the sweat and grime. It wasn't large or particularly deep, but the stream picked me up and I found a part of the current which, with some careful balancing, held me in position as I swam. Then I flipped on my back and let the flow carry me down into the shallow rapids and ground me in the sand, the water rushing over my shoulders and shins like a spa.

157

154

156

After a little doze in the dappled light of the rocky ledges I found a wooded weir pool about another mile or so downstream and camped there discreetly. As dusk gathered around me I sipped whisky and kept a silent vigil for bats and owls. As the evening drew late I thought I saw the luminescent blurs of will-o'-the-wisp in the shadows of the wood before I fell asleep under the trees, looking up at the pale midsummer night sky, with total darkness never quite descending.

Waking early I had a quick splash in the water in bright sunshine before trekking back to the car. I was heading ten miles downstream for the National Trust estate of Lanhydrock House. Once an Augustinian Priory, and the lowest crossing point of the Fowey, it was rebuilt as a great mansion by a Victorian industrialist and is now one of the Trust's most visited properties. The gardens are filled with magnificent magnolia and camellia and the estate stretches for many miles along the Fowey.

Downstream from Respryn Bridge there are bankside deckings which make a good place to change and swim. The water is fast-flowing and refreshing, about five feet deep in places and completely clear. I practised some shallow diving and then swam along the bank, searching for otter holes and examining the oak roots that grow down into the water.

As the morning drew on the path became busy with dog walkers and families playing Pooh Sticks so I got dressed and headed upstream to Bodmin Parkway railway station. This was the terminus of the first steam railway in Cornwall, built to bring lime-rich sea sand from Wadebridge for use as fertiliser. A discreet white gate in the corner of the station car park leads down to the old Lanhydrock estate driveway. A wooded stretch of riverbank near here is home to a dark but magical stretch of the river, completely overshadowed by trees and foliage. I swam and floated several hundred yards downstream and then had to tiptoe back barefoot through the undergrowth and creepers to find my pile of clothes. Here, only a mile from the mainline and the 08.35 to Exeter, you can pretend you're lost in a tropical jungle.

159

153 RESPRYN BRIDGE, R FOWEY
A lovely place on a sunny day, with dappled light reflecting on the river as it flows briskly through the woods. Wooden, bankside decks and a beachy shingle area by the lower footbridge (also good for Pooh Sticks). Up to 2m deep in sections and fun to swim against the current.

→ E on lanes from Lanhydrock House entrance. There is also a secluded, heavily wooded area with shingle beaches about 1 mile upstream, perfect for a skinny dip. Also accessible through white gates at end of Bodmin Station car park (50.4461, -4.6668).

10 mins, 50.4391, -4.6795 ⊞

154 CABILLA WOODS, R FOWEY
Mainly paddling in one of Cornwall's largest ancient woodlands.

→ 2 miles upstream from Respryn Bridge. 1 mile E of Bodmin Parkway station on A38 turn L signed Cardinham. Entrance on R after 300m.

5 mins, 50.4573, -4.6375 ⊠

155 GOLITHA FALLS, REDGATE, FOWEY
Here, the young river Fowey flows through ancient oak and beech woodland. Small beaches before the river cascades down over boulders and several falls to form a small plunge pool with golden sand. Good bluebells in spring.

→ 2 ½ miles W of Minions, then R at Redgate (signed Draynes/Golitha). Follow the path for 10 mins to top of cascades. Find a rough track which continues 200m down, beyond the mine ruins, to the shady secret pool at bottom. Slippery rocks!

15 mins, 50.4907, -4.5071 ⊠

156 TRETHURGY LAKES, ST AUSTELL
Popular chalk pit pool with turquoise water, but intermittently fenced off. **REPORTED PRIVATE / NO SWIMMING**

→ Just S of Penwithick A391, turn L off roundabout signed Eden Project/Innis Inn, and find wide track to Carclaze pit on R at bend (300m). Follow path up 200m then bear down L at top. For more chalk pit lakes follow the St Austell road out of Trethurgy and find track up to R after 400m (50.3643, -4.7650, 50.3627, -4.7670).

15 mins, 50.3659, -4.7703 🏃⊠ⓥ

157 GOLDIGGINS QUARRY, MINIONS
A secret, spring-fed quarry lake, out on the open moors but hidden in a small grassy amphitheatre. Flat rock ledges for jumping.

→ From the Hurlers car park follow the vehicle track which heads N onto the moor, past the stone circle. After 15 mins bear L at the junction and continue another ½ mile to find the quarry.

25 mins, 50.5248, -4.4711 ⊠⛰🍴ⓥ

158 THE PONY POOL, MINIONS
Beachy areas and gently shelving shallows make this small, sheltered lake perfect for kids. There's even a waterfall.

→ Follow as for Goldiggins but bear R at the junction. After the stream (about 300m) turn R off the track to find the lake and dam on the stream valley above.

20 mins, 50.5223, -4.4629 ⊠⊠

North and West Cornwall

Treading gingerly down the wet slate steps I descended into the veil of mist that rises from St Nectan's Kieve. Found in a hidden valley only a few miles from the Arthurian castle of Tintagel, deep in the shadow of the gorge, this 'kieve' – or basin – is part of an extraordinary double waterfall which for centuries was used for baptisms.

St Nectan, the hermit who lived here in the hermitage around 480ad, was one of the holiest of Cornish saints. It's easy to see why this place was revered. The flow of the water has sculpted a deep cylindrical well and a perfect man-sized hole through which the water spills. This upper pool is out of reach, but the lower pool is deep enough for an exhilarating splash and plunge.

The guardians of this site, who run the tiny tea shop above, don't mind bathing as long as it is done with sincerity and respect. This has long been a place of pilgrimage and immersion and it was here that King Arthur's knights were baptised before they set out on their quest to recover the Holy Grail. Today small shrines of cairns and photographs of loved ones have been set up on the surrounding rocky ledges. Little light filters down here, but hundreds of coloured ribbons tied to branches and rocks give the cavern a fluttering glow, like a pagan May Day.

160

162

165

Those interested in Arthurian legends should also visit Dozmary Pool, where the ghostly hand reputedly appeared to take the sword Excalibur when the knight Sir Bedivere returned it to the lake. Whirlpools are said to rage here to this day. On top of Bodmin moor on a sunny August day, clouds racing across the sky, Dozmary seems rather benign and the swimming a little shallow. The shores of Colliford lie across the field and provide a more satisfying swim. This is Cornwall's largest and highest lake. It is also situated close to the famous Jamaica Inn, setting for Daphne du Maurier's evocative novel of smugglers and pirates.

If you're looking for somewhere to stay then consider splashing out on a few nights in a romantic tipi by a turquoise quarry lake down near Port Isaac. The land has been in the same family for generations but when the quarry went out of business forty years ago the owner, Lizzie, decided to let it go wild, creating a network of forest clearings with tipis all around the lake. Now families come and stay throughout the summer.

Leaving my clothes in a heap I dived in to join the melee, the late afternoon light shining through the leaves. The underwater zone felt white, opaque and was flavoured with minerals. Almost before I had surfaced someone dive-bombed me from a tree and I raced for control of an abandoned Lilo. At the far end of the quarry a willowy boy stood alert at the prow of his canoe searching for trout below.

Later that evening we prepared a small fire and I retired to my tipi at the edge of one of the clearings. Towels were being hung out on the guy ropes to dry, swimming costumes adorned the totem poles and I could still hear the sound of splashing from the lake. This is a little lost world of canoes, swimming and Hiawathas.

'In the midst of the wild moors, far from any dwelling, there lieth a great standing water called Dosmery Pool. The country people said… that it did ebb and flow, that it had a whirlpool in the midst thereof, and that a faggot once thrown there into was taken up at Foy haven, six miles distant.'
from Richard Carew's Survey of Cornwall, 1602

161

160 ST NECTAN'S KIEVE, TINTAGEL

At the head of a wild glen a tall, slender waterfall falls into a high basin, flows through a circular hole and drops into a plunge pool (the kieve). This is a holy place with prayer flags, a shrine room above and lots of steps. Small tea room in hermitage. Entrance fee.

→ Find track with postbox, opposite telephone box, off B3263, in Trethevey, 2 miles E of Tintagel. Bear R and follow it for 1 mile, past St Piran's Well, down into the woods, and up along the pretty stream, finally climbing the steps up to the shrine entrance.

20 mins, 50.6644, -4.7168 ⛺🚻

161 ROCKY VALLEY, TINTAGEL

Downstream from St Nectan' Kieve. Pretty stream path leading down to waterfall pools by sea. Look out carvings of labyrinths, possibly 3,500 years old, behind old mill.

→ Park on B3263, just E of Bossiney, at layby by turn off to Halgabron. Find footpath opposite.

20 mins, 50.6740, -4.7299 🚻

162 CORNISH TIPI HOLIDAYS, ST KEW

The original tipi and wild-swimming campsite. 16 acres with its own beautiful, spring-fed quarry lake with canoes.

→ Tregeare, Pendoggett, St Kew, PL30 3LW, 01208 880781.

5 mins, 50.5813, -4.7705 🚻⛺🏊

163 COLLIFORD LAKE

A huge moorland reservoir, the highest and largest in Cornwall. Open access on the W side with beaches. Exposed.

→ Signed Colliford Lake Park/Warleggan, off A30, 2 miles SW of Jamaica Inn. Then continue ½ mile beyond the Lake Park.

2 mins, 50.5202, -4.5918 ⛺❓

164 DELFORD BRIDGE, R DE LANK

Pretty moorland stream and bridge with a nice shallow, sandy pool for children.

→ On lanes 2 miles N of Blisland (pass South Penquite Farm camping). Or turn R off A30 3 miles SW of Jamaica Inn, continue past Bradford and turn next R. Also Carbilly quarry pool close by at 50.5492, -4.6460.

2 mins, 50.5524, -4.6632 🚻

165 CARN MARTH POOL, REDRUTH

Old granite quarry amid heather, with smooth flat rocks and deep spring water, near summit of Carn Marth. Outdoor theatre. Great Flat Lode cycle route passes close by.

→ Near top of Lanner Hill (A393 between Lanner and Redruth) take Carn Marth lane (No Through Road) by the bus stop. Continue up, bearing R then L and park outside the old quarry/theatre.

10 mins, 50.2233, -5.2030 ⛺🖥️🚻🚲

166 BAKER'S PIT, NANCLEDRA

Open moorland spring-fed lake (once a china clay pit) with ruins of old mining works. Walk on to find Chysauster ancient village.

→ Turn L off the B3311 from Penzance at Nancledra. After 1 mile turn L to Georgia and park at the road end and walk SW on track.

10 mins, 50.1667, -5.5295 ⛺🏕️🏔️

Lower Ddwli Falls

Wales and Midlands

A region of waterfalls, woods, deep azure quarry pools and the famous gorges, cataracts and llyns of Snowdonia. This is a country of wild magical landscapes with rowan-clad plunge pools, mountain lakes and secret chasms in Tolkien-style profusion. The journey continues with the hill pools of the Malverns and the rivers of the Welsh Marches. Cheshire and Derbyshire provide rare meres, chalk dales and the mermaid's pools of the Peak District.

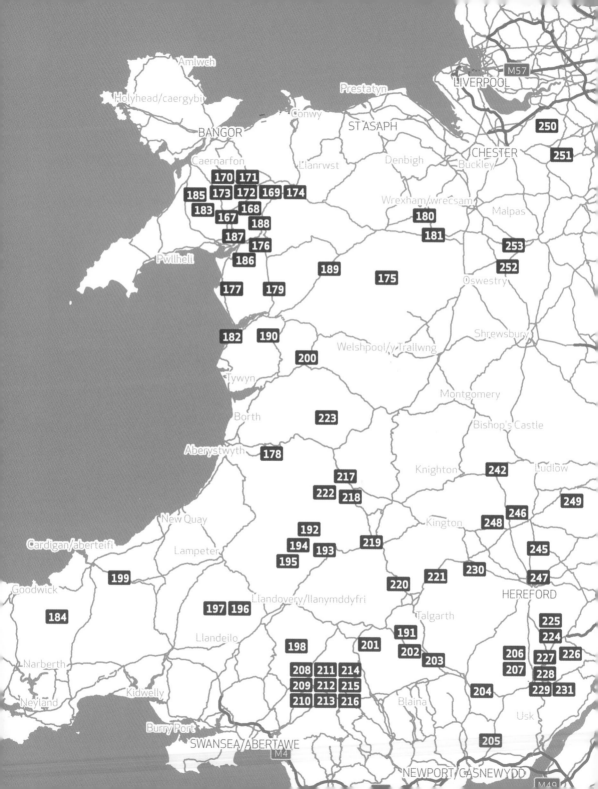

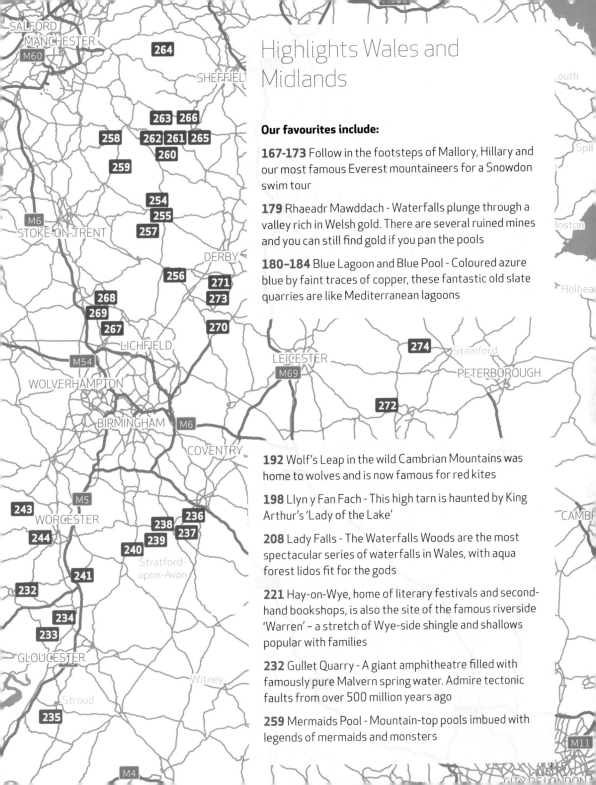

Highlights Wales and Midlands

Our favourites include:

167-173 Follow in the footsteps of Mallory, Hillary and our most famous Everest mountaineers for a Snowdon swim tour

179 Rhaeadr Mawddach - Waterfalls plunge through a valley rich in Welsh gold. There are several ruined mines and you can still find gold if you pan the pools

180–184 Blue Lagoon and Blue Pool - Coloured azure blue by faint traces of copper, these fantastic old slate quarries are like Mediterranean lagoons

192 Wolf's Leap in the wild Cambrian Mountains was home to wolves and is now famous for red kites

198 Llyn y Fan Fach - This high tarn is haunted by King Arthur's 'Lady of the Lake'

208 Lady Falls - The Waterfalls Woods are the most spectacular series of waterfalls in Wales, with aqua forest lidos fit for the gods

221 Hay-on-Wye, home of literary festivals and second-hand bookshops, is also the site of the famous riverside 'Warren' – a stretch of Wye-side shingle and shallows popular with families

232 Gullet Quarry - A giant amphitheatre filled with famously pure Malvern spring water. Admire tectonic faults from over 500 million years ago

259 Mermaids Pool - Mountain-top pools imbued with legends of mermaids and monsters

Swimming over Snowdon

Swimming over the iconic massif of Snowdon, with its pyramid pinnacle and stunning views, is the ultimate swim tour, with a range of dips from waterfall plunge pools to dramatic tarns.

The mountain has long been a place for wild bathing as well as mountaineering excellence. George Mallory, the ill-fated Everest explorer, was also a fanatical lake swimmer who used the mountain to train for the first British ascent. Accompanied by some of the finest thinkers of his time – E. M. Forster, John Maynard Keynes, the Huxley brothers, and other members of the Cambridge Apostles – an opportunity to bathe always rounded off a mountain day and complemented the new socialist ideology, which embraced a closer connection with the 'great outdoors'.

To swim over the highest mountain in England and Wales try this six-mile route from south to north, returning by bus and staying the night at the eccentric old mountain hotel of Pen-y-Gwryd. The route begins at Llyn Dinas under the precipitous rocky knoll of Dinas Emrys, a fifth-century castle stronghold where the original red dragon of Wales emerged from a pool and defeated the white dragon of the Britons. This crag-bounded lake makes an impressive and historic starting point and is lined with gnarled oaks, craggy outcrops and parched gorse.

Two miles up the road, at Nantgwynant, the Watkins Path begins. Within half an hour a series of large plunge pools

173

169

168

and waterfalls appears on the right. Cascading down the mountain, deep blue and decked with rowan, this sunny, south-facing stream is popular with Snowdon walkers.

As you continue you'll pass more pools and the Gladstone Memorial where in 1892 the elder statesman, after being prime minister four times, made a plea for justice for Ireland and Wales. The path turns and rises steeply up to the southern ridge of Snowdon and then on to the summit before heading over onto the Llanberis path that follows the course of the railway. From a mile below the summit you can drop down to the right, to the tiny tarn of Llyn Glas with its magical little wooded island. The tarn overlooks the Llanberis pass and the sea but it's a very rough, steep scramble (and 300-metre descent) to the plateau on which it's perched. Alternatively turn off left instead, to Llyn Du'r Arddu, a deep blue lake, stained by copper and set under the craggy cliffs of 'Cloggie' (Clogwyn du'r Arddu). This 100-metre sheer rock wall is legendary among climbers and rescue helicopter pilots. So fearsome is the location that legend says birds will not fly over the lake.

From here on down the River Arddu drains the heather moors for three miles and the path continues, tracking the railway, past Hebron mountain railway station. The road heads to the tree-line where you'll find another series of amazing plunge pools cascading into Llanberis.

You're almost home and after such an expedition you deserve a night at the classic mountain hotel of Pen-y-Gwryd, high on Pen-y-Pass. When Mallory and Irvine failed to return from Everest in 1923 it was 30 years before Hillary led the first ascent. Pen-y-Gwryd was where his team trained and it is filled with climbing antiquity. After a long day on the mountains enjoy the great Victorian bath-tubs, the outdoor sauna and swimming lake and a hearty five-course meal that appears on the dot at seven o'clock, announced by a gong.

"Perfect weather. Explored Craig-yr-Ysfa, three new climbs, bathing each time on the way back."

Mallory's letters, 1907. He and his climbing partners took to bathing with obsessive zeal and wondered if life would ever be so good again.

170

167 LLYN DINAS, BEDDGELERT

A mile long valley lake at the foot of Snowdon with stunning craggy backdrop. Accessible directly from the main road.

→ 2 miles NE of Beddgelert on A498. ½ mile after Sygun Copper Mine find parking on L. Cross road for footpath over footbridge to far shore.

10 mins, 53.0224, -4.0664 🏊

168 WATKINS PATH WATERFALLS

A series of pools and falls on Cwm Llan at the bottom of the Watkins path. Popular with walkers freshening up after climbing Snowdon.

→ From Beddgelert A498 continue past Llyn Dinas and park beyond Gwynant Chapel café (LL55 4NL, 01766 890855) on R. Explorers can also continue to the secluded pools on the nearby Afon Merch (53.0520,-4.0399). Also Llanberis waterfalls at 53.1115, -4.1255 on N side of Snowdon.

20 mins, 53.0441, -4.0551 🏊

169 LLYN GWYNANT

SW facing beach and lake with camping, near Watkins path.

→ Nant Gwynant camping (LL55 4NW, 01766 890853)

5 mins, 53.0519, -4.0167 🏊⛺🛶

170 LLYN DU'R ARDDU, CLOGWYN

A deep blue lake set under a 100m sheer crag (Cloggy) famous in climbing circles and in traditional folklore. Shaded in the afternoon.

→ Below the main Llanberis path, directly below Clogwyn station.

120 mins, 53.0813, -4.0894 🏊🛶🏔

171 LLYN GLAS, CRIB GOCH

An enchanting, wild tarn (the 'blue' lake) with an island on which grow two conifers, and a nest of gulls. On the N side of Crib Goch. Well worth seeking out.

→ If you are going here you better be able to read a map! Tiny Llyn Bach, above, is also special (53.0793, -4.0690).

75 mins, 53.0807, -4.0638 🏔🛶

172 LLYN GLASLYN, PEN-Y-PASS

Large lake, clear waters, great views. Ruins. Shelving shoreline.

→ A well-trodden path from Pen-y-Pass (Miner's Track) leads up and along this large lake (2 miles). Also Llyn Lydaw above (53.0712, -4.0448). The classic mountaineers' Pen-y-Gwryd Hotel is nearby for afterwards (LL55 4NT, 01286 870211)

45 mins, 53.0719, -4.0642 🏊ℹ️🍴🛶

173 GLAN-YR-AFON SLATE QUARRY

Very remote, deep old quarry lake now filled with crystal clear spring water. Difficult path down.

→ West side of Snowdon. Take footpath from Rhyd-Ddu (direction Snowdon ranger path), over railway line and on for a mile. Old quarry is above 300m. Also beautiful but dangeous quarry pool at 53.1256, -4.1439, above Llanberis, where many unexploded bombs were sunk in the Second World War.

30 mins, 53.0646, -4.1190 ⚠️🛶🏔❓

Fairy Glens, Gorges and Gold

During the eighteenth century the most northern part of Wales was still one of the wildest and least charted regions of Europe. Yet it was increasingly renowned for its beautiful waterfalls and was in vogue among the adventurous artists of the aesthetic movement searching for the ultimate 'picturesque' scene.

One intrepid travel writer keen to cash in on this trend was the eccentric Reverend William Bingley, a peripatetic pastor and naturalist from Suffolk who had taken it upon himself to bring tales of the wild waterfalls of Wales to London. *North Wales, delineated from two excursions through all the interesting parts of that highly beautiful and romantic country* was intended as a guide to future tourists. It was published in London in 1804 and sold over 300 copies.

One of his most memorable descriptions is of Rhaeadr Du – the Black Cataract – a 'deep and horrid chasm' in a little visited woodland near Maentwrog in the northern Rhinog mountains. The best time to go is in early September when the water has been warmed, the oak leaves are still green and blankets of moss cover the forest floor. Sheer, steep, rocky cliffs soar up, trees grow out sideways and buzzards circle above. Huge tangles of fallen trunks litter the river bed but a string of quiet pools lie between, as calm as glass.

The canyon is much more peaceful than when the vicar visited it 200 years ago. Upstream the gorge was dammed and the waters diverted in 1925 leaving the river almost empty. The result is eerie calm, but offers wonderful swimming and sunbathing on the large dried-up bedrocks.

178

179

176

Take the old coach road which stretches up the hillside past a slender and abandoned medieval coach bridge, overgrown with ivy. After a sweaty ten-minute climb, with the ravine on your left, you'll hear the gentle sound of falling water. Down through the trees a bobsleigh run of rapids tips a slender column of water over the chute of Rhaeadr Du and into a perfect plunge pool below. At midday the sun is high enough to light up the glade but the cold may be intense – you'll be lucky to do more than rocket around the pool a few times, squeal and scrabble out. With the surface of your skin dilating and blood reaching into the extremities of your body in a great rush this is cold dipping at its most therapeutic. Drying off in the tingling warmth, your skin stinging, the world seems sharp and clear with the muggy layers purged.

There are many other beautiful gorges and waterfalls in Snowdonia. The Fairy Glen near Betws-y-Coed has long been a place for the romantics, its picturesque qualities still much in evidence. A swim down its steep-sided gorge is a sublime and peaceful experience. And what could be more fairytale than swimming in rivers of gold? Deep in Coed-y-Brenin forest, accessible via the extensive network of mountain-bike trails, two waterfalls lie at the one-time heart of Welsh gold production. The gold from this valley near Dolgellau made Princess Diana's wedding ring and has been the royal choice since Roman times. The last commercial operation closed down in 1998 but there are still many old workings along the gorge. The most prominent are by the plunge pools of Rhaeadr Mawddach. The building here generated power for the mines and they say the old tailings still contain traces of gold. Why not try panning for some of your very own royal Welsh gold?

'In this cataract, which is surrounded with dark and impending scenery, the water is thrown with vast impetuosity… the banks closed in above my head, leaving but a narrow chasm, from which the light was excluded by the dark foliage on each side… I found myself entering, to appearances, into the mouth of a deep and horrid cavern…'

From Bingley's *North Wales*, 1804

176

174 FAIRY GLEN, BETWS-Y-COED

A picturesque gorge with access for £1.
The grassy junction pool is good for a
longer, sunnier swim and family picnic.
Upstream gorge has some large rocks to
sit on and a deep section down the middle
to swim through if water level is low.

→ 2 miles S of Betws-y-Coed on A470
(Blaenau Ffestiniog turning). Turn L
for Fairy Glen hotel (LL24 0SH, 01690
710269) just before bridge. Follow path
via river to grassy banks and large junction
pool (400m). Continue 300m on wooded
path to bottom of gorge.
15 mins, 53.0725, -3.7953 �

175 PISTYLL RHAEADR, BERWYNS

Highest waterfall in Wales plunges
down a vertical cliff and flows through a
circular hole. Pools for plunging below the
footbridge.

→ Well-signed off the B4391/B4580,
but in remote hill country between Bala
and Oswestry. Cosy cabin restaurant and
tearoom. Pleasant campsite (SY10 0BZ,
01691 780392).
5 mins, 52.8546, -3.3780 △♥♨

176 RHAEADR DU, MAENTWROG

The Black Waterfall. A beautiful wild
gorge with high waterfall and large
plunge pool, once admired by Victorian
travellers but now off the tourist track.

→ 1½ miles S of Maentwrog on A496
(Harlech road), at Magnox North power
station, find Woodland Trust path on
L up along the river (parking in layby R
200m before). Follow for 1½ miles up to
falls and bushwhack down steep forest
slope to reach plunge pool at bottom. The
adventurous like to find the ruined bridge
and more falls (52.9270, -3.9826) 500m
upstream. The Grapes Hotel (LL41 4HN,
01766 590365) is a good pit stop.
30 mins, 52.9302, -3.9850 ♥♨♦△

177 NANTCOL CAMPSITE

Deep ravine and falls with paddling too.

→ 12 miles S of Rhaeadr Du falls
(Maentwrog). Well signed (Nantcol
Waterfalls) from the Victoria Inn in
Llanbedr, S of Harlech on A496 (LL45 2PL,
01341 241209).
5 mins, 52.8205, -4.0663 △▼♥

178 RHEIDOL VALE WATERFALLS

Many gorges, deep pools and beaches.

→ Turn off A44 3 miles E Aberystwyth,
signed Cwmrheidol / Butterfly House.
Continue 5 miles to 'end of route' to find
parking, info boards and a gate down to
beach. Many pools, jumps and waterfalls
on route (e.g. Stakcraft sign, 52.3866,
-3.8710 and 52.3915, -3.9600).
2 mins, 52.3858, -3.8686 ♥♨

179 RHAEADR MAWDDACH

A large deep plunge pool at this huge
waterfall, set among gold mine ruins.

→ 6 miles N of Dolgellau on A470 (dir
Porthmadog) turn R at end of Ganllwyd
(where speed limit ends), cross bridge
and continue 1¼ miles to road end and
barrier. Park and walk ¾ mile on track
upstream to find Pistyll Cain down path to
L or much larger Rhaeadr Mawddach over
footbridge and through mine ruins to R.
Also accessible from the Coed-y-Brenin
mountain biking trails (LL40 2HZ, 01341
440728). Also another Rhaedr Du falls, on
other side of A470 (52.8021, -3.8956).
20 mins, 52.8301, -3.8777 ♨♥▼

182 Blue Pool, Friog

Snowdonia Blue Lagoons

The disused mine quarries of North Wales often fill with clear, blue water and appear like cobalt jewels on the mountainside. Two of the best known are the evocative Blue Lagoon near Llangollen and the Blue Pool close to Dolgellau. These old quarry holes were cut into the seams of Silurian slate, which often occur intermixed with deposits of copper. The copper inhibits algae growth – normally responsible for the green colour of natural lakes – and gives the waters an ethereal azure hue that is further deepened under a blue summer sky.

I had heard rumour of the Blue Lagoon near Llangollen in 2007 but had no exact directions and spent a thankless hour criss-crossing the mountain before the blue lake finally appeared in view, 100 metres below me, set deep in the core of a volcano-like crater. I scrambled down over scree with yellow hawkbit sprouting from ledges to reach the massive slate rocks that make up its shores. Swimming near to the cliff face wearing goggles was an experience that induced vertigo. The old quarry wall plunged down to a lunar landscape of moraine and boulders that appears far beneath, wobbling in the blue abyss with almost perfect visibility. At one end there was a sunken red car, abandoned by joy riders, its scale and depth strangely mutated by the water. Many divers came here to practise their deep-water skills but sadly the lagoon was filled in and destroyed using explosives as part of quarry restoration works in 2015.

184

183

185

Although there was quarrying here as far back as the seventeenth century, operations only intensified two hundred years later with the coming of the canal and then the railway to Llangollen. Traces of buildings are still visible: dressing sheds, a steam winding house and sawing mill. Many years after closure the quarry holes have stabilised and the risks from falling rocks are no more than in any upland mountain terrain. However, the quarry walls are exceptionally steep and the water obviously very deep. Even though this is a popular place in summer you should take great care.

Golwern Quarry, the Blue Pool, is fifty miles to the west set high above the Mawddach estuary with views out over Cardigan Bay, Cadair Idris and the Rhinog mountains. You can walk up from Fairbourne or drive in via a spectacular mountain road from Arthog past the Cregennen lakes, although you will have to open at least ten gates! The pool is accessed via a short, low railway tunnel which quickly opens out into an open-roofed cavern. This pool is smaller than Moel-y-Faen and almost perfectly rectangular with smooth straight rock walls that make it as close to a natural swimming pool as you can imagine.

The rich mineral seams of north Wales made many investors rich but just as many poor. The Prince of Wales quarry at the head of the remote and beautiful Cwm Pennant valley was a wildly optimistic undertaking. An entire village was built to house 200 workers, a tramway was routed for many miles up the mountain and a reservoir constructed to provide the constant water supply essential for running the machinery of a mine. You can still see the dam, a double-skinned dry stone wall that would have been filled with clay.

The remains of an old waterwheel is some way below next to the ruined dressing sheds. Here the water-powered machines would have helped split and grade the slate before it was loaded onto the mountain railway. Although 200 years have passed since the reservoir was built it still remains, its pool of unused water perfectly clear blue. Sheltered in its little valley it is serene and romantic, surrounded by the fading ruins of a long gone industrial age with steep banks of heather growing along its edge.

180

180 BLUE LAGOON, HORSESHOE PASS

A completely clear azure blue lake at the bottom of a spectacular quarry crater SADLY NOW CLOSED AND IN-FILLED.

→ Head for the Ponderosa Café (LL20 8DR, 01978 790307) 4 miles N of Llangollen (A542 signed Ruthin / Horseshoe Pass). Cross road and head up the hill on the main path. After 300m veer R into the quarry area. There are two huge hidden pits with warning notices. The second of the pits used to contains the 'lagoon' deep at the bottom of its crater.
20 mins, 53.0207, -3.2160

181 LLANGOLLEN, R DEE

Popular pools and rock ledges in the town centre or the horseshoe weir in fields two miles upstream.

→ Walk 300 m upstream from town bridge (via steps). Or head for Horseshoe Pass (A542) and take first L after a mile (Corwen, B5103) and find car parks after ½ mile (Llantysilio picnic area). Also try River Dee below old Pont Cysyllte aquaduct, 52.9704, -3.0875, LL20 7RH.
5 mins, 52.9707, -3.1749

182 BLUE POOL & CREGENNEN LAKES

A green-blue rectangular pool in a great quarry amphitheatre entered by a spooky railway tunnel. Lots to explore but TUNNEL ACCESS NOW BLOCKED.

→ Approach from above, along the amazing Cregennen Lakes road LL39 1LJ (amazing lakes but 'No Swimming' signs). Or from below: 7 miles W of Dolgellau (A493, dir Tywyn), and 300m S of Friog / Fairbourne church, turn L at telephone box, up narrow dead end lane (Fford Panteinion) to find steep track up to quarry on R (very limited parking). Find small grassy plateau at top with (currently blocked) tunnel.
20 mins, 52.6891, -4.0413

183 CWM PENNANT, GOLAN

A clear blue lagoon in a hidden cleft, at the head of one of the most remote and beautiful valleys in Snowdonia. Interesting old mine ruins of Ynys y Pandy mine.

→ From Penmorfa (A487 W of Porthmadog) follow the signs to Cwm Pennant via Woollen Mill, and continue 4 miles, through several gates, to road end and car park. Follow path 300m up to ruined mine manager's house above on R, then continue up, bearing R up old railway, to reach ruined watermill and factory 200m. Follow stream valley to find old reservoir 200m above. Bring a map!
20 mins, 53.0236, -4.1657

184 ROSEBUSH, MYNYDD PRESELI

Mysterious freshwater quarry with clear blue waters and rocks for diving.

→ Between Fishguard and Narbeth on B4313. Turn into Rosebush village to pink corrugated, traditional Tafarn Sinc tavern (SA66 7QU, 01437 532214). Then walk up the dead end lane, beyond the cottages, and after 500m find the lake among mounds on your R.
15 mins, 51.9359, -4.7959

185 DOROTHEA QUARRIES, NANTLLE

A wild ruinous site with a 100m deep quarry lake, also used by divers.

→ Park at roundabout, far E end of Talysarn (LL54 6AF). Follow access track E ½ mile.
30 mins, 53.0566, -4.2411

Llyn Eiddew-Bach

Llyns and Tarns of Wales

Tarns – or Llyns as they're known in Wales – are those magical lakes that appear as you're sweating your way to the top of the mountain. Swimming in them provides total immersion in the landscape and the ultimate sense of the wild.

My favourite is Llyn Eiddew Bach, part of a series of wild mountain lakes that is very dear to me. It's in the heart of the northern Rhinogs, Snowdonia's least-visited region, close to a 3,000-year-old roadway that once linked Ireland with Stonehenge. I spent some time living in the farm close by and I would always leave a bottle of bubbly stashed and chilling on the lake bottom, tied to a secret piece of string, in preparation for weekend picnics. On the shallow side of the tarn are grassy, sheep-mown banks perfect for playing frisbee and paddling in the water. On the deep side are cliff ledges for sun lounging and for those who like to jump. A backdrop of bronzed September bracken, bony stone peaks and glimpses of the Irish Sea completes the sense of awe and beauty.

To the north, on the great massif of the Moelwyns and Cnicht, between Blaenau Ffestiniog and Snowdon, is another network of mountain-top lakes. Llynnau Diffwys are a pair that are rather shallow, though this does mean they warm up quickly.

188

189

187

They stand at the head of Croesor's U-shaped valley, with views down the mountains, across the sandy flats of Traeth Mawr, and out to sea. You will also find nearby the crumbling remains of the mining town of Rhosydd, one of the largest, highest slate mines in North Wales. There are over twenty tarns up here, all within a couple of miles of each other and you can make a fantastic ten-mile mountain walk from Penrhyndeudraeth through Croesor to Blaenau Ffestiniog, taking the mountain railway back to your starting point.

Snowdonia is a glaciated landscape and contains many true 'cwm' lakes ('corries' as they are known in Scotland). They have been scooped out of mountain walls by 10,000-year-old glaciers and usually formed in a northern or easterly direction, in the shadow of the ancient afternoon sun. One of the most famous and dramatic is Llyn Cau in the deep cliff-faced cwm of the beautiful Cadair Idris near Dolgellau.

Getting in, and out, of a tarn like Llyn Cau is as much a part of the ritual as the swim itself. For me it has to be a dive. First I peer down to check for sea monsters among the rocky shapes of the dark bottom. Then, with a lurch of adrenalin, I leap in and am under the water, scrabbling up through a riot of rising bubbles towards the surface before breaststroking to the side, gulping little sips of the sweet spring water as I go. As I reach the shallows and wade out of the primordial depths my skin is already tingling. I may have only managed 50 yards but there's an unnatural sense of elation and achievement – my head is in focus, the world is in perspective again and all my grogginess has been washed away. No sooner am I dry than I turn to dive in again.

One branch of evolutionary theory suggests that humans spent millions of years evolving into uprightness as semi-aquatic waders and swimmers in the Indian Ocean – our subsequent life on dry land is a relatively recent and bereft affair. Here – in an expanse of wild water – I feel as happy as a salmon. The mountains tower higher, the sky stretches wider and the great unknowns of life wash over me. The rhythm and sensuality of the swim soothes the mind and carries stress away on its ripples.

190

186 LLYN EIDDEW-BACH, TALSARNAU

A beautiful tarn in the remote northern Rhinogs on Snowdonia, with cliffs for jumping and fabulous views of the sea. Stone circle and good hotel for après-swim cream tea.

→ Head for Maes-y-Neuadd Hotel (LL47 6YA, 01766 780200), off B4573 to Harlech. Turn R (by 'hotel 200 yards' sign) up narrow steep lane and continue ¾ mile to road end and parking. Follow track ¾ mile, across wall stile, and a further ¾ mile to reach lake on L. Bryn Cader Faner is a 3,000-year-old stone circle ¾ mile N. Or continue on the amazing mine track that winds up along the mountain wall a mile to reach little Llyn Du at the summit (52.8866, -3.9973).
30 mins, 52.8905, -4.0141 🏔🏊🎣🖼

187 LLYN MAIR, TAN-Y-BWLCH

Lily-padded lake with picnic area by road, on Ffestiniog mountain railway.

→ Turn L off A487 at Oakley Arms (LL41 3YU, 01766 590277) E of Porthmadog, and continue ¾ mile to car park on R.
1 min, 52.9519, -4.0072 🏊🚂🛶

188 LLYNNAU DIFFWYS, TANYGRISIAU

Two small shallow tarns at the head of Croesor valley, one with an island. Fantastic views of Cnicht and the sea. Many other lakes and the ruins of the Rhosydd mine. Also approachable from Croesor.

→ Head to top of Tanygrisiau village (A496 to Blaenau) and follow track path past Llyn Cwmorthin. Continue up 2 miles to plateau and mine ruins of Rhosydd. Break off to the R (NW) over moor to find island tarns ¾ mile. Nearby to the E are the old reservoir lakes of Corsiog and lovely Clogwyn Brith with cliffs (53.0007, -3.9909).
80 mins, 53.0027, -3.9987 🏊

189 LLYN TEGID, BALA

The largest natural lake in Wales with gravel shores and swimming freely allowed.

→ Good access from the picnic site at Llangower, B4403, 3 miles S of Bala or continue along shore for further remote beaches. Also good access at lakes Vyrnwy, Brenig and Alwen 10 miles to the S and E.
3 mins, 52.8742, -3.6329 🏊

190 LLYN CAU, CADAIR IDRIS

A huge, dramatic glacial cwm in the crater of Cadair Idris set beneath 400m-high mountain walls. It's a 350m ascent up from the car park, past numerous falls and pools, so even if the lake is cold you'll be warm when you arrive. Shady by afternoon.

→ 6 miles S of Dolgellau on A487, turn R after the Minford Hotel (LL36 9AJ) to find main car park on B4405. Cross bridge through woods and follow stream up hillside via major path to arrive at lake after 2 miles. You are about half way up Cadair Idris if you want to continue!
50 mins, 52.6942, -3.8987 🏊🖼

191 LLANGORSE LAKE, BRECON

Largest natural lake in South Wales. Reedy squishy entry but warm.

→ From behind church at Llangasty Tal-y-Llyn. Signed off B4560 N of Bwlch (A40 near Brecon).
2 mins, 51.9276, -3.2623 🏊🖼

Wolf's Leap and the Cambrian Mountains

Wolf's Leap is a tight rocky canyon on the River Irfon set above a series of deep river pools. Rugged and beautiful, the valley winds its ways down from the rooftop wilds of central Wales and is a sanctuary for the once rare red kite.

The canyon takes its name from the last wolf in Wales, allegedly seen jumping to freedom here in the sixteenth century. Wolves were perceived as vermin and hunted to extinction. The same fate almost befell the red kite, which was down to just a handful of breeding pairs by the end of the nineteenth century. These mountains were their lonely refuge but a huge conservation effort has led to their UK-wide recovery.

The journey to these hills can feel rather epic. I made it in a conkedout 1979 campervan, driving in from Tregaron in the west, up and over twenty miles of narrow mountain lanes. My van overheated and was saved by a call to the AA from the lonely telephone box that stands at the junctions of two mountain roads high on the moors of rhos pastures, a wetland mosaic of heather grass and bog.

The River Irfon appears as you descend down the Devil's Staircase, the landscape opening up into a wide crag-edged valley. The pools themselves are at the outflow of a small slot canyon, which forms the metre-wide Wolf's Leap. This narrow crack of churning water has cut deep down into the rock and eroded pot holes and chambers. The pool is small but deep with great sloping slabs of Cambrian rock, some of the oldest in the world.

Well known as a swimming river, the Irfon was once used by local churches as a place for baptisms. Downstream from the Leap is the wash pool, also used by drovers, for whom the river was the beginning of a cattle-herding routeway to East Anglia. Up to one thousand animals at a time would be brought by this pool, sometimes under the shepherding of just one man and his dogs.

198

193

200

Downstream, the tiny town of Llanwrtyd Wells was once famous for its natural springs. These days they have fallen into decline but in an effort to diversify and attract tourists, the town has introduced the world championship for 'bog snorkelling'. Competitors have to complete two lengths of a 60-metre trench cut through the peat bogs of Waen Rhydd in the quickest possible time, wearing snorkels and flippers, but without using any conventional swimming strokes. A triathlon has also been introduced, as well as mountain-bike bog snorkelling that involves cycling underwater through the trench. With over a hundred participants each year, entries have included snorkellers from Russia, Australia, New Zealand and Ireland.

At the southern end of the Cambrians is the Black Mountain, the most western end of the Brecon Beacons National Park. In this area of sinkholes and limestone karst, Llyn y Fan Fach is one of two high tarns that sit beneath the peak. For many centuries legend has told of a 'Lady of the Lake' who would rise shimmering on the first Sunday of August at two o'clock in the afternoon. Apparently she married a mortal, a nearby farmer, but returned to the lake along with his cattle after he hit her three times. In Victorian times the tale was so well known that whole families would climb up the mountain in the summer sun in the hope that she would appear.

I camped up here with a friend one midsummer. A wall of bare scree rises up on the south side of the lake and many miles of central Wales' most remote interior drops away in undulating vistas to the north. We ventured into the grey, glassy waters at the end of the day, just as the sun was becoming pink in the sky. Having reached the middle we watched in amazement as great sheets of summer mist began to roll in and surround us on the water. Our distant tents disappeared beneath the shrouded veil and great wisps of ghostly vapour rose slowly up the mountain wall. We made for the shore, feeling the lake might suddenly erupt in some supernatural horror and stood there shivering and waiting, peering out for our camp. And then, just as quickly as the mist had come, it was away, and the burning evening glow dried us as the sun sank like a fireball in the sky.

194

192 WOLF'S LEAP, R IRFON

A valley of wild beauty. A series of deep pools at the bottom of a narrow, sculpted slot gorge. Open, sunny with flat rocks.

→ From bridge at Llanwrtyd Wells (famous for its bog-snorkelling championships) follow signs to Abergwesyn, 4 miles, then L at postbox signed Lyn Brianne / Tregaron. Continue 1.7 miles to rockfall sign and see pools below L.

10 mins, 52.1788, -3.6949 🅰🔆🆅

193 WASH POOL, R IRFON

Large roadside pool with waterfall above.

→ As Wolf's Leap but half way to Abergwesyn find Forestry Commission sign and obvious pool on R. Great fun.

2 mins, 52.1362, -3.6678 🅰🔆🔆

194 LLYN BRIANNE LAKE, R TYWI

Beautiful wooded reservoir. This picnic and parking area has grassy shores and steep gravel beach.

→ Continue on road from Wolf's Leap up to pass and L down to lake at head of Tywi valley.

2 mins, 52.1482, -3.7416 🔆❓

195 YSTRADFFIN, R TYWI

Double waterfalls in wooded gorge. Hillock opposite is a wildlife reserve with legendary cave.

→ Descend from Llyn Brianne. Or take Cilycwm Rd from Llandovery and continue straight (signed Rhandirmwyn) about 10 miles. Finally turn L just after Gallt y Bere camping field, signed Troedyrhiw, and continue ¾ mile to find a flat grass and rock plateau above gorge. From here a path descends to waterfalls on L. Beware high water levels.

5 mins, 52.1049, -3.7861 🆅🔆🅰🅰

196 TALLEY ABBEY LAKES

Chapel and majestic ruins by a double lake. Follow the W shore to explore.

→ B4302, 6 miles N of Llandeilo.

5 mins, 51.9774, -3.9907 🔆🔆❓

197 ABERGORLECH, R COTHI

Super riverside pub with pool below.

→ Black Lion (SA32 7SN, 01558 685271). Pool below the little church hall. B4310, 3 miles W of Talley Abbey lakes.

2 mins, 51.9824, -4.0612 🅸🔆

198 LLYN Y FAN FAWR, GLYNTAWE

High, wild haunted lake in the shadow of the Black Mountain, legendary home of a lake nymph. Fantastic views to E. Shelving entry.

→ From Abercraf head N on A4067 (dir Sennybridge) and turn L after 4 miles at the old Tafarn-y-Garreg inn (signed Trecastle, SA9 1GS). After 3½ miles, at the top of the hill, find off road parking space on L and a rough track leading up the mountain beyond. Llyn y Fan Fach is further round to W but swimming is not allowed.

35 mins, 51.8795, -3.6965 🔆🔆🅰

199 CENARTH, R TEIFI

Waterfalls and large pool beneath old bridge. Coracle centre.

→ 6 miles E of Cardigan on A484.

2 mins, 52.0455, -4.5252 🔆❓🔆

200 CEMMAES, R DOVEY

Good riverside banks for paddling, picnic and a dip if no fishermen.

→ 8 miles E of Machynlleth, off A470.

2 mins, 52.6405, -3.7243 🔆❓

Nant Sere

Usk and the Brecon Beacons

The River Usk runs deep through the heart of the Brecon Beacons National Park, fed by the streams and pools of Pen-y-Fan and Cribyn. Carving through soft pink sandstone, it is a shallow river for much of its length, but occasionally opens out into beautiful hidden swimming holes.

One such area is around the little village of Llangynidr, halfway between Brecon and Abergavenny, nestling on the edge of the high moors. From the narrow medieval bridge the river runs rocky and shallow below, forming small rivulets between island clumps of butterwort and shingle. The bedrock is as gentle to the touch as soapstone but struck through with cream and red quartz bands.

Rounded eddy holes hold little piles of pebbles, and pillars of rock stand like miniature wind-carved tors, etched by the current and flow. Picking my way down the rough bankside path from the bridge I was searching for a particularly idyllic swimming pool discovered by a friend. Just as I was about to give up and return to the bridge the alto tinkling of the shallow

202

201

202

water began to lower into the baritone of a deeper pool. A few minutes ahead the river poured over a low ledge into an area of still water extending from bank to bank with flat sunny picnic ledges and sculpted stones on which countless local families must have hung their clothes.

This was perfect river swimming. I was surrounded by open fields yet shaded by a coppice of poplar trees hung with mistletoe. Scents of wild saffron and mown hay hung on a late summer breeze with early evening birdsong, all inducing a sort of hypnosis as the water sang on by. I came round to the sound of a lamprey blowing bubbles on the surface. Dangling my legs in the water, feeling tentatively for the bottom, I dived in then struck out, swimming gently against the flow and letting a trickle of sweet water into my mouth.

The Vale of the Usk is a wonderful valley in which to while away a weekend of wildlife spotting. Bats may be seen in the early evening swooping over the river, purple- and green-winged orchids can be found and in the spring there are crab apple, wild cherry and plum blossoms.

Some miles downstream you'll find Crickhowell, a medieval town beneath Table Mountain – Crug Hywel – from which it takes its name. There is good paddling and plunging in the pool beneath the bridge and a small weir by some stone steps. An old right of way stretches across the river and if you swim across you'll notice that the bridge appears to have seventeen arches from one side but only sixteen from the other.

Upstream the great escarpment peaks of the Brecon Beacons are like turrets above the Usk valley. The ridge path along Pen-y-Fan is popular on a summer day but few know about the waterfall that cascades down into the Usk, set into the side of the steep mountain and invisible from above.

The valley of Nant Sere is the most remote: a series of mosscovered waterfalls in a deep, sheltered vale filled with patches of ancient oak woodland and shallow pools among mountain bracken. At least five falls drop down this mountainside and after a hard walk up to the summits there's nothing more idyllic than to descend and dip in every one.

205

201 PEN-Y-FAN, NANT SERE, BRECON

A string of magical, moss-covered shallow waterfalls in fairy woodland under heather covered hillside beneath Pen-y-Fan.

→ Spectacular approach by bush-whacking down from Cribyn peak. Or from main road on W side of Brecon take turning by St David's Church (Bailyhelig Rd) and continue 2½ miles to road end, turning R at T junction. Follow wall all the way down to stream ½ mile (small waterfall) and continue up ½ mile.

20 mins, 51.8936, -3.4195 🏔️🚶

202 LLANGYNIDR, R USK

A beautiful river pool and low waterfall set beneath wooded crag. Fun rapids downstream. Private fishing rights so do not swim if fishermen present.

→ Signed off A40 between Brecon and Abergavenny. From medieval bridge follow river R bank footpath downstream ½ mile. More pools downstream. Also pools ½ mile upstream of bridge on path.

10 mins, 51.8746, -3.2234 ❓

203 CRICKHOWELL, R USK

A large pool, up to 2m deep, beneath the arched medieval bridge of Crickhowell. Rather public. Paddling, picnics and shallow pools upstream along riverside path. Private fishing rights so do not swim if fishermen present.

→ Access from steps below garden of Bridge End Inn (NP8 1AR, 01873 810338).

2 mins, 51.8561, -3.1405 🍺🚶

204 LLANVIHANGEL GOBION, R USK

Secluded corner pool with pebble and sand beach. Continue on along river for another mile and back by lane for a lovely circuit and more pools.

→ From Pant-y-Goitre bridge (B4598, between Abergavenny and Usk) walk downstream to Llwyn Corner. Also explore upstream of bridge. There is sometimes riverside camping at the Chain Bridge Inn on road back to Usk (NP15 1PP, 01873 880243).

20 mins, 51.7785, -2.9306 🏔️

205 NEWBRIDGE-ON-USK, R USK

Deep above bridge, beach and shallows below.

→ J24 / M4 at Newport then A48 then signed Catsash. The smart Newbridge on Usk inn is above (NP15 1LY, 01633 451000).

2 mins, 51.6487, -2.8900 🚶🛈🚴🏔️

206 SKENFRITH CASTLE, R MONNOW

Shallows and pools behind the ruined castle. Rope swing.

→ On the B4521 10 miles E of Abergavenny. Good food at the Bell Inn (NP7 8UH, 01600 750235).

5 mins, 51.8793, -2.7908 🚶🛈🏰

207 TREGATE BRIDGE, R MONNOW

Paddling, pools and picnics for a mile up and downstream of bridge.

→ Take turning next to Bell Inn / bridge at Skenfrith. Continue 2½ miles, then turn L to bridge.

5 mins, 51.8516, -2.7607 🚶

Waterfall Woods and Ystradfellte

Coed-y-Rhaiadr means 'waterfall woods' and you'll not find a more impressive network of forest lidos and falling water anywhere in Wales.

The route to the waterfalls near Pontneddfechan is found through an old gate inscribed simply 'Waterfalls' in wrought iron. Soon the sound of rushing water fills the woods. If you follow the trail for twenty minutes or so you'll come to a large rocky outcrop on the right above a mini canyon through which you can snorkel, with clear views of the underwater rock formations in the abyss below. Further on there's a large junction pool beneath a footbridge where families swim and older children jump.

Like many wooded waterfalls in Wales this valley has its share of legends. It was from a cave by the riverside here that Elidorus, a fourth-century priest, found a passageway to a secret land from which he tried to steal a golden ball. The next waterfall along, Sgwd Gwladys, or Lady Falls, is named after the daughter of King Brychan who ruled here in the tenth century. The falls occupy a giant amphitheatre rimmed with a lip of dark black gritstone.

210

209

212

The great bowl holds a wide pool of gentle water and shingle beach. Moss and fern grow in profusion in this misty microclimate and many say this is the most beautiful waterfall in Wales. I arrived at midday and the sun was high enough to light up the sunken woodbine and ragwort-draped glade. A slender chute of water was falling from a high ledge beneath slopes of oak and beech. Tiptoeing into the pebble shallows, I dived into the deeper parts of the plunge pool and swam underwater in the peaty darkness, hearing the drone of the water hum between my ears and the movement of the falls vibrate across my skin. Breaking the surface close to the far wall I clambered out onto a ledge of wet rock that leads around behind the falls.

Lady Falls is variable: sometimes it can be a roaring cascade, at other times a trickle. If you're well equipped and have time you may be able to bushwhack your way up a further kilometre through the forest above Lady Falls to find the falls of Einion Gam, named after Gwladys' lover. This is twice as tall, and its pool is cut into a sheer-sided ravine. Back at the footbridge and junction pool a rather precipitous path leads on to the Horseshoe Falls and two perfectly elliptic pools, like emerald lidos, lying deep in the forest.

In the parallel valley of the Melte, leading up to Ystradfellte, there are yet more waterfalls. At one of the most famous, Scwd yr Eira, an ancient drovers' road passes behind the flow. In another the entire river disappears into the caverns of Porth yr Ogof, one of the largest cave systems in Europe.

This extraordinary landscape was laid down in layers of time. The oldest limestone was formed from the shells of sea creatures that inhabited the early tropical seas and these soft layers have been eroded into the plunge pools. The harder red sandstones and gritstones above were compressed out of the desert sands that covered the earth just before the dinosaurs and these form the hard lip at the top of the falls. Finally there are the carboniferous, or coalbearing, seams, the remains of the first forests that colonised earth once the seas and deserts receded. Warped, compressed and contorted, all these aeons of time are visible in the waterfalls.

211

208 LADY FALLS, R NEDD FECHAN
A graceful column of water falls 10m into a deep, large plunge pool. Set in a wooded amphitheatre. You can also climb behind the fall and dive back in. Take care!

→ Pontneddfechan is off the A465 from Swansea. From the Angel Inn (SA11 5NR, 01639 722013) follow the river on a good path up through the woods, just over a mile, to arrive at a junction pool with footbridges (good jumps here). Cross first bridge and bear L to the falls, 300m.
25 mins, 51.7714, -3.6011 🏊🍴

209 EINION GAM FALLS, R PYRDDIN
Wild, very tall waterfall about ¾ mile further upstream from Lady Falls.

→ Climb above the falls and bushwhack along stream another 500m.
45 mins, 51.7719, -3.6083 🏊⛰️

210 LITTLE CANYON, R NEDD FECHAN
A little gorge, right by the path. Jumps.

→ About half way to Lady Falls from Pontneddfechan, 300m before the picnic tables. A rocky flat area for watching.
15 mins, 51.7639, -3.5978 🍴

211 HORSESHOE FALLS, R NEDD FECHAN
A fantastic set of large, deep forest plunge pools beneath a horseshoe-shaped waterfall. The top pool has a tree and high cliff you can jump from.

→ From the junction pool and footbridge (for Lady Falls) bear R and follow the main stream a further ½ mile.
35 mins, 51.7742, -3.5936 🍴⛰️🚶🏊

212 LOWER DDWLI FALLS, NEDD FECHAN
Another fantastic pool under a wide-arced cascade.

→ Continue on from Horseshoe Falls another ½ mile. By this point it is easier to park at Pont Melin-fach car park (51.7826, -3.5853, off the Ystradfellte road) and walk back downstream.
10 mins, 51.7771, -3.5876

213 POWDER TRAIL, PONTNEDDFECHAN
Huge pool beneath ruined weir and gunpowder ruins at bottom of Mellte.

→ Bear R at Dinas Inn and continue on to village hall. Walk another ¾ mile to footbridge.
20 mins, 51.7637, -3.5679 🚪🍴

214 ISAF CLUN-GWYN, R MELLTE
Pools below the main falls in the adjacent Mellte valley, a steeper but more dramatic waterfall valley than Nedd Fechan.

→ On the Ystradfellte road from Pontneddfechan – after the Pont Melin-fach turning but before chapel and telephone box – find parking area by cattle grid and bridleway. Go down past Clyngwyn Bunkhouse (SA11 5US, 01639 722930) bearing R to bottom of gorge. You can also start from the amazing Porth yr Ogof river caves (51.8004, -3.5557, visitor centre) and walk 25 mins downstream.
15 mins, 51.7838, -3.5625 ⛰️🚶

215 SGWD Y PANNWR, R MELLTE
Secluded and enchanting waterfall.

→ Just off the path another ¼ mile downstream from Clun-Gwyn.
20 mins, 51.7813, -3.5631 ⛰️

216 SGWD Y EIRA, R HEPSTE
Path runs behind these falls! Large pool.

→ A mile further downstream on main path from Clun-Gwyn falls.
35 mins, 51.7784, -3.5546 🏊

219 Pen-Ddol Rocks, River Wye

Upper Wye and Elan

The Elan Valley is sometimes known as the Welsh Lake District and was the romantic inspiration for Shelley's early years. It is also the Welsh Wye's first major stop on its journey from its source in the Cambrian Mountains towards the literary haven of Hay-on-Wye.

Shelley – the idealist, revolutionary and great romantic poet – first visited his uncle's estate in the Elan when he was 18, walking there from Sussex over the course of a week. Already having a reputation as a strange but fun-filled young man, he used to bathe in the mountain streams and sail toy boats down the currents, sometimes with a cat on board. He fell in love in the valley and tried to make a life there with his first wife but when they failed to acquire a house the marriage collapsed. She drowned herself in the Serpentine in London two years later. He lost his life at sea in Italy aged 29.

The Elan stream in which Shelley used to bathe and both the valley homes he loved so much – Cwm Elan and the manor house Nangwyllt – were also drowned by a series of Victorian reservoirs in the late nineteenth century. These impressive dams and vast lakes were created to supply water to Birmingham at the height of its population growth. While swimming is not officially allowed in the reservoirs it is still

223

218

217

possible to swim in the Elan at the pool where it meets the Wye a few miles downstream. In the spring the water flows in from the top layers of the reservoir and is not too icy. In summer the authorities begin to release water from the bottom sluices and it drops in temperature dramatically.

The Wye continues south from the Elan junction, often shallow but sometimes pooling where it meets rocky seams. Pen-doll Rocks at Builth Wells is a particularly impressive series of pools and rapids. Wildlife along this stretch includes ravens, red kite, buzzards, herons, kingfishers, peregrines and otters.

As it reaches the north escarpment of the Brecon Beacons the Wye is forced to turn abruptly north-east and arrives in the charming, bookshop-filled town of Hay-on-Wye, a place that loves to swim. The Warren, a twenty-minute walk upstream from the town centre, is the place to paddle, skim stones or watch hapless canoeists negotiate the rapids from the long pebble beach. Further upstream the river is deeper and a longer swim is possible. During the Hay Festival you'll find it packed with people from all over the world, propped up on one elbow reading with their picnics and Pimms.

These grassy banks had been used to catch rabbits since medieval times but in the 1970s a scheme was proposed to convert the Warren into a caravan park. Local businesses and residents were so horrified they decided to club together to purchase the field.

A '20 Club', set up to find twenty supporters, quickly mushroomed into the '300 Club' that continues to run to this day. The outpouring of community spirit that was catalysed by this swimming hole led to other community initiatives and restoration projects. Anyone can join the Warren Club and membership is still £13, as it has been since 1973, though non members are free to use the area.

'Rocks piled on each other to tremendous heights, rivers formed into cataracts by their projections, and valleys clothed with woods, present an appearance of enchantment…'

Shelley, on his walk to Rhayader, 1811

221

217 PONT MARTEG, R WYE

Ancient wooded gorge with paddling and pools in nature reserve below road.

→ 3 miles N of Rhayader (A470) find layby on L just after R turn to St Harmon / Gilfach. This leads to footbridge, clear pools and paddling. Or for the explorers, head downstream about 1½ miles to 52.3227, -3.5453, via lane on the opposite bank (cycle route 8, cars cross via next turning on L) to find grassy avenue down to footbridge with white pebble beach and wonderful deep gorge pool and rope swing / jump, where old railway used to cross.
5 mins, 52.3320, -3.5403

218 ELAN JUNCTION POOL, R WYE

A wide deep junction pool with deepish pools and shallower paddles upstream by bridge. Reservoir water - very cold. Leave if fishermen. NO SWIMMING SIGNS.

→ 10 miles N of Builth Wells on A470 turn L signed Llanwrthwl. Continue through village ¾ mile then R at T-junction, and another mile to find footpath / track to R leading to junction pool after 50m.
5 mins, 52.2788, -3.5160

219 PEN-DDOL ROCKS, R WYE

An exciting stretch of the Wye narrowing through rocky cliffs near Builth Wells. Downstream are safe white sandy bays. Upstream the water deepens through a small gorge with rock formations.

→ 1 mile N of Builth Wells (A470) to find small layby opposite entrance to Penmaenau Caravan Park. Style in fence leads down steep bank to river.
2 mins, 52.1613, -3.4195

220 ERWOOD, R WYE

Deep, wide secluded corner pool.

→ 1¼ miles walk downstream of Llanstephan (lovely suspension bridge). Signed off A470 at Trericket Mill (great eco bunkhouse / camping, LD2 3TQ, 01982 560312) a mile S of Erwood.
25 mins, 52.0541, -3.2803

221 THE WARREN, HAY-ON-WYE

A popular stretch of commoners' meadow with long white shingle beach and shallows below the rapids, and deeper section above. Tree shade. Good for paddlers. Beautiful setting.

→ Heading S through Hay turn R at the Swan Hotel, past St Mary's Church, then after 500m, at speed restriction, drive / walk down bumpy track on R to car park at bottom. www.haywarren.org.uk.
5 mins, 52.0761, -3.1369

222 ELAN LAKES

Series of spectacular reservoir lakes. Penygarreg has a picnic area and island at top end. Craig Goch above is open access along its NW shore below Pont ar Elan.

→ Follow Elan Valley signs from Rhayader for 10 miles. Turn R over dam wall of Craig Goch to Penygarreg picnic area or continue towards Pont ar Elan and drop down from roadside. Cycle route 81. No swimming, but people do, well away from dams.
10 mins, 52.3020, -3.6190

223 LLYN CLYWEDOG, LLANIDLOES

Stunning reservoir lake which twists through deep valleys with many beaches.

→ Signed off the B4518, 3 miles NW of Llanidloes. Good roadside access along SW shores. No swimming, but people do.
2 mins, 52.4847, -3.6290

230 Bredwardine, River Wye

Lower Wye and Herefordshire

I spent my early childhood close to the Herefordshire Wye, near Hoarwithy. We were two families and a gang of five children. I was the youngest and would trail along behind as rafts were built and lanes explored by bicycle. It's easy to be nostalgic about a river when it flows through the heart of your formative years.

When I tried to remember some of the places I had swum on the Wye, however, I realised many were lost in the fog of early memories, so I decided to return to Hoarwithy for a week and retrace old steps. I based myself at Tressacks campsite, a plain but pleasant stretch of riverside with a little beach, roaring campfires and an excellent gastro pub. Each morning I tiptoed sleepily down to the river and plunged groggily into the shallow waters and was brought to life with a judder of adrenalin. I had played near here as a young boy, I thought, though the river seemed so much wider and deeper then. On really big expeditions we would cycle the three miles to Sellack Common and it used to take all day. The height of excitement was standing on the white iron suspension footbridge, bouncing up and down to see if it would swing and dropping blackcurrants on canoes as they went by.

The Wye is lucky to be one of the several rivers in England with an Act of Parliament that enshrines the right to navigate, and to swim. Some suggest that all rivers navigable by small

225

227

224

craft have automatic rights of navigation but even here on the Wye, one of the most famous canoeing rivers, there are still occasional conflicts between fishermen and other river users.

From Sellack Common the river completes a five-mile loop to Backney through mainly private fishing estates, but a mile-long lane, over the brow of a hill, cuts off the corner and brings you to Backney Common. This area of meadow has age-old commoner rights and occupies the inside of a large, deep meander. A wide pebble beach has been deposited over time on the inside bank and large deep swimming holes have been eroded on the outside. The sand and pebbles are beautifully graded so you can even bring your bucket and spade.

Some seven miles downstream the river comes to its most splendid reach as it enters the great wooded ravine of Symonds Yat. Beechforested cliffs climb up on all sides and King Arthur's and Merlin's Caves can be spied high on the limestone walls, cut by the river many thousands of years ago. The village is squeezed onto the narrow rising banks of the gorge and the east and west side are joined only by two rope ferries. It is possible to swim across but most inhabitants use canoes. Many homes – and even the church – have river landing stages which double up for river swimming in the summer. The village is equally famous as a place for learning about rivers and the great outdoors: the Biblins forest camp in Symonds Yat has been giving inner city children wild experiences for over 50 years.

The Wye is the most popular canoeing river in Britain and many companies will arrange everything needed for a few days canoecamping through the countryside. There is also the beautiful Wye Valley Walk and it was at Symonds Yat that I met an elderly couple from Lincoln who had walked for over thirty miles, swimming along the way. They had come rather unstuck skinny-dipping one lunchtime just as a flotilla of canoes helmed by a stag party in fancy dress came by! Despite that, they had a strict routine of swimming three times a day: 'Before breakfast, lunch and tea we agreed – its very good for you, you know, going in the cold water. And we haven't missed an opportunity yet.'

226

224 BACKNEY COMMON, R WYE
Ancient common land and pasture in tight loop of Wye. Large shingle and sandy beach shelving to a large pool. Large swan population, with droppings.

→ From A449 Ross take A49 Hereford road then first R, signed Backney. After 2 miles, bear R to Foy and find car park on R after 300m. Adjacent is a track to meadows, continue ½ mile upstream beach.
15 mins, 51.9390, -2.6009 🏊🏖⛺

225 SELLACK BRIDGE, R WYE
Beautiful open common by small church with shingle beach shelving to deep section on far bank. Elegant white suspension footbridge. Limited parking.

→ As for Backney but L for Sellack Church, instead of Foy, then R at sign after a mile. Or approach from King's Caple bank, over bridge. Good riverside campsite (Tressacks) and pub (New Harp Inn, HR2 6QH, 01432 840900) upstream at Hoarwithy.
10 mins, 51.9483, -2.6323 🏊🏖ℹ⛺

226 KERNE BRIDGE, R WYE
Canoe launch steps. Stone landing stage if you explore upstream through meadow.

→ 3 miles S of Ross on B4234 and 300m after the Inn on the Wye (HR9 5QS) pull into village hall / old railway parking on R.
2 mins, 51.8662, -2.6089 🏖🏊

227 SYMONDS YAT, R WYE
Small sandy bay and meadows, shelving to pool. Large rock on far bank.

→ Follow signs to Symonds Yat West. Follow path behind Paddocks Hotel or walk upstream 300m from Ye Olde Ferrie Inn (HR9 6BL, 01600 890232). Also Symonds Yat East. Swim from campsite (HR9 6JL, 01600 890836) or canoe steps below Saracens Head Inn. (HR9 6JL, 01600 890435). Tricky parking.
10 mins, 51.8479, -2.6431 🏊🏖ℹ🍴

228 THE BIBLINS, R WYE
Beach under wooden bridge by Scout Camp among forests.

→ Follow river downstream 1½ miles, on either bank .
30 mins, 51.8266, -2.6553 ❓

229 REDBROOK, R WYE
Grassy banks, deep water, good pub.

→ 2 miles SE of Monmouth on A466, park by old railway bridge and cross to other side. Swim anywhere downstream of tiny Boat Inn (NP25 4AJ, 01600 712 615).
5 mins, 51.7849, -2.6739 ℹ🏖🏊

230 BREDWARDINE, R WYE
Beach and deeper pool beneath bridge.

→ Signed of A438 7 miles W of Hereford.
5 mins, 52.0966, -2.9698 🏊🏖🏊

231 CANNOP PONDS, FOREST OF DEAN
Two wooded lakes and picnic areas. Warm water, beaches and pontoons, just set back from roadside. Very tempting in summer. Most ignore the no swimming signs but don't disturb anglers.

→ B4234 from Lydney, a mile N of Parkend. For something more discreet try Woorgreens Lake (51.8118, -2.5377) 100m N off the Cinderford road (B4226).
5 mins, 51.7897, -2.5700 ❓

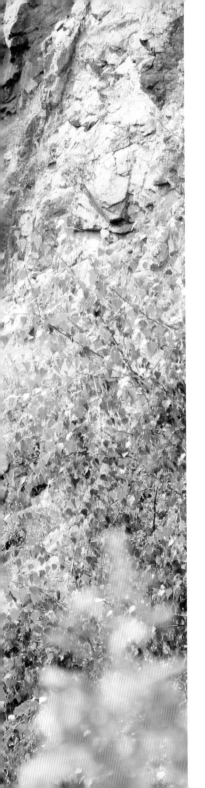

Gloucestershire, Malverns and Warwick Avon

The Malvern Hills in western Gloucestershire rise suddenly and steeply affording views out of proportion to their modest height. From here you can see across the plains of the Severn and towards Shakespeare's Avon and the Midlands.

The rocks of the Malverns are hard and resilient and some of the most ancient on the planet, formed more than 600 million years ago. The curative powers of the spring waters that well up beneath them are some of the best known in the world: Tennyson came here after a nervous breakdown, Florence Nightingale stayed in 1897 and Charles Darwin visited three times.

The waters were first bottled over 150 years ago and have been drunk by the royal family for more than a century. If you want to drink the water there are over 70 drinking fountains dotted across the hills, but if you want to swim in it, there is only Gullet Quarry. This old stone quarry opened in 1818 as a source of stone for Malvern town. The cliffs and crevices that surround it have quickly returned to nature in the thirty years since it closed, and the famous spring waters have filled it to create an aquamarine amphitheatre over 100 metres wide.

153

239

241

234

This is a deep and wild place like journeying to the centre of the earth. As I swam under the tectonic folds and curling faults laid down during the earth's early formation buzzards circled high above, alighting on the cliff-top trees and – as I pondered the aeons of time and great subterranean forces condensed in the tiny crucible around me – I felt rather small and insignificant.

The Vale of Gloucester stretches beneath and carries the wide meanders of the River Severn in its final stages before reaching the estuary. It's the longest river in the UK and I was keen to try swimming in it. There are a number of pleasant spots, such as the 11th century Odda's Chapel at Deerhurst and the Tithe Barn and riverside pub at Ashelworth. As there hadn't been much rain the current was very gentle.

I was also keen to explore Shakespeare countryside from the twisting perspective of the Warwickshire Avon. Much of the river is navigable, which means the water is always deep and there are no problems with access, but large boats cannot pass beyond Stratford. Up to the Warwick the river is wild and beautiful.

I set off late in the day from Charlecote Mill, one of only a small handful of surviving commercial working watermills in the UK. Most of the processes are as they would have been over 200 years ago and wherever possible grain is still sourced from local farms. I dawdled downstream, long into the warm evening, then stopped for the night among tall grasses on a remote section of bank.

That summer night, as darkness came, I strung up the hammock and watched a full moon rise across the meadows. Then, at around eleven o'clock, when the moon was bright, I slipped into the water. The river was silent, and the swans were sleeping in the reeds. There was just the soft sound of the water trickling as I broke the pool of silver light. Unzipping my tent early the next morning the sweet fresh river beckoned me in for another swim. Dew had covered everything but was burning off quickly as I struck camp, and I covered several pre-breakfast miles before arriving at Stratford-Upon-Avon for a superb riverside brunch.

240

232 GULLET QUARRY, EASTNOR
Spring-fed quarry lake in great natural amphitheatre of Malverns. NO SWIMMING SIGNS. COLD WATER.

→ 3 miles E of Eastnor (A438), turn L at crossroads (Hollbush). Continue a mile and turn L at top of hill to find bollards in road. Park and follow this road 500m. Popular with local young people; several fatalities.
5 mins, 52.0406, -2.3483 🟦🟦

233 ASHLEWORTH QUAY, R SEVERN
Green pastures, tiny lanes, a little pub and NT tithe barn. A pretty place to dip in the Severn. Watch out for boats.

→ Signed from A417 N of Gloucester. Boat Inn (GL19 4HZ, 01452 700272).
2 mins, 51.9239, -2.2648 🟦🟦

234 ODDA'S CHAPEL, R SEVERN
The great wide Severn moves slow and deep beneath the grand 11th century chapel. Swim across to the Yew Tree Inn at Chaceley but mind the boats. Also at Haw Bridge downstream on B4213.

→ Signed off A38, 2 miles S of Tewkesbury.
10 mins, 51.9672, -2.1941 🟦🟦🟦

235 WOODCHESTER LAKE, STROUD
Four lakes in wooded parkland below haunted mansion. NO SWIMMING SIGNS.

→ Woodchester Mansion (GL10 3TS, 01453 861541) is signed off the B4066 between Dursley and Stroud. Walk down to Middle or Kennel ponds. Be discreet.
20 mins, 51.7077, -2.2512 🟦🟦🟦🟦

236 HAMPTON LUCY, R AVON
Large pool in quiet fields above mill.

→ From A429 S of Warwick cross bridge and take track immediately on R. Press red button to pass through gate, alongside garden and along river banks. Charlecote Mill, still working and milling, is open to visitors (CV35 8BB, 01789 842072).
15 mins, 52.2142, -1.6223 🟦🟦

237 ALVESTON, R AVON
Idyllic riverside below village.

→ From the Ferry Inn (CV37 7QX, 01789 269883) pass down Ferry Lane and continue along footpath or descend by old ferry steps (Swiffen Bank).
5 mins, 52.2049, -1.6525 🟦🟦

238 STRATFORD-UPON-AVON
Recreation and picnic area. Good access.

→ Signed on R ½ mile out of town on A439.
2 mins, 52.1991, -1.6936 🟦🟦🟦

239 WELFORD-ON-AVON
Quintessential line of thatched cottages lead to down to beautiful, riverside path, upstream of weir.

→ 4 miles W of Stratford. From Bell Inn (CV37 8EB, 01789 750353) head past church to bottom of Boat Lane.
10 mins, 52.1679, -1.7910 🟦🟦

240 MARLCLIFF, BIDFORD-ON-AVON
Deep wide corner pool beneath cliffs.

→ A mile's walk downstream from Bidford or signed Marcliff from B4085 (continue down The Bank to parking).
20 mins, 52.1535, -1.8649 🟦🟦🟦

241 ECKINGTON BRIDGE, R AVON
Roadside picnic area by medieval bridge with easy access to river.

→ Signed off A4104 S of Pershore.
2 mins, 52.0782, -2.1133 🟦🟦🟦

Bodenham, River Lugg

Welsh Marches: Teme, Lugg and Arrow

The Teme – part Welsh, part English – means 'the dark one' in ancient Celtic and is one of several rivers that drain the Welsh Marches. It is wild and beautiful and is locally known for its annual coracle regatta at Leintwardine.

Coracles are one of the oldest boat designs in Britain, and were used by bronze-age Britons and invading Romans alike. They are oval in shape, rather like half a walnut shell, and traditionally made from interwoven willow rods tied with willow bark, covered in horse or bullock hide and sealed with a thin layer of tar. Designed for use in swiftly flowing shallow streams, such as those on the Welsh border rivers, they don't have a keel and only need a few inches in which to float. This makes them very light – perfect if you're a poacher and need to flee – and very manoeuvrable.

It's just as well that the Teme at Leintwardine is an excellent swimming river because the coracle's manoeuvrability makes it inherently unstable – spinning round on the spot and all too easily tipping you in. If you haven't yet honed the necessary skills, the Leintwardine coracle regatta is the perfect place to combine some training with plenty of opportunity for an involuntary river dip. The village's main swimming stretch runs from the road bridge upriver past the rope swing to a largish pool where the River Clun joins the Teme. With gardens running right down to the river, these backs have a rather civilised and homely feel. A little further on the meadow opens out and the river runs fast over wide pebble rills with some deeper holes and lively currents.

The Teme, which eventually joins the Severn, is just one of the many rivers that drain down from the Radnorshire hills and form this historic stretch of the Welsh Marches, a borderland of battle grounds and fiefdoms that the Normans attempted to

245

246

244

control from 1066 onwards. The River Lugg runs parallel a few miles to the south and eventually joins the Wye. At its valley head stands the church of Pilleth, meaning 'the pool on the hill'. In 1402 it was the site for one of the bloodiest and most important battles in a thousand years of Welsh independence wars. Despite the great massacre here, and the burning of the church, its holy well is still revered for its healing powers. Tadpoles and great crested newts also seem to thrive in its shallow waters.

It was not until we'd travelled another twelve miles downstream of Pilleth, way past Presteigne, that a friend and I actually found somewhere for a proper swim in the Lugg. Just outside Leominster near the village of Eyton, in a perfect rural landscape, you'll find several weirs and river pools. The Arrow runs close by and we started searching for a shallow ford that was the location of an idyllic toddlers' picnic party he had attended thirty years before and which he wanted to relocate. We found the site, homing in using a photo as a guide, and a mile upstream discovered a long weir pool, which provided a deeper swim in dark, peaty water through a tree-lined avenue of emerald alders.

The Arrow eventually joins the Lugg downstream of Leominister and we stopped for an afternoon dip at Hope under Dinmore before continuing on some miles to Lugg Meadows near Hereford. These are the largest known modern example of 'Lammas' meadows in Britain, with ownership divided into strips marked by dole stones. The meadows are still managed in accordance with this medieval system and an active commoners' association controls the grazing rights. With its intermittent gravel beaches and deeper pools we part swum, part waded the length of the Lugg that evening, floating in the low light past banks awash with cow parsley and meadow shank.

'Upon the glittering stream behold, Those fishermen, of courage bold, In numerous pairs, pursue their trade, In coracles, themselves have made; Formed of slight twigs with flannel cas'd, O'er which three coats of tar are plac'd. And (as a porter bears his pack) Each mounts his vessel on his back.'
With reference to the River Teme, 1794

242

242 LEINTWARDINE, R TEME

A stretch of open common with pub, bridge, church and rope swings. Little beaches and fun currents upstream.

→ 6 miles W of Ludlow on the A4113. Walk upstream from bridge to rope swing and beach. Lion Hotel (SY7 0JZ, 01547 540203). Also, a secret weir and pool upstream at 52.3523, -2.9190.

5 mins, 52.3595, -2.8777 🚽

243 KINGSWOOD COMMON, R TEME

A secret stretch of riverside with old weir, beach and pools.

→ Look out for the footpath sign on L off the B4204 on the steep hill from Martley down to Ham Bridge.

15 mins, 52.2405, -2.3752 ⛰🏊

244 BRANSFORD BRIDGE, R TEME

A deep meander with tree swings and jumps from high earth embankments. Popular with local kids.

→ Park at the Fox Inn (WR6 5JL) and walk ¾ mile upstream from bridge, on near bank.

15 mins, 52.1772, -2.2984 🍴🏊

245 BODENHAM, R LUGG

Long sandy beach and river pools in meadows behind church. Beautiful gravel lake too.

→ Signed off A49 7 miles N of Hereford. Follow path behind church. Cross bridge to far side of river, then downstream 200m. Or stay on near side of river and follow meadow upstream to find lake on R after 400m.

15 mins, 52.1535, -2.6892 🏊🏊

246 EYTON, R LUGG

Over a mile of deep pools and beaches with shallows meandering through open pasture with little wooded glades. Very pretty and rarely visited.

→ Heading N from Leominster (B4361), turn L to Eyton after a mile, then L (signed Aston / Lucton) after another. Find double steel gates on L, before first house (no footpath sign, but it is) and follow track 400m, bearing R at end, towards to river and bridge 400m. Cross bridge and head downstream for deeper sections and second weir.

15 mins, 52.2474, -2.7849 ⛰🏊🏊📷

247 LUGG MEADOWS, HEREFORD

Meadows and common land on outskirts of Hereford. The meandering Lugg bores deep holes in the bends with plenty of little beaches.

→ Follow A465 out of city (direction Worcester A4103), past college and Nuffield Health, to big car park at bottom of Aylestone Hill. Cross over onto meadows to river 500m ahead.

20 mins, 52.0686, -2.6869 🏊

248 PEMBRIDGE, R ARROW

Pretty paddling by bridge and downstream for ½ mile (follow R bank).

→ 7 miles W of Leominster on A44, turn R just before the old world New Inn (HR6 9DZ, 01544 388427).

5 mins, 52.2212, -2.8935 🏊🚽

249 KYRE POOL, HANLEY CHILD

Secret fishing lake on bridleway / byway.

→ Heading N on B4212 from Bromyard, find track on R, 200m after turning for Kyre Park gardens on L, and continue ¾ mile.

10 mins, 52.2803, -2.5420 ❓🏊

West Midlands: Meres, Mosses and Dales

The West Midlands' meres and mosses are some of the last remaining fragments of ancient peat bogs in the country. They form one of our most important habitats in Britain with new species still being discovered.

There are important lakes near Ellesmere and Colemere but Delamere – the forest of the meres – is Cheshire's most important area of wetland. The lakes were laid down 10,000 years ago at the end of the last ice age. As the melt took hold, huge iceberg-sized chunks fell away from the undersides of the glaciers and became trapped in pockets of earth and mud on the newly revealed ground. When they finally melted and collapsed they left large depressions – kettle holes – that evolved into freshwater lakes. Some were then colonised by sphagnum moss, which would entirely fill the shallows, soaking up rainwater and swelling like a sponge to many times its original size to form higher wetland areas called 'mosses'. These endangered lowland bogs have unique flora and fauna and have been drained, farmed or destroyed in many other parts of the country.

Hatchmere, nestling in the corner of Delamere, is a serene, reed-banked lagoon that has been popular with wild-swimmers for generations. A small bay leads to sandy shallows that can reach 24 Celsius at the height of summer. Late afternoon sun filters through the forest canopy. Dark, dappled green waters reach out ahead and jewel-blue dragonflies whirr low over the water.

254

251

253

This area is particularly well known for dragonflies – including the White-faced Darter and the Southern Hawker – and swimming in the lake is a fantastic way to get up close without disturbing them. As you glide through the water, nose peeping up from the surface, you are just another part of the lake's ecosystem. Hatchmere has always been a popular place for families and there is little evidence to suggest that swimming in the lake has a detrimental effect on wildlife.

This site, however, was the centre of a major struggle between local people, a private fishing club and the wildlife trust that bought the lake in 1998. The trust, unaware of the lake's use as a summertime swimming hole, initially gave an exclusive license to the fishing club who, in turn, tried to fence out the swimmers. A huge campaign ensued with local families and media lobbying for the people's right to swim and paddle. Now fishermen occupy one end of the lake and families the other. Signs say 'swimming not advised' – to cover liability issues – but dipping in the water is lawful and popular again.

To the west another popular uprising by working people seeking access to their countryside took place over 75 years ago. On 24 April 1932 over 600 walkers from nearby cities took to the moors, then reserved only for grouse shooting, in the Kinder Scout Marches mass trespasses. Six were arrested but their campaign eventually led to the establishment of Britain's first ever national park – The Peak District – in 1951.

The Peaks form the headwaters of the Dove, one of the most beautiful rivers in the Midlands, beginning at Dovedale, a truly spectacular limestone gorge. Here the river is mainly shallow but there are deeper sections under the ancient rock caves and limestone cliffs of Dove Holes and Raven's Tor. At Lover's Leap a young women, hearing that her fiancé had been killed in the Napoleonic Wars, threw herself from the cliff but was saved when her billowing dress caught in the trees. The entire White Peak area is made of old coral that used to lie at the bottom of a 350 million-year-old tropical sea. You can still find fossils of ancient crinoids or 'sea lilies' by the stepping-stones at the south end of the dale and Thorpe Cloud Hill is actually the remains of an old tropical atoll on the seabed.

250

250 HATCHMERE, DELAMERE FOREST

A shallow, warm lake in the nationally important wildlife area of Delamere Forest. A grassy area with beach is next to the road. Plenty of room for a long swim. Long campaign of access. Be respectful to fishermen.

→ 7 miles S of the M56 (J12) on B5152. Find beach next to The Carrier's Inn (WA6 6NL, 01928 787877). Woodland walks and bike rides around adjacent Delamere Forest Park.

2 mins, 53.2446, -2.6698 🏊🚻🚲🅿️📷

251 LITTLE BUDWORTH POOL

Pretty lakes with grassy banks. Good for a swim if no fishermen.

→ W of Winsford off A54. The Red Lion (CW6 9BY, 01829 760275) is a pretty pub.

5 mins, 53.1867, -2.6022 🍴❓

252 COLEMERE COUNTRY PARK

In an area of glacial meres, this is an easily accessible lake with quiet shore path and small sailing club. Blue–green algae possible. Be discreet.

→ Signed from the A528, 2 miles S of Ellesmere. Swim from beach near car park, or follow path around to wooded N shore for quieter spots. Some also swim from NW shore of Ellesmere (52.9122, -2.8815).

5 mins, 52.8910, -2.8402 🏊❓📷

253 HANMER MERE

Sandy bay at edge of woods. No boats or fishermen, just solitude and water that can reach 20 degrees in summer.

→ 7 miles W of Whitchurch (A539). Follow footpath by Glendower Place for 500m through woods.

10 mins, 52.9474, -2.8146 🏊

254 DOVEDALE, THORPE

A deep limestone gorge with caves, rock spires and shallow pools. Popular stepping stones perfect for paddling and picnics.

→ Signed off A515 2 miles N of Ashbourne, then continue through Thorpe. Deeper pools beneath Dive Holes upstream (53.0795, -1.7883) nearer Milldale.

15 mins, 53.0597, -1.7760 🏊🥾

255 OKEOVER BRIDGE, R DOVE

Famous annual Christmas bridge jump and raft race. Pretty in summer too.

→ 2 miles NW of Ashbourne. Walk over from the pleasant Okeover Arms (DE6 2AB, 01335 350305).

10 mins, 53.0302, -1.7570 🍴❓🏊

256 TUTBURY CASTLE, R DOVE

A deep rural stretch of the Dove above a weir, with view back to Tutbury Castle on the bluff.

→ Park in Tutbury Mill picnic area (signed off roundabout by river) and follow path behind, over meadows, along millstream to weir, ¾ mile.

15 mins, 52.8613, -1.6986 🏊

257 ELLASTONE, R DOVE

Pools in river near home of George Eliot.

→ Follow path upstream of river bridge. Shallow becoming deep above weir. Duncombe Arms gastropub (DE6 2GZ, 01335 324275). Also Toad Hole footbridge with pools, on bridleway W of Snelstone (52.9905, -1.7877).

3 mins, 52.9786, -1.8198 ❓🏊

163

Three Shire Head

Derbyshire Peaks and East Midlands

On Axe Edge Moor, high in the Peak District at the headwaters of the Dane, there's a riotous little creek that gushes down the hillside along narrow grassy banks before dropping into a pool beneath two medieval bridges. This is Three Shires Head, so-named because the three counties of Derbyshire, Staffordshire and Cheshire have their boundaries on the old packhorse bridge.

The residents of nearby Flash, the highest village in the country, used to put this giddy political geography to good use, holding illegal boxing matches on the no-man's land of the bridge where no county sheriff could arrest them. Renowned for making counterfeit 'Flash' money they came to Three Shires Head to exchange it for goods.

The moor was deserted as I approached across the hillside, squelching through the legacy of a week of summer rains. Dark clouds had blocked out the sun again and a warm westerly wind whipped at my coat. The storms of the previous days had enlarged the mountain tub to a raging, frothy cauldron. Giant ferns were billowing about like the bendy palms in a tropical typhoon and great bubbles the size of footballs were moving in circles around the pool. Overheated and sweaty after the walk I stripped and plunged, buffeted by currents of the wild jacuzzi. A cluster of bubbles took off in a gust, floated down the valley before being caught on the gorse.

That night, at the remote Mermaid's Inn, that looks over The Roaches from some miles away, they told me about the legend of a local beauty who was accused of witchcraft by a spurned admirer and was drowned in another nearby tarn: the Mermaid's Pool, also marked on maps as Blake Mere. Three days later the man was also found dead in the pool, his face

259

273

262

torn by talons. Now no animal or human will dare go there. In Celtic times small pools and standing waters were viewed as a doorway between the terrestrial and spirit worlds. Generally these pools were seen as bringers of life and of fertility but the spirits could be unpredictable. The next morning the Pool made a chilly wakeup call but I emerged unharmed. Rain clouds were rolling in from the west again as I set off in search of more recent history.

There can be few more popular screen moments than when Colin Firth, playing Mr Darcy in the BBC's *Pride and Prejudice*, goes swimming in the lake at Pemberley, to emerge dripping from the waters, his shirt unbuttoned and clinging to his chest, his breeches sodden and his dark hair a tangled mess. The scene helped turn Firth into a romantic icon. Both Lyme Hall and Chatsworth House have played Pemberley but Chatsworth's River Derwent is the more popular location for a summer swim. Landscaped by Capability Brown, the mountain river was deepened and straightened between two weirs. Soft red sands line the banks and with the light low, once the coach crowds have departed, the still waters allow for a long and most aristocratic swim.

The Derwent and all the rivers of the southern Peaks flow eventually into the great River Trent, artery of the great coalfields and industrial heartlands of the East Midlands. Just shy of the Thames in total length, it passes through some lovely swimming scenery. Essex Bridge, the longest packhorse bridge in the UK, with 14 of its original 40 arches remaining, was built in 1550 for Queen Elizabeth I. Above is the forested Crannock Chase, with a series of lakes and secret pools. Downstream, near Derby, seek out the extraordinary caves of 'Anchor Church' carved out by the river and inhabited by hermits and saints since the sixth century. In earlier history the river was a major transport route for the coalfields but since their demise the National Forest project has begun regeneration of former colliery pits and slag heaps. One of the prettiest is at Oakthorpe, a perfect vision of regeneration. This once humming colliery is now meadow and woodland and where the land subsided from a subterranean mine collapse, a wild lake has now formed, waiting for you to take a dip.

260

258 THREE SHIRE HEAD, R DANE
Packhorse bridge, waterfalls and shallow pools in small wild valley, famous for counterfeit money and skulduggery.
→ Many possible approaches but why not start from the New Inn pub in Flash (SK17 0SU, 01298 22941, off A53 Leek - Buxton) the highest village in England. Take footpath at Spring Head Farm.
30 mins, 53.2138, -1.9869 🏔

259 MERMAID'S POOL / BLAKE MERE
Tiny moor-top pool by roadside. Steeped in legend with views of The Roaches.
→ 6 miles N of Leek (A53) turn R before Winking Man pub. Continue 2 miles to find pool just below on R by junction. Continue on for remote Mermaid Inn (ST13 8UN, 01538 300253).
2 mins, 53.1486, -1.9418 🖼🏔

260 LATHKILL DALE, MONYASH
River emerges from a cave into limestone valley. Shallow weirs and pretty waterfall.
→ Descend on path, by toilets on B5055, ½ mile E of Monyash..
30 mins, 53.1880, -1.7303 🡇

261 ASHFORD IN THE WATER, R WYE
Riverside pools above weir.
→ W of Bakewell on A6. Footpath leads downstream ½ mile from the old bridge, on R as you enter village.
10 mins, 53.2223, -1.6939 🡇❓

262 MONSAL DALE, R WYE
Weir waterfall with rocky pools above and below.
→ ½ mile downstream of the viaduct. Drop down from Monsal Head Hotel / viewpoint by woodland path on L bank, ¾ mile. Cross on footbridge then return for a circular loop.
20 mins, 53.2395, -1.7353 🏃🚲

263 CRESSBROOK, R WYE
Wonderful big pool above weir and old mill in limestone gorge.
→ Walk, cycle or drive a mile upstream from Monsal Head and take the footpath at the back of Cressbrook Mill development 200m to weir. Also lovely paddling, stepping stones and gorge walk along Chee Dale (53.2586, -1.8141) 4 miles upstream.
5 mins, 53.2525, -1.7433 🚲

264 SLIPPERY STONES, R DERWENT
Deep pool on pretty stream with grassy banks, busy at weekends.
→ Drive (or take bus at weekends) to the head of Howden Reservoir (signed Derwent Valley Dams off A57). Then walk about a mile upstream to find pool 300m above footbridge. Some also swim in the lakes too. I swam below the layby, A57 (53.3735, -1.7221).
25 mins, 53.4547, -1.7471 🡇

265 CHATSWORTH, R DERWENT
Long river pools with fantastic Chatsworth parkland vistas. Red, sandy river bed, lawns for picnics. Be discreet.
→ Park at Calton Lees car park ¾ miles S of house (£2). Drop down to river and walk upstream. There is also a long stretch of sheltered, secluded river upstream of house and bridge (53.2289, -1.6174).
10 mins, 53.21990, -1.61254 ❓🖼

266 CALVER BRIDGE, R DERWENT
Deep and long, but shady and cool!
→ Below bridge , A625 to Froggat
3 mins, 53.2748, -1.6342 🡇🍴

268

267 FAIROAK POOLS, RUGELEY
Sandy lakes in open heath and woodland of Cannock Chase.

→ Birches Valley Forest Centre and GoApe are well signed 1½ miles W of Rugeley. Walk or cycle on new path behind car park up valley to find two lakes, followed with two more ½ mile further up.

20 mins, 52.7432, -1.9801 🚴♿❓

268 ESSEX BRIDGE, R TRENT
Narrow medieval packhorse bridge with paddling and pools above and below on grassy banks of Shugborough Estate.

→ Great Haywood is 5 miles NW of Rugeley (A51). Turn down little Trent Lane, past post office and under railway bridge, 300m.

5 mins, 52.8007, -2.0085 ♿🍴

269 BROCTON POOL
Old gravel pit with pools and cliffs.

→ 6 miles N of Cannock (A34) turn R at Brocton, signed Katyn Memorial. ¼ mile on L find footpath through woods along cliff top, down to pool on far side.

10 mins, 52.7654, -2.0473 ❓🅥

270 OAKTHORPE COLLIERY
Reclaimed colliery and meadow lake.

→ Follow Ashby Rd E from Donisthorpe. After a mile see blue colliery gates on R with picnic sign. Park and go through Willesley Woods 300m to open grassland.

10 mins, 52.7244, -1.5089

271 ANCHOR CHURCH, R TRENT
Extraordinary carved grotto cave with safe swimming on offshoot of Trent.

→ 2 miles N of Ticknall (A5006). Follow footpath from Ingleby (on road corner) a mile down to and along river to reach the crag. In high water you may need to take the path above the crag and drop down.

20 mins, 52.8415, -1.4975 🖼♿

272 COTTINGHAM, R WELLAND
Sandy pool beneath bridge.

→ From Cottingham take the Ashley Rd. After ½ mile, bear R by foot down track.

10 mins, 52.5103, -0.7679 🚴

273 CARVER'S ROCKS, FOREMARK
Beautiful secret sandy bay in woods on S shore of Foremark reservoir lake. No swimming, but people do.

→ 1½ miles SW of Ticknall, descending hill, find wide locked double gate on R with room to park. Follow track to old car park and find footpath down through woods on L. Follow lake shore R for 200m to cove. Also below Calke Abbey on Staunton Harrold lake (52.8016, -1.4465).

20 mins, 52.8032, -1.5081 ⛺♿❓

274 SYKES LANE, RUTLAND WATER
Huge horseshoe reservoir with shoreside cycle track around it. Warm with gently shelving shores. An official swimming beach is due to open thanks to the progressive attitude of Anglian Water.

→ At Sykes Lane tourist centre, signed off A606 E of Oakham. Hambleton peninsula is also lovely to explore, with views to the submerged church.

10 mins, 52.6625, -0.6174 🍴🖼

Lakes and Dales

The Cumbrian Lake District, home to Wordsworth's daffodils and *Swallows and Amazons*, is a place of volcanic mountains and lakeland islands. The nearby limestone karst country of the Yorkshire Dales provides a stunning assortment of waterfalls, gills and swimming rivers.

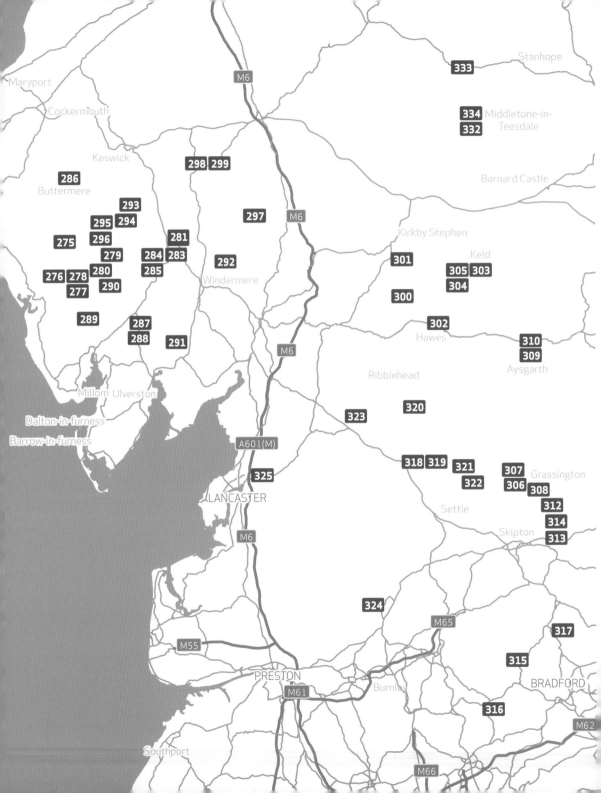

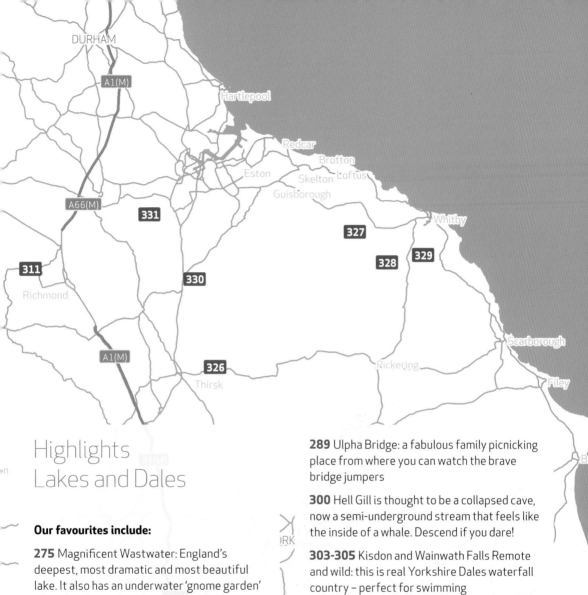

Highlights
Lakes and Dales

Our favourites include:

275 Magnificent Wastwater: England's deepest, most dramatic and most beautiful lake. It also has an underwater 'gnome garden'

277-280 Eskdale: a magical series of pools leading up to Scafell Pike. There's nowhere better to be on a hot day in the Lakes

281-282 Buckstones Jum - William Wordsworth's mountain pools with view across Rydal Water

287 Peel Island - Swim across to Wildcat Island of Swallows and Amazons fame

289 Ulpha Bridge: a fabulous family picnicking place from where you can watch the brave bridge jumpers

300 Hell Gill is thought to be a collapsed cave, now a semi-underground stream that feels like the inside of a whale. Descend if you dare!

303-305 Kisdon and Wainwath Falls Remote and wild: this is real Yorkshire Dales waterfall country – perfect for swimming

307 Ghaistrill's Strid - a gentle cataract great for 'tubing' – rafting the rapids on rubber rings

312 With two pubs, a river campsite and a tiny island, Appletreewick is an idyllic wild-swimming village

313 Set next to the ruins of Bolton Priory, this stretch of river becomes Costa-del- Bolton on hot summer days

West Lakes: Wastwater and Eskdale

The sun was falling in golden pools in a small bay where a group of walkers and swimmers had congregated to catch the last rays of the day. Steep white scree slopes plunged 500 metres into the lake on the opposite shore.

Scrambling down to the shoreline, grimy from a day of driving, the cool water instantly quenched my skin. Striking out over the white quartz lake bed the water was as clear as the Mediterranean. Small clumps of freshwater grass were soon waving beneath me and the mountains of Whin Rigg and Illgill Head rippled in broken reflections around.

There are many little white bays along the three-mile length of Wastwater, several fringed with great boughs of Scots pine. The whole area is tinged with the pinks and blues of the white volcanic granite that underlies the area, a material so pure and hard that it creates virtually no sediment or nutrients, keeping the lake free of algae and the clearest in the Lake District.

This valley of Wasdale is certainly a place of extremes: Wastwater, England's deepest lake, is overlooked by Scafell Pike, its highest mountain. It even contains the country's smallest church so perhaps it's not surprising that it's also home to some of its tallest tales. The World's Biggest Liar competition was first won by Will Ritson, landlord of the Wasdale Head in 1872. The competition was resurrected by Copeland Borough Council in 1974 and has attracted

275

275

279

competitors from Australia and Canada with classics such as the foxhound that could fly because its mother mated with a golden eagle (1989 winner) and turnips so huge that the Lakes folk could quarry sheep pens from them (1992).

You'll understand, then, why I didn't believe a story about a garden of gnomes that lives 50 metres down at the bottom of the lake, guarded by a picket fence. As it turns out, the story is true. The lake is popular with divers because it's so clear and deep. However, because there isn't much for divers to do or see on the way down, a series of extraordinary artificial 'sites' have been built up to keep them amused. Apparently the underwater gnome garden is growing.

The next morning I headed east to Boot in Eskdale on the other side of the great scree slopes, an area that shares the same bright white geology and crystal waters as Wasdale. Down near the road, a short walk from the pub, is a beautiful wooded pool called Gill Force. It's just upstream from a riverside church. The Esk is renowned for the magical pools and waterfalls along its 15-mile length and the higher you go the more dramatic they become. The next day I made a day trip high into the mountain to the legendary 'Tongue Pot' and Esk Falls, sampling many of the dips on my way.

Tongue Pot is just beneath the packhorse bridge at the head of the dale, about an hour's walk from the road. Here, in a cleft of the mountain burn, a long emerald pool has formed beneath a waterfall at the meeting of two rivers. A pebble beach shelves down on one side and an oak tree overhangs. On each side sheer rock walls rise up, making the place famous for jumps. The oak's knotty roots create excellent handholds for scrambling out of the water before diving back in.

Climbing higher, through Esk Falls, a series of perfect plunge pools extends right up to the Great Moss mountain plateau above which a shimmering Scafell Pike looms. Further smaller pots link back down again via Lingcove Beck, the rocks grey and sinuous, streaked with white quartz. Each forms a perfect place to lie in the sun as the waters roar by. When the sun is shining there is no better place on earth to be.

279

275 OVERBECK BRIDGE, WAST WATER

England's deepest lake with white, quartz beaches and clear water. Road access all along the NW shore. Dramatic mountain backdrop. Good pub and NT campsite.

→ Signed Santon Bridge / Wasdale from the A595 W coast road between Barrow and Whitehaven. Or from Ambleside and Eskdale via the dramatic Hardknott Pass. 2½ miles on from the youth hostel, there's a good beach at Overbeck Bridge, with car park on L by stream. Continue to end of lake for Wasdale Head Inn and camping (CA20 1EX, 01946 726229)

2 mins, 54.4501, -3.2838 ⛰ 🍴

276 BLEA TARN

Popular swimming tarn above Eskdale. A steep walk up. A beachy area on S side. The water is peaty and a little brown. Amazing sunsets.

→ Follow the path up from behind Beckfoot Station, Eskdale.

40 mins, 54.3967, -3.2870 ⛰ 📷

277 GILL FORCE, ESKDALE

A small rocky gorge and pool on the Esk, close to the village of Boot. Shady. Deep section with rocks to jump from.

→ From Boot Inn (CA19 1TG, 01946 723711) continue back down to the road junction (200m) and cross directly over down track leading to St Catherine's Church by the river (700m). Turn L, following river upstream for 250m to find narrow gorge and footbridge with pools below. Or arrive by the steam railway from Ravenglass

10 mins, 54.3902, -3.2663 🚉 📷

278 DALEGARTH BRIDGE

Tree swings into deep water in mini gorge below old bridge by road.

→ Turned R opposite old school 200m W of Dalegarth Station. Parking is ¼ mile beyond bridge. You can also head up track ¾ mile from car park to Stanley Force with pool in shady ravine (54.3849, -3.2727).

2 mins, 54.3922, -3.2769 📷

279 TONGUE POT, ESKDALE

There's a series of lovely pools up the Esk. Tongue Pot is the best, set beneath an ancient packhorse bridge with high jumps possible into deep water. Many more pools 200-300m above at Esk Waterfall and on Lingcove Becks.

→ Park by telephone at bottom of Hardknott Pass and follow riverside path up through Brotherilkeld Farm for 2 miles to confluence and bridge.

45 mins, 54.4236, -3.1907 📷 ⛰

280 KAIL POT, ESKDALE

A sunny, shallow, secluded pool off path on way up to Tongue Pot. Low waterfall with jumps.

→ As for Tongue Pot, but ¾ mile after farm, and 200m below path. 250m after joining of Scale Gill and 200m before wall boundary.

20 mins, 54.4106, -3.2073 📷 📷

281 Buckstones Jum

Central Lakes: Rydal and Elterwater

The mountains, rivers and waterfalls of the Lake District were the literary inspiration for William Wordsworth and many of his influential circle. The area around Rydal Beck was the setting for many of his walks, swims and musings.

Rydal Mount was Wordsworth's base for eight years, his most beloved home, and the place from which he courted his future wife, Mary Hutchinson. There are many pools in the parkland and fells above Rydal but one was so special to him he named it after Mary and dreamed of building a cottage there.

We may never know the pool's true identity but he described it as 'far among the ancient trees' and I have wondered whether Buckstones Jum could be the place, set in open fells on the edge of the wooded estate. It's a perfect triangular pool with a shingle beach in a bay between two flat slabs of granite, the water pouring in over the rock lip and scouring out a deep pool, perfect for swimming. From up here a wide lakeland vista opens up, stone walls criss-cross down the valley and Rydal Water glints below.

Wordsworth believed that nature was the crucible through which we must pass before our spirit can be independent. Many people who travelled to visit him in his remote home were touched by a sense of liberation and joy as they immersed themselves in the landscape. 'I have satisfied myself that there is such a thing as that which tourists call romantic... It was a day that will stand out like a mountain, I am sure, in my life', wrote Charles Lamb after spending a day wading up waterfalls and streams. But returning to London he soon spiralled into depression. 'You cannot conceive the degradation I felt... from being accustomed to wander free as air... and bathe in rivers without being controlled by any one... I had been dreaming I was a very great man.'

286

285

282

There is an even more hidden pool above Rydal Mount, a grotto lost within the woods, and this might also be Mary's pool. As you climb from the edge of the park the faint path begins to twist through a dingle of small mountain ash and yellow iris. You can hear water rumbling and a rocky outcrop appears, dotted with yew, hawthorn and rowan. On coming close a carpet of moss leads down to a small stone bank, carefully constructed by previous pilgrims. The cleft is narrow and dark and the pool incredibly deep beneath the waterfall. Rock walls on either side provide places from which to plunge, and ivy and mistletoe hang down from the trees. Swimming in this deep bower, with the roots of the ancient yew dipping in the water, awakens a sense of wonder and intense elation.

Samuel Taylor Coleridge and Thomas De Quincy were also visitors to this area and Wordsworth would take them on rambles and boat journeys as they recited poems to each other. His sister records a July day in 1800: 'in the afternoon Coleridge came. Very hot. He brought the second volume of the Anthology. The men went to bathe, and we afterwards sailed down to Loughrigg.'

Loughrigg Tarn is still an idyllic setting, now with a campsite providing the most basic facilities. The tarn itself is a relatively small, warm and shallow lake, set in a grassy dell with rocky bluffs and woody copses under a backdrop of the Langdale Pikes. On one summer night I remember the sun setting in great streaks over the Tolkien skyline. Small groups had gathered. Some stood together whispering, others sat with guitars but one couple had slipped into the water and their bodies were sending perfect ripples across the still lake. Then they turned on their backs and just floated, gazing up at the sky as the clouds turned magenta.

'Oh! many a time have I, a five years' Child, A little Mill-race sever'd from his stream, Made one long bathing of a summer's day, Bask'd in the sun, and plunged, and bask'd again Alternate all a summer's day...' From *The Prelude – Childhood* by William Wordsworth, 1850

283

281 BUCKSTONES JUM, RYDAL BECK

A deep triangular plunge pool with huge rock slab. High on the edge of the fells. Large pebble beach. Views down to Rydal Water. Occasionally marked private, but on open access land.

→ 1½ miles NW of Ambleside on A591, turn R entering Rydal for Rydal Mount. Park and continue up lane / track 1¼ miles, beyond last cottages and due N. As track flattens into base of valley you will see an obvious triangular pool on R.

30 mins, 54.4611, -2.9788 ⚲ ⛺ ▢

282 RYDAL BOWER, AMBLESIDE

Hidden deep in the woods with magical qualities. A narrow dark cleft between rock walls and a waterfall, crowned with rowan. Very deep and cold with cliff to jump from.

→ From Buckstones Jum continue downstream 400m through various waterfalls to come to a large rocky outcrop, through which the stream flows. There is a small grassy entrance below and a tree to hang your clothes on.

35 mins, 54.4567, -2.9786 ⚲ ⛺ ▢

283 LOUGHRIGG, SKELWITH BRIDGE

Beautiful small tarn, relatively warm, set against the backdrop of the Langdale Pikes. There is a basic but scenic campsite adjoining. Great sunsets.

→ Signed High Close off the A593 at Skelwith Bridge. Then track on R (Tarn Foot Farm) after ½ mile. The campsite (LA22 9HF, 01539 432 596) is through yard onto field. If not camping or campsite closed, find footpath on R at 54.4315, -3.0158, half mile further up lane.

10 mins, 54.4300, -3.0090 ⚲ ⛺ ▢

284 ELTERWATER, R BRATHAY

An easily accessible and perfectly picturesque lake shore, backed by ancient woodland and the Langdale Pikes skyline, with wide river pools and waterfalls downstream.

→ An easy 1½ mile walk from Skelwith Bridge (path by bridge) upstream past the waterfall, along lakeshore via Rob Rash wood and on to Elterwater village.

30 mins, 54.4295, -3.0244 ⚲ ⚲ ▢ ▯

285 HODGE CLOSE QUARRY

An exciting flooded quarry in a deep, seemingly inaccessible amphitheatre. Scramble down into dry quarry pit 100m to the N, then pass through tunnel to the water's edge.

→ 4 miles S of Skelwith Bridge (A593) turn R signed 'Hodge Close only'. Continue to parking at road end. Also explore amazing Cathedral Quarry (54.4161, -3.0587) a mile to N.

10 mins, 54.4062, -3.0538 ⚲ ⚲ ▢

286 CRUMMOCK WATER, HAUSE POINT

Very easy access beach by road with parking and small crags to dive from.

→ 1½ miles NW of Buttermere on B5289 find gravel beach by road with Rannerdale parking on R. Continue 1¼ miles on, beyond next parking area, to find a stile and gate on L leading down to and along a much wilder shoreline (54.5664, -3.2995). Lovely lakeside camping and boat hire at Dalegarth Guesthouse / Harness, 1¼ miles S of Buttermere (CA13 9XA, 01768 770233).

2 mins, 54.5530, -3.2962 ⚲ ⚲ ⛺ ▢

289 Ulpha Bridge

South Lakes: Coniston and Duddon

Peel Island – Wildcat Island in *Swallows and Amazons* – can be found off the south-east shore of Lake Coniston. Old woodland, gravel beaches and rocky promontories provide superb swimming, walking and canoeing.

Swallows and Amazons by Arthur Ransome tells the stories of the Altounyan family who visited the Lakes over several summers during the 1920s. The adventures of Titty, Roger, Susan and John have captured the imagination of children and teenagers for generations since. Their adventures begin when they sight the distant Wildcat Island and mount an expedition to reach it. After learning to sail their clinker dinghy, Swallow, they eventually reach the island and camp there, settling into a routine watching for enemies, making campfires and fetching milk and eggs from shore. Eventually they meet another group of children on the island who have a boat called Amazon, and they get up to various mischiefs together, drink ginger beer, go swimming, fight and bother Captain Flint on his houseboat.

Peel Island is now owned by the National Trust and camping and fires are no longer allowed, though you will see many people sailing and canoeing there in summer. It is no more than 100 metres long and has steep rocky sides but in the south-west corner you'll find both the 'Secret Harbour' and the beach described in the books. Anyone who has taken a boat in here, manoeuvred around the submerged rocks, splashed ashore and scrambled over the rocks needs little convincing that they are on Ransome's island. It's from the beautiful rocky headlands in

290

289

288

the woods at Low Peel Near that you can swim to the island, a crossing of some 100 metres.

There are several other swimmable bays up the east coast but the most popular beach is on the western side along the grassy banks of Brown Howe, close to where the Amazon family had their home. Arthur Ransome was inspired by his own childhood holidays spent in the Lake District. Each summer as he and his siblings arrived they would rush down to the lake, dip their hands in the water and make a wish. When they left they were 'half drowned in tears'. Nibthwaite, the tiny village where they stayed, is at the south end of Lake Coniston and still retains an air of simple, carefree summers. Parallel to Lake Coniston, only eight miles to the west, is another valley rich with childhood memories. Ulpha Bridge on the River Duddon has also been a favourite for family swimming for generations. The grassy banks and cherry trees provide a choice of shallows or deeper pools. The little post office sells sandwiches, coffee, newspapers, ice creams and fishing nets. Many families while away whole days here and the bridge jumping – from a respectable fifteen foot – provides ongoing entertainment through the afternoons.

Further up the Duddon valley, craggy hills create a rugged backdrop as the road twists and turns, meeting the river here and there. Beyond the hamlet of Seathwaite are the rocky pools of Birk's Bridge on the edge of Dunnerdale Forest. Set in a canyon overshadowed with dappled sunlight and beneath an old packhorse bridge, the water is still, deep and clear. It's possible to swim right up and under the bridge into a small gorge underneath a waterfall. The road continues on and up to Hardknott Pass and the old Roman Fort, eventually connecting up with Eskdale and its string of swims, creating a perfect wild swimming driving tour.

'There are no natives on the island now,' said Roger. 'They may have been killed and eaten by other natives,' said Titty. 'Anyhow, this is the best place for a camp,' said John. 'Let's put the tents up at once.'

Arthur Ransome, *Swallows and Amazons*

287

287 PEEL ISLAND, LAKE CONISTON

A stretch of wooded shore with beaches and crags. Swallows and Amazons Peel (Wildcat) Island is 100m offshore with a little bay to swim out to.

→ Turn off the B5285 E of Coniston (signed Brantwood / E of Lake) to follow the E shore. Continue 4 miles to Rigg Wood parking then another ½ mile by foot to a beach by the road and Peel Woods.

5 mins, 54.3175, -3.0849 🌊 🏖 🛶 🖼

288 BROWN HOWE, LAKE CONISTON

Car park, slipway, toilets, grassy banks and a long stretch of beach make this popular with families and those with small boats.

→ On W shore (A5084) 2 miles S of Blawith. Coniston Hall campsite (LA21 8AS, 01539 441223) is a few miles further N, with a great shoreside location, though can be busy.

2 mins, 54.3105, -3.0906 🏖 🛶 ⛺ 🌊

289 ULPHA BRIDGE, DUDDON

A popular, pretty area of grassy riverside with a long deep section under bridge, good for jumps. Shallows downstream. Easy parking. Village post office and shop nearby.

→ 1 mile W of Broughton-in-Furness (A593) turn R for Ulpha and continue 4 miles.

2 mins, 54.3263, -3.2366 🌊 🍴 🏨

290 BIRKS BRIDGE, DUDDON

A deep gorge, with crystal clear water, under an old packhorse bridge. Swim upstream from the rocks to the waterfall. Shady.

→ From Ulpha Bridge continue N on lane, through Seathwaite and 2 miles beyond to reach Birk's Bridge car park. Continue 2 miles further for Hardknott Pass and Eskdale. Seathwaite Tarn is to the E for those seeking a really big swim (54.3806, -3.1521)

5 mins, 54.3837, -3.1808 🍴

291 HIGH DAM, WINDERMERE

A pretty man-made tarn above Lakeside with many coves and a few places to jump in. Peaty but clean. Sheltered.

→ From Newby Bridge head to Lakeside and follow signs on through for Stott Park Bobbin Mill (½ mile) bearing L at fork on bend. Turn R up into woods after 300m and park. Walk uphill for about 15 mins, past the first, smaller lake, and you will arrive at a larger lake. Turn right over the wooden bridge and there are numerous entry points.

20 mins, 54.2903, -2.9813 🏖 ⛰

292 KENTMERE TARN

A very secluded hidden lake with a small pontoon, interconnected with the river Kent.

→ Follows signs to Kentmere, from Staverley, (A591 E of Windermere). After 2 miles turn into Kentmere Pottery / factory area on L and follow footpath upstream a mile.

30 mins, 54.4215, -2.8415 🏖 ⛰

North Lakes: Borrowdale and Ullswater

Borrowdale is considered by some to be the most beautiful valley in the Lakes. A steep-sided vale, running ten miles from its sources beneath Scafell down to the shores of Derwent Water, it is spectacular and remote, with waterfalls, deep pots and high tarns.

An old lady who lived on St Herbert Island in Derwent Water once told Beatrix Potter the story of a squirrel that swam out from the mainland to collect nuts each summer. The lake is scattered with wooded isles and the story and location became the inspiration for *The Tale of Squirrel Nutkin*, in which the squirrel and his friends built a raft of twigs and used their tails as sails to reach the island. Now the lake is a little too busy with ferries for my liking, though there are still plenty of places to bathe along the shore, and squirrels do still swim here.

My favourite swim is further upstream, near Seathwaite. From this tiny village, centred around the very civilised Langstrath Country Inn, a steep track leads to camping fields along the banks of Langstrath Beck. Just 15 minutes further upstream is Galleny Force, a series of river pools, sparkling as they overflow, overshadowed by twisted and teal-green mountain oaks. They are not deep, no more than three feet in places, but make a great place to snorkel with their hypnotic array of underwater light and shade. Galactic bubbles stream over the waterfall and sunbeams laser across the sandy river

299

295

298

floors. I spent much of my first afternoon in Borrowdale floating about in these crystal clear pools, burning my back in the sun as I chased minnows and gazed down on the great wobbling underworld.

Beyond Galleny the valley walls steepen, peregrine falcons soar above the fell and the map marks the remote bluffs of Eagle Crag, Heron Crag, Bleak How and Great Hollow. Climbers report several caves in this vicinity and, a couple of miles ahead under the mountain eye of Scafell Pike, lies Blackmoss Pot, a cliff face above a wide cavity in the rock and a deep, clear cauldron of water.

The best way into Blackmoss is to swim upstream. The pot walls gain in height gradually so you have time to admire the curves and gain your bearings. This pot has long been a place of initiation, legend and superstition. In recent years teenagers have gathered here from Whitehaven and Cockermouth most weekends to swim in circles in the pool and dare their friends above to jump. It's not particularly high or dangerous – about fifteen feet – but many stand for hours trying to summon up the courage in vain. As any old hand will explain, you should make your decision to jump during a thorough reconnaissance beforehand. Then, as you approach for the real thing, you can clear your mind and step out, relaxed in the knowledge that there is nothing left to consider. If you dither at the edge, looking down and filling your head with dizzy vertigo, hours can pass in torture.

Beyond Blackmoss you can follow the river for several more miles as it becomes wilder and higher with more 'pots' and pools to find. If you follow it to its source you can complete the highest swim in England, on the edge of Scafell Pike at Lambsfoot Dub. Unfortunately it's only three feet deep so nearby Styhead Tarn and Sprinkling Tarn are more satisfying, far larger and just as spectacular. The temperatures can be chilly but no worse than a mountain stream, and the water tends to heat up through the day. Sprinkling Tarn has a small swimming island near the edge, linked to land by a causeway of stepping stones. From up here the views down Borrowdale to Derwent Water are sublime.

294

293 GALLENY FORCE, STONETHWAITE

Two sets of pools and cascades, with grassy knolls and ancient rowan trees. Fun for plunging, snorkelling and picnics.

→ 6 miles S of Keswick (B5289), after Rosthwaite, turn L at postbox to lovely Langstrath Country Inn (CA12 5XG, 01768 7 77239). If camping continue on rough track up hill for further 600m to Stonethwaite riverside campsite (CA12 5XG, 01768 777234). Continue beyond campsite on path above woods ½ mile to find first set of pools on L, followed by more after ¼ mile on bend.

20 mins, 54.5069, -3.1226 🄰🛈🦮

294 BLACKMOSS POT, LANGSTRATH

A deep pot / gorge with 15 foot cliff for jumping. Interesting rock formations. Teenagers at weekends. Fun, open, sunny.

→ From Galleny continue along the river path a further 1½ miles, 300m after Blea Rock (the house-sized boulder on far L). Many more pools upstream a mile at footbridge (Swan Dub, Tray Dub)

40 mins, 54.4892, -3.1335 🍴

295 SPRINKLING TARN, ROSTHWAITE

A high tarn in the shadow of Scafell Pike with island and excellent swimming at 550m altitude. Good for wild camping.

→ Seathwaite is off B3289 a mile after Stonethwaite. Park at road end and continue upstream a mile, bearing R up Seathwaite Fell to reach Styhead Tarn (420m altitude). Continue further 800m SE up to Sprinkling Tarn.

60 mins, 54.4725, -3.1922 🄰🖼🄰

296 LAMBFOOT DUB, SCAFELL PIKE

Tiny, shallow, remote pool on route to England's highest peak (650m).

→ 100m above the Corridor Route.

90 mins, 54.4653, -3.2037 🄰🖼🄲

297 SWINDALE BECK WATERFALLS

Excellent series of high falls and deep pools in very remote valley.

→ M5 J39 head to Shap, then L to and through Rosgill. Continue on to Bampton Grange by back lane and turn L signed Swindale. Park at road end, walk up to farmhouse, then follow beck up for a mile.

60 mins, 54.4956, -2.7591 🄰

298 AIRA BECK

Series of pools and deep pots for ½ mile above well-known Aira Force.

→ Take the Dockray road, signed off the A592, Ullswater. After a mile, and beyond the Aira Force car park, find large double layby. Park and walk down to find the first of a series of falls and plunge pools. Continue downstream to wooden bridge, and finally stone bridge at Aira Force itself.

15 mins, 54.5793, -2.9289 🍴

299 KAILPOT CRAG, ULLSWATER

A high, gnarly crag plummets into deep water. Great for jumps and snorkelling. Wood behind, beach alongside.

→ Take the ferry to Howtown and follow the shore path a mile SW. Or take Howtown turning from Pooley Bridge, N of Ullswater, and follow it 4 miles to Howtown pier (tricky parking) or Sandwick. You'll pass several beaches on route and Park Foot camping (CA10 2NA, 01768 486309) has lakeshore pitches. Or try Side Farm in Patterdale (CA11 0NP, 01768 482337).

25 mins, 54.5763, -2.8734 🍴🄰🖼

Hell Gill

North West Dales: Eden and Upper Swaledale

I stepped down on to a remote and windy station halt. The train pulled away with a judder, creaking higher on the 'long drag' over the Settle-Carlisle moors. From here I would attempt to descend through the watery bowels of Hell Gill.

Hell Gill is a collapsed limestone cave system, now a deep slot canyon and geological curiosity. It provides the opportunity to plunge and paddle down an old underground river system, about 500 metres in length, without the need for specialist knowledge.

My local guide was Rob, an outdoor instructor. We climbed up Lunds Fell together, past Hell Gill waterfall and Hell Gill farm to a small medieval bridge spanning a deep fissure. This has long been the county border between Yorkshire and Cumbria: Dick Turpin leaped to freedom across it on Black Bess and Mary, Queen of Scots was escorted this way to her imprisonment at Bolton Castle. Satan himself is said to have created this gash which, though only a few yards wide, is like a fault line opened up by an earthquake. Ash trees overshadow crumbling sandstone cliffs, which almost touch in places. The water gushing in narrow chasms and pools below is heard rather than seen.

We entered further up where the stream tumbles down into the gorge via stepped pools. The sky was overcast but no rain was forecast and the whole stream catchment was within view, an important consideration when entering a slot canyon. The brown limestone karst walls were curvaceous and plump, undulating like an ileum, pitted with dimples making the water echo and our voices boom, as if we were inside Jonah's gut.

300

301

305

The walls of the canyon rose higher as we descended, the light dimming, but the sky and trees remained reassuringly visible above.

I was only out of my depth at one point in a deep plunge pool that you must swim after sliding down a boulder by a waterfall. There is usually a rope tied to help you back up, should you wish to retreat, although if this is not there you should return and enter from the bottom of the gorge instead. There are also some accessible upper ledges to escape to in case of unexpected rains.

This brown limestone karst is found across the moors in Upper Swaledale too. The village of Keld has five excellent waterfalls with plunge pools. So remote is this region that in the seventeenth century the nearest consecrated land was over three days away. After following the river below you can walk the 'Corpse Road' back over the high limestone plateau.

Kisdon Force is the most spectacular set of falls with two huge pools beneath great basalt-like pillars, thundering deep down in the woods. The high pool is the larger, at least 100 metres across with ledges around its edge, while the lower pool is the deeper: dark and frightening with steep walls.

At Park Lodge campsite in Keld, behind the café and down a track to a river, you will find several shallow falls flowing across hot, flat rocks with shallow pools that heat up nicely during the day. At night the campsite's riverside fires send reflections shimmering across the river pools and in the morning you can swim in your own private plunge bath.

Finally Wain Wath falls, a mile beyond Keld, is the most popular and accessible of the Keld swims. Prettily situated under limestone cliffs there's even a garden, a little gate and a bench on which to hang your towel.

Slot canyons with long catchments are particularly dangerous as unseen localised rainfall upstream can create flash floods. Kolob in Zion Park in USA gained international notoriety in 1993 when a group of scouts lowered themselves into a flooding canyon with no means of retreat.

303

300 HELL GILL, GARSDALE HEAD

A deep, almost enclosed chasm and stream with impressive rock formations, descending steeply to a dark waterfall and deep plunge pool. Good scrambling skills required. Safer to climb up the gorge.

→ From Garsdale Head (Moorcock Inn, LA10 5PU, 01969 667488) follow B6259 N towards Kirkby Stephen. After 2 miles at the Cumbria border sign turn R onto track; there's parking for one car at end. Cross railway and turn L. Hell Gill waterfall is 100m on, below you on L, but continue up track 600m to farm, then 300m to stone bridge. 100m below is Hell Gill exit. Or follow wood boundary 250m up hillside to find Hell Gill entrance. Never descend if you cannot reclimb.

15 mins, 54.3669, -2.3300 🟥 🟥 🟥 🟥

301 PENDRAGON CASTLE, R EDEN

Amazing wild ruined castle with secret pools in river downstream.

→ 4 miles beyond Hell Gill on B6259, turn L at Pendragon Castle and after ½ mile, at cattle grid, follow footpath track (signed Wharton). After 5 mins you'll spot a corner pool with beach below. Many more beyond.

10 mins, 54.4269, -2.3389 🟥 🟥 🟥

302 COTTER FORCE

Tiered rock slabs flow down to a deep wide plunge pool.

→ 3½ miles E of Garsdale Head. Head E on A684 to find stone bridge over river, parking and tarmac path along river. Follow path upstream ½ mile.

10 mins, 54.3235, -2.2346 🟥 🟥 🟥

303 KISDON FORCE, R KELD

Two spectacular waterfalls deep in a woody gorge. One is 5m high with 80m-wide plunge pool, open and awe-inspiring. The other is 12m high with a 50m-wide plunge pool, deep, dark and terrifying!

→ From Keld village follow Corpse Road path dir Muker ½ mile then drop down to find Kisdon Force waterfalls in trees below.

15 mins, 54.4043, -2.1584 🟥 🟥

304 PARK LODGE, KELD

Riverside campsite with campfires and café with impressive falls and pools upstream.

→ Enter site through farmyard gate, to L behind Keld teashop. Descend to river and find many pools and falls upstream in the ravine up to Hogarth's Leap.

5 mins, 54.4082, -2.1731 🟥 🟥

305 WAIN WATH WATERFALL, KELD

A wide waterfall, about 3m high, with pleasant plunge pool and open aspect by roadside. Limestone cliffs in valley and grassy banks for picnics. Interesting river and rock shapes downstream and good paddling.

→ Continue beyond Keld (dir Kirkby Stephen) to find falls on R, 200 m after turning to W Stonesdale. Continue on a mile for pleasant riverside campsite, just before bridge on L.

2 mins, 54.4095, -2.1803 🟥

193

Upper Wharfedale and Eastern Swaledale

Upper Wharfedale is the classic Yorkshire Dale: rectangular hay barns in every field, green meadows filled with wild flowers and beautiful rivers dotted with pools and falls.

High up on the fells of Moss Top and Chapel Moor the headwaters of the Wharfe begin to collect, filtering down through sinkholes, trickling through cracked limestone fissures before reappearing in tiny tributaries and streams. The Wharfe gathers pace through Langstrothdale then flows through the pools of Amerdale Dub before arriving at Grassington, one of Yorkshire's most picturesque swimming villages.

Most people gather on the river meadows to the south of the village. Here you'll find families in rubber dinghies and children wielding fishing nets. At the weir people slide down the smooth chute or swim in the larger clear pool above. Further down there is a waterfall by a footbridge and stepping stones to a riverbank church. The connoisseurs, however, head upstream of Grassington to Ghaistrill's Strid, a series of cascades and

306

311

306

rapids: the perfect place to while away the day swimming in rocky pools, chasing minnows and 'tubing' the rapids. Above the falls, and alongside an idyllic grassy knoll, the river is forced down a 100-metre bobsleigh run. Only a modicum of skill is needed to navigate the chute – the current takes care of the rest. The best method is to lie down head first on the ring so you can steer yourself with your arms – if you sit on the ring you tend to spin round and round. Our group was soon running time trials for sets of three descents, including the run back up the hill. If you're very daring, and the river is low, it's possible to surf the white water without a ring at all, though you may end up bruising a knee or an elbow. Keep your head down, eyes up and arms in front. Stay streamlined but flexible and let the current curl you around the corners and guide you around any obstacles. The trick is to move with the flow like an eel and make only small body adjustments.

The walk from Grassington downstream follows an avenue of sycamores and oaks before arriving in the outskirts of Burnsall at Loup Scar, a faintly Jurassic-like limestone scar. You might well be disturbed by the spectacle of young men throwing themselves off the cliffs of the scar into the plunge pool below as part of a well-known local rite of passage. The small pool is certainly deep enough for those who wish to test their mettle, but the full jump requires a degree of judgement as an overhanging cliff must be cleared. There have no doubt been serious accidents here. If there are no jumpers the pool is also excellent for a gentle swim and you can sit with your legs dangling in the water over its perfect edge almost as if you are at a properly excavated swimming pool.

Just below the rapids there is a larger river pool before passing behind the old Anglo-Saxon church of St. Wilfred's and heading on to the village bridge. On hot days the village green in Burnsall heaves with families. The field next door is turned into a large car park and the river is choked with a flotilla of the kiddy dinghies sold from the village shop and various makeshift stalls. The shallows below the bridge are popular with children, while upstream, alongside the pub, you can even find grown men drifting around in toy boats while ordering drinks from the bar.

308

306 GRASSINGTON WEIR

A large grassy area of riverside common with two weirs, a water slide, a waterfall, an ancient church and stepping stones. Popular, fun and safe.

➔ Grassington is on B6265 9 miles N of Skipton. Park in Grassington village centre and walk down to the river via Sedber Lane (200m), or park S of the village (signed Linton Falls and church) on Church Lane and cross on footbridge. Best swimming is above higher weir. There's a smooth chute (slide) on far side by ruined millhouse – fun with inflatables. Head downstream 10 mins to the stepping stones and the twelfth century riverside church of St Michael and All Angels.

10 mins, 54.0668, -2.0016 🏊🍴🚻

307 GHAISTRILL STRID, GRASSINGTON

Exciting rocky pools and rapids. Lower pools have interesting snorkelling and a large reach for a longer swim. Also little tubs of warmer standing water in rockpools. Upstream rapids have a chute which is fun on rings but be careful!

➔ From the Grassington bridge follow river upstream on river's L bank for a mile to come to the flat rocky ledges and pools beneath rapids. Watch out for submerged ledges. The upper section (200m) is accessed by riverside footpath behind hedges, and has a fine long cataract / chute, picnic spot and pool. In low water you can try shooting the chute on a rubber ring. Continue another 300m into Lower Grass Woods.

15 mins, 54.0766, -2.0153 🔺⛰️

308 LOUP SCAR, BURNSALL

A fantastic stretch of grassy riverside incorporating the limestone cliffs and plunge pool of Loup Scar with a terrifying jump above. There's a large, shallow, grassy river pool just downstream.

➔ Burnsall is 2½ miles S of Grassington on a lovely riverside walk, or on B6160. Follow riverside path upstream from village / Red Lion (BD23 6BU, 01756 720204) about ¾ mile, past church, to Loup Scar gorge with a very deep rectangular plunge pool beneath cliff.

15 mins, 54.0517, -1.9558 🍴🔺ℹ️🏊

309 WEST BURTON, WALDEN BECK

Two beautiful village waterfalls with good pools. Lower falls beneath bridge are deeper.

➔ At bttom (N) end of village green turn down narrow lane to find some parking, the bridge and the upper falls by the old mill.

2 mins, 54.2760, -1.9712 🏊

310 LOWER AYSGARTH, R URE

Mighty and impressive tiered cascades. Great fun in low water. Many pools below.

➔ ½ mile downstream on river path from Aysgarth bridge.

10 mins, 54.2951, -1.9736 🔺

311 RICHMOND, R SWALE

Pretty riverside swimming hole with beach upstream, waterfalls beneath the ruined castle downstream.

➔ Follow the river path up upstream from the older upstream bridge (Bridge St) ¾ mile, for grass and deep pools. Or head downstream beneath the castle for the waterfalls themselves.

15 mins, 54.4040, -1.7518 🏊🚻🔺

Lower Wharfedale and Hebden Bridge

Appletreewick is a delightful stretch of Lower Wharfedale with two pubs, some houses and a pleasant lane that leads down through grassy fields to a river pool with an island.

Bathing morning and dusk in this peaceful place became the routine of our days. I had arranged to explore the area and test out the local swimming holes with a group of friends. Emerging from our tents we would slowly gather at breakfast time beneath the old hazel, dive into the cool peaty waters and swim several lengths of the long pool. Then we would loll about on the short grass and dry in the morning sun, sipping tea and reading papers, sometimes putting up a hammock between the trees if we felt energetic. Soon we were planning the day's excursion but by dusk we would re-congregate, sometimes lighting up the island with candle lanterns and swimming silently in the inky waters beneath the rising stars.

Downstream of our happy home at Appletreewick is the Bolton Abbey estate and we made several expeditions to test the waters and teashops there. The great ruins of this major monastic enclave sit on a bend of the river above a stretch

317

314

313

of pebbly beaches. During the hottest days it becomes a Yorkshire Costa del Sol: a mass of swimmers and sunbathers mixed with suntan lotion and sloppy ice cream. Upstream the river is deep enough for swimming, downstream it is shallow enough for paddling and stone skimming. Taking the water, ruins and landscape together it's not surprising it attracts so many people.

Some miles upstream the 'Strid' section of river is less crowded. The river here runs through a notorious cataract with fantastical curving rock shapes. The water is so deep that it is almost motionless on the surface. When in flood the level rises quickly creating treacherous under-surface eddies. Although the Strid is very narrow it is 20 feet deep in places and its profile is hourglass shaped. Underwater there are many hidden caves and pockets in which you would not want to get trapped.

A 'strid' in old provincial English literally means 'a narrow passage between precipitous rocks or banks, which looks as if it might be crossed at a stride'. A number of people have died trying to jump the gap, or venturing too close to the edge, and the dangers are particularly acute during heavy rains.

We peered into the Strid respectfully and decided to swim several hundred yards below it instead, where the river has returned to its normal width. The bluebell-rich beech and oak woods have been opened up by a series of tracks and are a Site of Special Scientific Interest, renowned for summer migrants from Africa including the wood warbler, redstart and pied flycatcher. Arriving by the middle of May they find the insect-rich vegetation and mild valley climate irresistible. The yellow and white wood warbler nests at ground level and can be hard to spot, though its call of a whistle followed by a harsh trill is difficult to miss. The pied flycatcher is scarce, though nesting boxes have been placed around the woods.

We swam breaststroke under the lush beech trees while a warbler whistled sweetly from the bank. Some of us swam up close to the Strid and peered in from the safety of our downstream position. The curving rocks rose up above us and we thought soberly of the water's potential power and fury.

312

312 APPLETREEWICK, R WHARFE

A pretty rocky pool in the river with a small island and bay and rapids upstream. Rope swing on far side, grassy banks and field for picnics. Large shingle beach on far bank downstream too. The water has many submerged underwater rocks, which makes diving dangerous.

→ Appletreewick is 2 miles off the B6160 via Bolton Abbey and the A59 from Skipton. Pool is in field below the New Inn (BD23 6DA, 01756 720252) but access is via footpath just before Mason Farm campsite (BD23 6DD, 01756 720275), then follow back downstream. Craven Arms (BD23 6DA, 01756 720270), just up the road from the New Inn, is highly recommended.

10 mins, 54.0332, -1.9213 🚗🍴ℹ️⛺

313 BOLTON ABBEY, R WHARFE

A popular stretch of river in front of the priory ruins. Upstream of stepping stones and bridge is deeper section where people sometimes use boats. Downstream are the shallows but underground rocks make swimming difficult and diving dangerous.

→ Well signed off A59 6 miles E of Skipton. Park car on L, cross road and descend into estate through gates. River is in front of ruin. Tearoom and restaurant upstream at The Pavillion.

10 mins, 53.9839, -1.8865 🚗🍴

314 STRID WOODS, R WHARFE

A deep, shady stretch of river through nature reserve and woodland. Above is the Strid gorge (do not swim in the cataract itself). Wide river, shelving gently to 3m. Stony bottom. Dappled and glorious on a sunny day. A long swim possible up to entrance of Strid and downstream until it shallows. At weekends the path alongside river can be busy.

→ 2 miles beyond Bolton Abbey, find turning R into The Strid car park and visitor area. Pay for parking and walk down through woods to admire the cataract. Follow path downstream to about 300m beneath end of the cataract and drop down to rocky riverside.

10 mins, 54.0024, -1.9019 🏊▼

315 LUMB HOLE, HEBDEN BRIDGE

Picturesque waterfall and plunge pool surrounded by ferny cliffs.

→ On Crimsworth Dean Beck near Stone Booth Farm, N of Pecket Well. Or walk / cycle up from Hardcastle Crags car park (bottom of Midgehole Rd N of Hebden Bridge).

40 mins, 53.7790, -2.0132 🚗

316 GADDINGS DAM, TODMORDEN

High and wild, this old reservoir is a well-known local swim with a pub at the bottom to reward your efforts.

→ Climb track by Shepherd's Rest inn (OL14 6JJ, 01706 813437), just W of Lumbutts, S of Todmorden.

20 mins, 53.6992, -2.0793 🏊ℹ️⛺🖼️

317 HARDEN BECK, GOITSTOCK WOODS

A mighty waterfall and a good pool along this woodland walk near Bingley.

→ Take footpath a mile upstream from bridge in Harden (B6429 to Cullingworth).

20 mins, 53.8263, -1.8844 🚗

318 Stainforth Force

Ribblesdale, Ingleton and Malham

The Yorkshire Dales have more waterfall plunge pools than anywhere else in England. The south-west corner of the Dales, around Settle and Ribblesdale, is one of the bestknown areas.

At Stainforth on the River Ribble, just a few miles north of Settle, a caravan park has grown up around one of the river's most popular swimming holes. It's always busy through the summer and deservedly so. There is a series of shallow rapids by an old packhorse bridge where children fish and paddle. The water then tumbles down a waterfall into a deep, black, smooth-sided plunge pot with an old iron ladder. On any day in summer you can sit and watch the antics of children and parents alike testing their nerve by jumping into the cauldron from higher and higher vantage points. Downriver, fields open

322

319

323

out in a wash of peace and buttercups, and further large pools provide a place for longer swims.

Catrigg Force is just a mile's walk from Stainforth but much more secret. Water squeezes down through a slot in the tall rock structure via an upper pool, into which you can climb, and down into the lower pool. It's only large enough for a quick plunge but the cathedral-like setting deep in this wooded glade more than makes up for that in awe and wonder.

The reason for all these waterfalls is the limestone geology and the legacy of glaciation. At Gordale Scar, ten miles away, a 400-footdeep ravine is all that remains of a great underground river cave the size of the Channel Tunnel, while nearby at Malham Cove a waterfall with the power of Niagara once flowed over a vast inland cliff. This cliff can still be seen, stained grey and overgrown with ferns and shrubs. Several miles upstream, Malham Tarn, a mile-wide lake, is all that remains of the great river that once fed it. It is now a wildlife reserve with possibilities for discreet swimming among the curlews, mallards and greater crested grebe that live there.

For more waterfalls than you can possibly swim in a day you should try the Ingleton Waterfall Walk, with a really superb series of falls and plunge pools. The Walk was established in 1885 and thousands of visitors travelled by the new railway from Manchester and Bradford to see its geological wonders. By 1888 it was attracting over 3,000 visitors a day, even with an entrance price of 2d.

On the western side Pecca Falls and Thornton Force are now on open-access land though no one will thank you for attempting to park in these narrow lanes. Thornton Force is the more popular, a classic strata waterfall with an upper layer of 330 million-year-old carboniferous Great Scar limestone and lower layers of 500 millionyear- old Ordovician sandstone. The pool is open, south-facing and on a hot day you will find many people wading, swimming and clambering on the rocks. Pecca Falls below flows through a woody glen and its many plunge pools will be attractive if you're a Gollumtype that likes to scrabble on the rocks and dive in and fish among the dark pools.

318

318 STAINFORTH FORCE

A series of river pools and falls set beneath an old packhorse bridge. Grassy banks and good paddling. A deep cauldron into which the brave jump. Longer river pools. Set below a caravan park though peaceful stretches in the field downstream. Peaty water.

➔ Stainforth is 3 miles N of Settle (B6479). Park in village and carry on up main road 200m on foot. Turn L down Dog Hill Brow and descend 400m to bridge (where there is some limited parking in the off-season). Main fall is 200m downstream. Continue down to find further deep river pools and more open countryside.
20 mins, 54.0997, -2.2791

319 CATRIGG WATERFALL

An atmospheric waterfall set in woodland on edge of moor with small pool beneath towering rocks.

➔ From post office in Stainforth continue to green (100m) and turn R up lane, becoming a track up hillside. After ¾ mile falls are below on L at top of woodland.
20 mins, 54.0994, -2.2580

320 BIRKWITH CAVE, RIBBLESDALE

Amazing subterranean river deep inside cave system. Only for the properly equipped.

➔ 3 miles N of Horton-in-Ribbersdale.
15 mins, 54.1880, -2.3023

321 MALHAM TARN

Large, windswept natural lake; a remnant puddle of the river that once flowed over Malham Cove waterfall.

➔ Take the Arncliffe road from Malham village and turn R after 3 miles. You can see the lake. There's a large carpark off the lane. Tarn is 300m up footpath on L, access from E bank only.
10 mins, 54.0922, -2.1625

322 JANET'S FOSS

Lovely little clear plunge perfect for families. Cave to explore.

➔ Signed downstream of Gordale Bridge, about a mile E of Malham on route to Gordale Scar.
5 mins, 54.0657, -2.1365

323 THORNTON FORCE, R KINGSDALE

Famous waterfall with overhang and large pool popular with bathers.

➔ Off A65 on Ingleton Waterfall Wrail (fee charged) but also on open access land / public footpaths, from lanes N of Ingleton. Also Beezley Falls, a huge deep cauldron pot further along on the Waterfall Walk (54.1727, -2.4690).
30 mins, 54.1727, -2.4690

324 CLITHEROE, R RIBBLE

Edisford Bridge with picnic area and parking. Pretty beach and paddling.

➔ 1 mile W of town on B6243.
3 mins, 53.8679, -2.4180

325 CROOK O' LUNE

Just off the motorway, this is a wide stretch of mature river with beaches and long swims. Easy access.

➔ M6 / J34 take A683 towards Caton and turn L after 2 miles, signed 'Crook O' Lune Picnic Site'. Beaches below bridge or river walks up and down stream.
5 mins, 54.0763, -2.7312

Gormire Lake

Yorkshire Moors

Sutton Bank offers the finest view in England according to the real James Herriot. From here you can see for miles across the Vale of York to the Dales. Halfway down the escarpment, romantically nestled in the woods, is the emerald oval of Gormire Lake.

The water of Gormire Lake is pretty warm and you'll most likely be the only person swimming there when you go This is a quiet and secluded place to visit among broad-leaved woodlands: a breeding place for coot, great grebe and mallard, sheltered by higher ground. A steep path leads down Sutton Bank, the top of the escarpment. Alf Wight, better known by his fictional name James Herriot, had his veterinary practice in Thirsk (Darrowby in the books) about five miles away. He often visited Gormire Lake.

The tarn was formed 20,000 years ago by glacial erosion, and folk tales and legends of Gormire abound, many involving horses. One tells of a local knight who tricked the Abbot of Rievaulx into lending him his white mare. The mare would not respond to his commands, jumped off Sutton Bank and plunged him into the lake with the Abbot behind transformed into the devil. Ambitious schoolmaster John Hodgson was so inspired

326

328

331

by this tale and a recent trip to the white horses of Wiltshire that in 1857 he and 31 volunteers decided to carve out their own horse from the escarpment. It was badly damaged by a hail storm in 1896 and fell into disrepair after the First World War but was renewed in 1925 and today is the most northerly white horse in England.

The steep, twisting road that leads up to Sutton Bank threatens horrible things to caravans as it rises onto the Yorkshire Moors proper. From here 40 miles of heather and gorse flow in undulating ridges to the sea. There are few large rivers but several smaller becks and woodland waterfalls near the coast at Whitby. One of the best falls is just below the famous village of Goathland, through which the North Yorkshire Moors Railway steams. Goathland is the setting for TV's *Heartbeat* and the station was also used for Hogsmeade Station in the Harry Potter films – the shop on the platform was transformed into the Prefects' Room and the Ladies toilets became the Wizards' Room. The Thomason Foss waterfall is approached from the picturesque Becks Hole pub and bridge a mile down the road. It's a short walk up through woods to a west-facing rocky pool in a sunlit glade, where families often come to play in rubber dinghies and swim under the falls.

Even closer to Whitby, on the other side of the A169, is Falling Foss, romantically set in deep woods by the fairy-tale cottage of Midge Hall. Set over a deep black chasm into which a small stream flows, smoke was billowing from the chimney and in the evening light it was a scene reminiscent of *Hansel and Gretel*. It's a fair trek to reach the bottom of the falls, backtracking and then picking a way along the overgrown stream bed. Standing on the shingle beach looking up, the waterfall flows down the jet black cliff like a white veil, breaking into hundreds of competing rivulets.

We dived in and swam over to sit on the ledges beneath the water. In the cooling evening air this was certainly a cold dip but the dark green mosses and jungle-like setting made this place feel strangely exciting: like finding a secret passageway to a lost world.

329

326 GORMIRE LAKE, SUTTON BANK

A large, warm and little-visited lake set in woodland beneath the spectacular Sutton Bank escarpment. Squidgy leaf mulch at first but water shelves quickly, deepening to about 5m offshore. Beautiful views back up to escarpment.

→ 6 miles from Thirsk (E from A170), at the top of the long climb, park and pay at main Sutton Bank car park (café here too). Walk along escarpment and after 300m follow signs to nature reserve, descending via track on L into woods. After 500m find lake shore among trees. There are public footpaths around whole lake and a permanent right of way on the south side.

20 mins, 54.2427, -1.2283 🏊🏕️🖼️🍴

327 LEALHOLM, R ESK

Pretty paddling and dipping by the village green with train station, little pub, excellent bakery and coffee shop. Yum!

→ Deeper pool is just upstream of bridge on bend behind the Board Inn (YO21 2AJ, 01947 897279)

2 mins, 54.4583, -0.8257 🚂🚻🍴🚉

328 THOMASON FOSS, ELLER BECK

A rocky plunge pool set beneath an impressive waterfall in woods up from Beck Hole and its inn.

→ Beck Hole is down narrow lanes a mile N of Goathland station (North Yorkshire Railway or off A169 Whitby/ Pickering road). From Birch Hall Inn (YO22 5LE, 01947 896245) cross bridge and take path on R ¼ mile upstream. Mallayan Spout is also pretty (no pool) about a mile downstream (54.3978, -0.7323).

10 mins, 54.4081, -0.7289 🚉🚉

329 FALLING FOSS, RUSWARP

A tall plume and small deep plunge pool at the head of a wooded gorge. Shingle beach. Overlooked but feels secluded.

→ Follow B1416 from Whitby S and take the 'middle' R after 3 miles, signed Newton House / Falling Foss. Follow lane for a mile to car park. Continue down through woods on foot. To reach base of falls walk downstream, scramble down into gorge, then follow stream bed back up. Also small pool upstream of Midge Hall (50m).

10 mins, 54.4190, -0.6327 🏖️

330 COD BECK, OSMOTHERLEY

Pretty stream for paddling leads down to a lovely roadside lake with shoreside footpath and picnic parking. No Swimming signs, but many do. Cycle route 65.

→ Come off A19 for A684 Northallerton but follow signs to Osmotherley. Turn L in village and continue 1½ miles.

2 mins, 54.3854, -1.2829 🚲❓♿

331 NEWSHAM HALL, R TEES

Secretive and bucolic meander of the great river Tees. Good access but banks can be quite overgrown.

→ Take the Aislaby road from Egglescliffe (S of Stockton-on-Tees) and bear L (straight on) for Newsham Hall, and drop down to river path on open access land after ½ mile and explore downstream. More manicured access from Preston Park Museum 6 miles downstream (A135, Eaglescliffe, 54.5357, -1.3362).

5 mins, 54.4909, -1.4102 🏊🏕️

333 Westgate, Weardale

North Pennines and Hadrian's Wall

Heading north from the Yorkshire Dales, along the spine of Lune Moor, great long trails of pink cloud were reaching into the sky. I camped by moonlight in a large meadow on the banks of the River Tees, close to Low Force, before continuing on to Hadrian's Wall. The plan was to find the shrine of the water goddess Coventina and swim in the same spots as the Romans at Chesters Fort and Broomlee.

The North Pennines traditionally marked the last frontiers of Roman Britain; a great march of barren hills and plunging dales growing more desolate as they reached the border with the Picts. For the southern Mediterranean Roman soldiers stationed here in the second and third centuries AD the wet climate must have been very different from their dry and dusty homeland. They brought with them an adoration for springs, running water and river gods, all of which were to be found aplenty in ancient Britain. At Brocolita Fort on Hadrian's Wall they built one of the best preserved 'nymphaeum' shrines in the country. The water temple consisted of three altars to the part-Celtic, part-Roman water goddess Coventina. The inscriptions show her reclining with flagons and palms, protecting the three springs with her nymph assistants.

The great wall was begun in 122ad and acted as a working defence for over two hundred years. Its remains run

334

337

335

intermittently across the countryside, in some places a ragged ruin – much was taken to build the roads of Newcastle in the eighteenth century – but in more remote parts there are miles of surviving fortifications with milecastles and forts still standing among crags and tarns. In this central Pennine section the wall hugs a long dolerite escarpment, a natural defence, with lakes forming in the depressions below.

The Romans were very keen bathers and, though there was a bathhouse at Brocolita, it couldn't compare to that at Chesters Fort, three milecastles down on the River Tyne. With its endless supply of river water they were able to build a large bathing house complex. Its sixteen interconnecting chambers contained warm, hot and steam rooms and, of course, the cold plunge pools that are so central to Roman hydrotherapies.

There was once a great Roman bridge here and you can now paddle in the stream among the original bridge stones, scattered around like blocks from the Colosseum. Some years ago old Roman coins were found among the rocks and there are doubtless other treasures lurking in the riverbed.

The Romans were also excellent swimmers – it was a requirement of entry for the Roman soldier to be able to swim across a river in spate with full battle kit – but they would have had little challenge here. The river is mainly shallow in the vicinity of the ruined bridge, but there are deeper holes if you explore a little way downstream on the far bank.

The main Roman swimming was at Housesteads Fort, the most extensive and best preserved of Roman wall fortifications, and three milecastles to the west of Brocolita. Broomlee Lough is just 500 yards down from the fort, across the moor into no-man's land. Today the local farming families still gather here once a year for their summer swimming party in the overhanging eaves of Dove Crag. The tarn is large, mainly shallow and surprisingly tepid but at this crag end the water is deeper and the cliffs provide enough shelter from the wind for the mallard, tufted duck, golden eye and coots that make forays out from the reeds to paddle under the great Northumberland sky.

333

332 LOW FORCE, R TEES
This is the little-known sister of thundering High Force, about 2 miles downstream. There's a deep, calm pool on a side channel by a wooded island and a long gorge beneath a suspension footbridge.

→ 4 miles NW of Middleton-in-Teesdale on B6277 (15 miles SE of Alston). Park at telephone box / layby, by junction, 200m after Bowless Visitor Centre sign. Follow path down to bridge and falls (300m). Good basic riverside camping 1½ mile downstream on opposite bank at Low Way Farm, Holwick (DL12 0NJ, 01833 640506).

5 mins, 54.6464, -2.1505 ▲ ▼

333 WESTGATE, WEARDALE
Very pretty meadow side pool with falls

→ 200m upstream of A689 (Stanhope Alston road) river bridge, W of Westgate at turning for Side Head. Continue up to Side Head and on footpath beyond for remote circular tarn (54.7480, -2.1501) with sensational sunset views, and interesting ruins and pools in valley below.

2 mins, 54.7372, -2.1659 ✿ ▢

334 GIBSON'S CAVE, BOWLEES
Several pretty woodland plunge pools with paddling, leading to a waterfall and a large great cave overhang.

→ Follow sign to Bowlees from Low Force and follow well-marked path upstream.

10 mins, 54.65284, -2.14149 ✿ ✿

335 CRAMMEL LINN, R IRTHING
Huge waterfall with pool on wild moor.

→ Continue a mile W of Gilsland, over bridge and up hill and past Gilsland Spa. Go on another 1½ miles and take 'no through road' R turn over cattle grid. Find signed footpath down on R after a mile, on far edge of forest

10 mins, 55.0202, -2.5637 ▲

336 PLANKEY MILL, ALLENDALE
Beautiful wooded riverside walks. Local beauty spot. Occasional campsite.

→ 3 miles SW of Haydon bridge on A686, follow sign Plankey Mill / Lough Green, then 2 miles. Best pools are ¾ mile walk downstream. Upstream to NT Allen Banks is mainly paddling.

15 mins, 54.9468, -2.3170 ✿ ▲

337 BROOMLEE LOUGH HALTWHISTLE
Large open moorland tarn set beneath one of the great forts of Hadrian's Wall. Marshy, shallow shore in places but deeper in SE corner beneath Dove Crag.

→ Housesteads Fort is well signposted along the B6318 wall-road. Follow path up to fort (no need to pay) and join Hadrian's Wall path heading E. Continue ½ mile to milecastle 36 and bushwhack down over open-access land 300m.

20 mins, 55.0215, -2.3234 ▣ ▲ ▢

338 CHESTERS FORT, NORTH TYNE
Deep section of Tyne upstream of Chollerford bridge / weir, or follow path downstream to collapsed ruins of Roman Bridge and some pools. Interesting Roman bathing complex on opposite bank, within Fort bounds.

→ Chollerford is 3 miles N of Hexham. Find footpaths before bridge on L and R, by lights (no parking).

10 mins, 55.0315, -2.1144 ▣ ▣

River Etive

Scotland and Borders

This vast region takes us from Northumbria and the Cheviot Hills up into the great mountain massifs of Scotland. From Glen Coe to the Isle of Skye, Findhorn to the Royal Dee, Loch Ness to Loch Lomond, we explore the legend and history of Scotland's wild swimming waters.

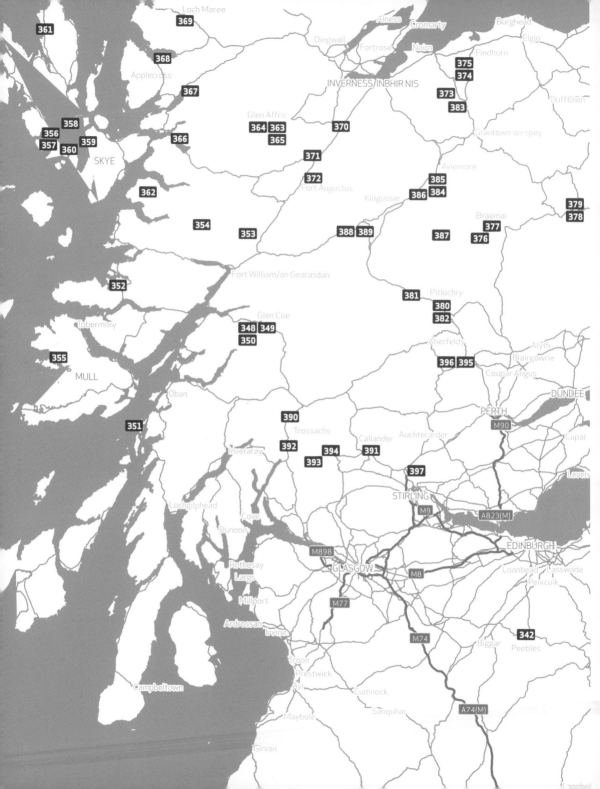

Highlights
Scotland and Borders

Our favourites include:

343 Union Bridge - swim across the border from England to Scotland at Union Bridge, one of the oldest suspension bridges in the world

345 Linhope Spout - The bottomless plunge pool of Linhope Spout in the grand Cheviot Hills

348-350 The magical Glen Etive is the less visited offshoot of Glen Coe, good for wild camping by its fantastic series of river pools

356-359 The Faeries and Faerie Pools of Skye, the clearest water in Britain

365 Plodda Falls - Scotland's second highest waterfall with a dramatic plunge pool too

370-372 Bathe with the Loch Ness Monster by the ruins of Urquhart Castle

384 Swim across to a ruined castle island on Loch an Eilein

392 Find Rob Roy's secret cave on the bonnie banks of Loch Lomond

397 Sheriff Muir - the closest thing to Highland pools without going north of Stirling. There's a good pub nearby too

390 Swim in Rob Roy's giant bathtub at the Falls of Falloch

Sillmoor, River Coquet

Cheviots and the Tweed

To the north-east of Hadrian's Wall lie the Cheviot Hills and a Northumberland borderland contested for centuries by chieftains and smugglers. Deep remote valleys are rich in river pools and on the northern edge you can swim to Scotland across the River Tweed.

All is peaceful in the county now and much is protected in the fabulous and remote Northumberland National Park with Kielder Forest and the Cheviot hill range. Three river dales drain the Cheviots: the Harthope, the Breamish and the Coquet. The best-known pool on all of these is Linhope Spout on the Breamish, renowned for its unfathomable depth.

It's a long walk to the Spout but the high plume is worth it. It tips down a straight chute into an almost perfect cylindrical plunge pool on the edge of a wooded Breamish dale. Popular with walkers and families cooling off in the summer, there is a fun six-foot ledge from which you can jump. For the wildlife enthusiast, Linhope Burn attracts breeding birds like the dipper and grey wagtail – always on the move in their search for caddis-fly and other aquatic invertebrates. You may well also see an oystercatcher scurrying along the river bank.

The River Coquet is easier to reach, but feels just as remote. A winding mountain lane runs for many miles to the head of the dale. Here it meets the Scottish border and the remains of Chew Green Roman Fort, an old staging post on the road from York to Scotland.

I followed the road to Linbriggs and Sillmoor and a stretch of perfect river pools bounded by grassy moor. The current was just strong enough to pick me up and propel me down the chute of the mini-waterfall. Although the river is generally shallow, it's possible to swim down for at least half a mile, mainly

345

342

347

carried by the flow, with a few strokes here and there to keep up the momentum.

Harthope is in the emptiest of the Cheviot valleys with a long approach walk. It's in the valley north of Linhope and the Breamish. The plunge pool is magical, deep and cave-like with mosses climbing up the steep black grotto walls. Finding Harthope Spout, hidden in the crevice of a wooded hollow, is quite an achievement and it makes a wonderful place to skinny-dip.

The Harthope and Breamish rivers both join the Till, which flows north into the Tweed. This, in turn, forms the border with Scotland in its final 20 miles. The Union Bridge was the longest suspension bridge in the world when it opened in 1820 and finally linked the east coasts of England and Scotland. Oddly the Scottish end is actually south of the English side! It has long been famous for eloping couples keen to wed under more liberal Scottish law: marriage on the Scottish side is legal even without the the 'reading of the banns' for three Sundays prior to the ceremony.

Given all this border history it seemed a good place to attempt to swim across the frontier. A friend and I arrived late one August afternoon for the challenge, the meadow beneath the bridge awash in head-high crimson balsam. Parting the flowers to find the riverbank we stepped down into the pebbly river shore and began to walk out into the alarmingly brisk current. The wide stream proved shallow enough to wade but after a little orientation – swimming breaststroke against the flow and practising landing ourselves on the bank – we began our migration attempt, striking out at an upstream angle to try to hit the opposite side square on, and checking from time to time that we could still feel the riverbed with our feet. The passage was remarkably easy and the feeling of running the stream invigorating – so much so that we swam between the two countries several times before finding somewhere to get a cup of tea.

'Says Tweed to Till Whit gars ye rin sae still? Says Till to Tweed Though ye may rin wi' speed And I rin sla For aye one ye droon I droon twa!' Traditional poem

345

339 SILLMOOR, R COQUET
Open meadows and moorland. Some rapids, a waterfall and pools.

→ Follow the Coquet from Rothbury and B6341 to Alwinton. Cross river Coquet at Linbriggs farm and continue ¾ mile to park by river. Continue on another 10 beautiful miles to the Roman border fort of Chew Green high on the Cheviot ridge.
5 mins, 55.3593, -2.1735 🏊⛺📷

340 THRUM ROCKS, R COQUET
Gorge with plunge pools and flat rocks, popular with lads who like to jump.

→ 1 mile E of Rothbury on the river path.
20 mins, 55.3084, -1.8929 🏊

341 WARKWORTH HERMITAGE, COQUET
Swim across the pretty River Coquet to the amazing hermitage, carved out of the rockface. Pretty river with beaches.

→ From behind Warkworth Castle follow the path upstream along the river 300m to where the little ferry boat usually waits to cross. Beaches upstream.
10 mins, 55.3465, -1.6210 🏊📷🏖️

342 PEEBLES, R TWEED
Broad grassy meander beneath Neidpath Castle, with pools, rapids and tree swing.

→ 1 mile W of Pebbles on A72 or follow river footpath a mile up from town centre.
5 mins, 55.6516, -3.2162 🏊📷🍴

343 UNION BRIDGE, R TWEED
Wide, shallow, fast flowing stretch of Tweed downstream of famous suspension bridge. Swim against current and cross to Scotland! Very strong current.

→ 5 miles SW of Berwick-upon-Tweed on A698, turn R signed Horncliffe / Norham Castle, then immediately R, through Horncliffe, then L signed Union Bridge. Also below Norham Castle, 3 miles upstream.
5 mins, 55.7561, -2.1073 🚗🏖️

344 BOTHAL WEIR, WANSBECK
Pretty wooded weir with fun salmon leap pools. Deep, long river section above.

→ Turn L signed Bothal off the A196 from Morpeth to Ashington. Take track on L after the bridge, on footpath 200m to weir. WEIR DESTROYED 2017, POOLS REMAIN.
5 mins, 55.1700, -1.6346 🏊🍴🏖️

345 LINHOPE SPOUT, R BREAMISH
A 'bottomless' plunge pot beneath a tall spout in a pretty glade that is ideal for picnics. Paddling in shallows of beck.

→ From A697 (between Wooler and Rothbury) follow signs to Ingram / Breamish Valley (3 miles) then on through village, past pretty paddling and picnic spots, to end of public road. Then 1¾ miles by foot through hamlet and onto open moor. Signed to spout below on R.
45 mins, 55.4477, -2.0671 🍴⛺

346 HARTHOPE LIN, WOOLER
Magical, deeply hidden waterfall and plunge pool in tiny wooded gorge.

→ Signed Harthope Valley from the Anchor Inn in Wooler. 2 mile walk from road end up the Harthope Burn.
40 mins, 55.4759, -2.1159 ⛰️🌲

347 LESBURY WEIR, R ALN
A pretty weir pool near Alnmouth.

→ Just N of Alnmouth roundabout (A1068) find footpath / gate on L, 100m before swanky new river bridge.
10 mins, 55.3966, -1.6371 🏊🏖️

Long Canyon, River Etive

Glen Coe to Loch Arkaig

Glen Coe is famous for its wild and dramatic scenery, but it is a little known valley running to the south that holds its most spectacular swimming pools and gorges. A haven for climbers and wild campers, Glen Etive is a place you could spend many days exploring.

Picking up a friend in Glasgow on her first visit to Scotland we drove north past Loch Lomond in the evening light before climbing up through the craggy lakes of Rannoch Moor as dusk fell. Arriving at King's House Inn at Glen Coe we pitched our tents in the darkness with the black outline of Aonach Eagach towering over us against the indigo sky. Apart from catching the occasional glint of foam flashing in our headlights, we could only hear the nearby river and hope we hadn't camped too close to its edge.

The whole valley was still in shadow when we awoke the next morning but the sun had caught the top of the mountain and was playing with wisps of cloud. Here, under the dark guardian of Buchaille Etive Mor – The Great Shepherd of Etive – we found ourselves by the most fantastic series of river pools you can imagine. A few yards away our grassy bank dropped into a gentle river lido in a wide meander with a shingle beach and a

351

353

354

hundred yards downstream it tumbled into a long gorge with deep lagoons and purple-streaked cliffs.

It was to this beautiful glen that Deirdre, foremost heroine in Irish mythology, came to escape Conor Mac Nessa and his warriors. Her twisted yellow tresses and grey–green eyes were said to lure the gods and mesmerise the mortals. That morning, as the shadow line edged down the mountain wall and the sun broke the high peaks with blinding rays, there was something of her colours in the dawn sky. The tiny road follows the river for over eight miles down to the remote and enchanted sea loch of Etive. The gorge by which we camped remains my favourite place but there are many other swimming holes as well. A mile upstream there are good shallows for children with a small island and further on the river plunges through a waterfall to open onto a long pool. Two miles before the road head of Glen Coe are deep plunge bowls scooped out of the blue stone, each a bathing place to while away a whole day.

Thirty miles to the north of Glen Coe, on the other side of Fort William, you'll find the Dark Mile, a long line of beech trees and a stone bridge across the Caig Burn. To the right the Eas Chia-aig Falls tumble into a deep, dark pool known as the Witch's Cauldron. An old woman was accused of casting her evil eye over Lochiel's cattle, causing them to fall ill and die. When she fell into the pool and drowned the cattle miraculously began to recover from their illness. There are three tiered pools and, while the lower is the largest, the upper two have wildly contorted rock striations that are particularly noteworthy. There may have been some witch-like trickery going on the day we were there. Having dipped in the Witch's Cauldron we headed further up the remote lane to find somewhere to swim in Loch Arkaig. We quickly passed an unusually early crop of red and white toadstools on the roadside, the magic mushroom Fly Agaric. Suddenly a stone on the road cut open not one but two of the tyres on the car. We had no phone reception and were stranded by the loch overnight. This gave us plenty of time to explore the white shingle beaches and swim but we couldn't help but feel we had been tricked by the Witch's Cauldron and her toadstools.

348

348 HIGHER GLEN ETIVE POOLS

A dramatic glen with many wonderful pink rock river pools, easily accessible from the little road. Great wild camping. This first set of pools is one of the best.

→ Heading NW on A82 (Glen Coe) turn L a mile after the Kings House Hotel (PH49 4HY, 01855 851259). After 2 miles the first main waterfall with plunge pools is visible on L near road.

3 mins, 56.6252, -4.9052 ⛺🚻⛺▽

349 EAS AN FHIR MHOIR, R ETIVE

Also known as Right Angle Falls, this is a much higher falls with large tub above, hidden from the road in a gorge below.

→ Continue a further mile from Higher Glen Etive pools and there's a pull-in and ladder stile. A rough, steep path leads down. Or carry on until the road reappears and explore by wading and swimming upstream.

10 mins, 56.6184, -4.9239 📷

350 LONG CANYON, LOWER R ETIVE

A long river canyon with high cliffs and deep water. Popular wild camping spot.

→ Continue on from Eas An Fhir Mhoir and 1¼ miles past the Alltchaorunn farm bridge on L there's kink in river by road with large river pool in bend and space to camp next to it. Just downstream the river flows into 150m long deep rocky canyon. Also more waterfalls 500m downstream. NB For a real campsite try the Red Squirrel 7 miles further along the A82, Glen Coe (PH49 4HX, 01855 811256).

5 mins, 56.6160, -4.9682 🏊⛺

351 EASDALE ISLAND, SEIL, OBAN

Many old steep-sided slate quarries now filled with Mediterranean-blue water, right next to the sea.

→ Off A816 S of Oban, follow signs to Seil (B844) and Easdale. From Easdale cross on to island and walk NW to quarries, 400m. The L-shaped one is the usual swimming one.

15 mins, 56.2927, -5.6615 ⛺🏊📷

352 CASTLE TIORAM, MOIDART

Large, deep river pool beneath bridge.

→ By roadside on L, on lane to the castle.

2 mins, 56.7562, -5.8065 ⛺

353 THE WITCH'S CAULDRON, CLUNES

Eas Chia-aig. A series of three falls and pools set in quick succession by roadside. Interesting rock formations.

→ Follow the Lochy river N of Fort William (B8004 / B8005) for 12 miles, bearing L at Gairlochy. 1 mile beyond Clunes forest find the bridge and picnic spot. The first pool by the bridge is deep and large. Above are more pools accessed via footpath, with more 500m up footpath.

5 mins, 56.9548, -5.0012 ⛺🏊▽

354 LOCH ARKAIG

Swim wild from the enchanting and remote white pebble beaches of Loch Arkaig. Perfect wild camping.

→ Continue 7 miles on from the Witch's Cauldron.

5 mins, 56.9760, -5.2917 🏊⛺📷

355 EAS FORS, BALLYGOWN, MULL

Cliff-top plunge pools overlooking sea.

→ 10 miles S of Calgary on B8073, 2 miles N of Oskamull. Pools above and below road leading down to main fall into sea.

5 mins, 56.5031, -6.1541 📷📷

1956 Faerie Pools

Skye & Knoydart
Faerie Pools

The Faerie Pools on the Isle of Skye are so clear you have to stare to see if they have water in them at all. They lie serenely in a sheltered glade of lilac rocks and rowan trees while the misty towers of the Black Cuillin kingdom rise menacingly above.

Skye attracts visitors from all over the world for its breathtaking scenery with some of the most inaccessible wilderness left in Britain today. Rising like great Gaudi spires above giant basalt cliffs, the Black Cuillin Mountains are the remnants of huge volcanoes made up of gabbro, an intensely hard, old, green igneous rock usually found under the ocean. Now ribbed by deep scars and ridges, the combination of millions of years of constant rain and the extraordinary geology, they contain some of the clearest and most colourful waterfalls in the UK, plunging down the mountains to the ocean. High in the hills are several 'Faerie Pools', renowned in local folklore for their association with enchanted beings. The best known are on Allt Coir a Mhadaidh in Glen Brittle. I arrived in the evening just as the peaks above had cleared for the first time in days. A crimson light was glowing on An Diallaid peak and the waterpipe gully that runs from top to bottom gaped open like a liverish wound. A mile up from the road the first

359

362

356

sunken glade appeared like a safe haven within the mountain. The waterfall, pool and stream were all banked with berries and ferns and sheltered from the wind.

The pools, some tinged with pinks and greens, are lined with smooth rock like the inside of a woodturner's bowl. Two are linked by an underwater arch and, with goggles on, I swam back and forth examining the faerie underworld. The rock face was encrusted with pieces of quartz and there was an almost phosphorescent emerald glow. Deep down on the pool floor ingots of rock shimmered on the sandy bed. I stayed in the water mesmerised for almost twenty minutes before realising how chilled I had become and rapidly made home in the dusk.

It's not difficult to understand how this scenery became so imbued with fairy myth. Skye legend tells of local chief MacLeod who fell in love with a Faerie princess. The King of the Faeries, Oberon, agreed to a marriage, but only on condition that after a year and a day the princess must return to her own people. The marriage took place, and a son was born but the princess had to return to the Land of Faeries. She abandoned her child at Faerie Bridge near Dunvegan but the infant's crying tormented her so that she returned periodically to comfort him, wrapping him in her shawl. The shawl can still be seen today at Dunvegan Castle, now the flag of the MacLeod clan.

If you're still searching for faeries, you will find further pools off the Glen Brittle road and more in the burns draining the Red Cuillins on the Torrin side. Don't forget to visit the Talisker Distillery nearby, where the whisky is made with faerie water, or the gorge just south of Sligachan, where there are yet more pools. Then, up at Uig, north of Dunvegan Castle, find Rha Falls, a large plunge pot, and a mile further into the hills, the famous Faerie Glen, a glacial curiosity potted with many small, conical-shaped hillocks overgrown with thick, green turf rising several metres in height. The landscape is littered with bleating sheep and occasional strange yellow mushrooms of unknown power or use. I found a tiny loch there with a small brook running through it and a circle of stones, shaped like a spiral. According to legend, girls who dance naked on the spiral will have their dearest wishes fulfilled, but that day the circle lay bare.

358

356 FAERIE POOLS, GLEN BRITTLE

Famous 'Allt Coir a Mhadaidh' pools and waterfalls, tinged with pink and blue hues, set under the mystical peaks of the Black Cuillins. Crystal clear water and underwater arch to swim between pools.

→ From Sligachan Hotel (A87) follow A863 / B8009 and turn L (signed Glen Brittle) just before Carbost (Talisker Distillery - yum). After 4 miles find 'Fairy Pool' car park on L. Cross road and follow clear path down and then up valley, keeping to L of stream for ¾ mile to find several pools. Good jump into the underwater arch pool.

20 mins, 57.2497, -6.2554 🏴 🖼️

357 ALLT A' CHOIRE GHREADAIDH

Also in Glen Brittle, parallel but further S, this is a less visited set of pools on mountainside.

→ Further S along the road to youth hostel and Loch Brittle. Also try Coire na Banachdich waterfall and pools (57.2113, -6.2763) and Brittle river itself, in pools alongside road. Great seashore campsite and hostel (IV47 8TA, 01478 640404).

20 mins, 57.2243, -6.2823 🏔️ 🔄 🔺 📷 🖼️

358 ALLT DURAICH BURN, SLIGACHAN

Pretty pool and waterfall at base of interesting slot canyon with deep pots above for those who like scrambling.

→ Cross old bridge and main river from Sligachan Hotel (IV47 8SW, 01478 650204) and bear R up stream 600m.

15 mins, 57.2863, -6.1636 ℹ️ 🔺 🖼️

359 FAERIE POOLS, BLA BHEINN

Dramatic waterfall gorge and pools on route up to Bla Bheinn, East Cuillins.

→ From Broadford (A87) follow B8083 (Elgol). 2 miles beyond Torrin find bridge and follow path up R of stream to find main waterfall (Alt na Dunaiche) after ¾ mile. If ascending search out Loch Fionna Coire on the edge of the world (57.2145, -6.0795)

20 mins, 57.2181, -6.0574 🔺 🖼️

360 LOCH CORRUISK, ELGOL

The wildest loch in Britain? Surrounded by the high mountain walls of the Cuillins.

→ Accessible by half and full day boat trips from Elgol (Bella Jane, 0800 7313089)

200 mins, 57.1993, -6.1579 🔺 🚣 📷 🖼️

361 RHA BURN, UIG

Magnificent double waterfall with large plunge pool, just out of town.

→ As you enter Uig from S, bear R on A855 Staffin road, then find footpath and steps up on R, just before bridge. Follow path through deep glen for 5 mins. Many more waterfalls up the valley. Also visit the enchanting Faerie Glen with fairy mounds, basalt columns and a little roadside pond. Back S from Uig on A87, turn L after a mile, signed Shaeder (57.5837, -6.3266).

5 mins, 57.5935, -6.3602 🏴

362 EAS O CHAORAINN, KNOYDART

Waterfalls and deep pools in the heart of Knoydart. Perhaps the remotest waterfall swim in Britain? Great tavern when you return. Good campsite.

→ From the Old Forge Inn in Inverie (PH41 4PL, 01687 462267) turn R and find forest track on R after 30m. Follow for 2 miles, bearing R at junction, another 2 miles down to the Guiserein river. Camping is 15 min walk from pub (PH41 4PL, 01687 462560).

90 mins, 57.0738, -5.6449 ℹ️ 🔺 🔺 🖼️

Glen Affric & Wester Ross

Glen Affric is a refuge for one of Scotland's largest remaining stands of rare, ancient Caledonian pine. You'll also find Scotland's second highest waterfall here and a loch with an archipelago of forest-clad islands.

Scots or Caledonian pine once made up the great ancient forests of Scotland. This magnificent old tree is entirely different from the regimented rows of conifers you now see in forestry plantations. Baobab-like in its grace, statesmanlike in its size, its boughs make graceful open arcs and its bark is gnarled and red. No two are ever the same. The Affric woods proper start as you approach Dog Falls, where several old pines stand cantankerously by the riverside. Ten minutes downstream you'll come to plunge pools ideal for bathing with hot rocky shelves to lay out a towel and dip in a toe. Further below are the main falls, a narrow plummeting chute into a gorge. A footbridge crosses some way down and from here it is possible to swim in the deeper water and explore the cliffs on either side.

The lane winds further up into the glen. At a sudden brow there is a promontory peeping out through the trees and Loch Beinn a Mheadhoin opens up, covered by a scattering of closely

369

366

364

interconnected forest islands. There is something about an island, a place of adventure yet retreat, which I've never been able to resist.

The thought of island-hopping creates even more excitement. Examining the map we located a point on the shore where the straits narrowed to only a hundred yards. With our inflatable canoe it was possible for two people to swim safely across to this refuge, with wide beaches and watery vistas. From there we circumnavigated the nearest island in an afternoon – part swimming, walking and boating – then struck out to the second.

The road actually ends as Loch Affric begins. From here truly wild territory begins, reaching into the heart of the Highlands, where the forest has stood for over 8,000 years, since after the last ice age. Bonnie Prince Charlie hid here after the Battle of Culloden and many of the trees are over 500 years old. Roe, sika and red deer are all present. Watch for them at dawn or dusk on the open hills above the tree line. Pine marten have increased in numbers over the past ten years, although their nocturnal habits make a sighting unlikely. Red squirrels, otter, brown and blue hare may be found too. Keep an eye open for buzzard, golden eagle or dipper by the water's edge. You may even encounter a wildcat or adder.

After a day of island-hopping and dipping at Dog Falls we camped in deep forest near Plodda Falls in the parallel valley of Abhainn Deabhag. Here is one of the most spectacular falls in Scotland, yet we were alone as we descended through the forest of Douglas fir the next morning. From the old Victorian viewing platform, on the edge of a 150-metre high precipice, miles of woodland open out across a great tropical gorge. A treetop dawn chorus was in full swing and down below we could see a giant pool. The path to the bottom of the falls was slippery and difficult but the pool was still and calm, with wood sorrel on the banks and only a small stream flowing into it from way on high. Once upon a time many people must have visited this place – an old wrought-iron walkway is still visible around the edge – but we swam in the great gorge as if no one had been here for years with just a circling buzzard above and the birdsong through the trees.

365

363 DOG FALLS, GLEN AFFRIC
Beautiful stretch of river among woods of Scots pine in this famous glen. Good plunge pool in stretch above falls or deep canyon below falls.

➔ From Cannich (A831) follow the Glen Affric road for 5 miles to find the Dog Falls forest car park on L. Admire the Scots pines by the river and follow path downstream 250m to find rapids and fun plunge pool, and then another 200m to footbridge and deep canyon below main falls (access further down, swim back up).
5 mins, 57.3133, -4.8456 ⓥ

364 LOCH BEINN A MHEADHOIN
Stunning islanded lake, rich in original Caledonian pine. Many places to swim from shore and potential to swim out to islands if you are in a group.

➔ Continue past Dog Falls car park and after a further 3 miles up Glen Affric look out for sharp L track leading to parking. 500m further on there is car park / picnic spot and a 100m channel swim to one of the islands.
5 mins, 57.2951, -4.9137 🏊🏞️🖼️

365 PLODDA FALLS, GLEN AFFRIC
Deep, large, black plunge pool (30m) at base of Scotland's second highest waterfall. Remains of Victorian viewing gangways around pool. Tricky scramble down into this forested canyon.

➔ Tomich is signed L at the power station off the Glen Affric road from Cannich (A831). Continue 3 miles beyond Tomich hotel, eventually on forestry track, to Plodda Falls forest parking. Drop down through woods, to view-bridge to admire panorama and the pool below, then down via steep, slippery path for a plunge.
15 mins, 57.2723, -4.8593 🏞️🖼️

366 COIRE DHUINNID, LOCH DUICH
Dramatic SW facing valley and switchback waterfalls above famous loch-side Castle Eilean Donan.

➔ Pass Eilean Donan (A87) heading SE. After 4 miles, at Inverinate, turn L (signed Carr Brae viewpoint). Cross bridge (½ mile) and after another 300m find cottage and track on R. Follow track up valley for ¾ mile. Also loch side by castle.
20 mins, 57.2588, -5.4586 🖼️🏞️

367 STRATHCARRON GORGE
Wooded gorge with pools. The best is hidden at the head, by two waterfalls, at the confluence of two streams.

➔ From Strathcarron level crossing and station (A890) follow river bank upstream for 1½ miles, above gorge, to eventually drop down to confluence (also path via Achintee). Or simply explore gorge at river level until you can go no further. Also pools at nearby Coulags (57.4576, -5.4118).
30 mins, 57.4197, -5.4041 🖼️

368 BALGY FALLS, LOCH TORRIDON
Falls on path to Loch Damph secret beach.

➔ Take path through small gate, 50m E of Balgy Bridge (A986 E of Shieldaig) and continue ½ mile to falls. Another ¾ mile (cross river) leads to jetty and beach.
10 mins, 57.5230, -5.5932 🏊🖼️

369 LOCH MAREE ISLANDS, GAIRLOCH
Another Scots pine forested archipelago with superb swimming and wild camping.

➔ Bushwhack N to shore off A832 about a mile E of Loch Maree Hotel (IV22 2HL)
60 mins, 57.6815, -5.4753 ⛺🏞️🏊🖼️🏕️

Dulsie Bridge

Findhorn and Loch Ness

High above Loch Ness, in the Monadhliath Mountains, the enchanted River Findhorn gathers its waters and prepares to carve out a string of gorges and river pools inhabited by gods and satyrs.

As you leave Glen Affric it's impossible to avoid the Loch Ness Monster tourist bonanza centred on Drumnadrochit and it seemed a little churlish to miss the chance for a swim with Nessie. The ruins of Urquhart Castle seemed the most impressive place to dip but, determined to avoid the crowds and coaches, I walked up the road a way and dropped down through a steep field of yellow mullein and butterflies to reach a more peaceful section of the shoreline. A lochside ruin can never fail to impress in Scotland. More than once during its troubled 700-year history Urquhart was able to hold out because it could be re-supplied by ship. As I swam a little way out into the castle's hidden bay I had a fish-eye view up to the battlements and could see at first hand the great rocky bluff on which it had been built.

If you really want to swim with Nessie, though, she'll undoubtedly prefer the many more peaceful bays on the far

372

371

373

south side of the Loch. I decided to leave her alone and head on to explore the Findhorn, one of the longest rivers in Scotland and one that rises in the Monadhliath Mountains above Loch Ness. Famous for its mystical qualities and great legends it has associations with *Macbeth* at nearby Cawdor Castle (where King Duncan is said to have been murdered) and more recently the spiritual eco-village of Findhorn, where residents believe the river is sacred and marks a border between the earth and the spirit worlds.

At Randolph's Leap, a narrowing gorge overlooked by shelves of yew and Scots pine woodland, the black peaty Findhorn water twirls and swirls through fissures. It passes over large river stones carved and curved by flood eddies and opens onto a wide calm pool dotted with islands and bays. On the sunny afternoon I was there it did indeed seem like the place to meet Pan and his nymphs and to frolic and gambol with the satyrs.

As you wander around these woods look out for the two flood stones, protected in iron cages, which look a little like gravestones. They mark the upper reaches of the great Muckle Spate of 1829, probably the greatest British flood ever.

After a sultry week in August a thunderstorm began over the Monadhliath Mountains. It rained for three days and three nights and all the bridges except nearby Dulsie were washed away. The position of the stones show how high the waters rose, climbing over 10m and consuming vast tracts of land on both sides of the valley.

The bridge at Dulsie only survived because the gorge that it spans is so high. Yet the spate came to within a foot of its central keystone. This is a well-known beauty spot. The path above the bridge leads down to rocky shallows. Below the bridge there is a large area of calm, deep water where a waterfall joins from the right bank beside a small sandy bay. Silver and downy birch shade the river banks, with rowan, willow and bird cherry, and there are great stands of aspen, now rare in Scotland. Dippers and osprey are also sometimes seen and, if you look carefully, there is a rock remarkably similar to a rhinoceros bathing in the pool below.

370

370 URQUHART CASTLE, LOCH NESS

Britain's longest lake and home to Nessie. Trek down through these fields to find this secluded place to access the shoreline and swim out to Urquhart Castle, far away from all the crowds.

→ Park at the huge Urquhart visitor centre just S of Drumnadrochit. Continue up main road 300m on foot (NE, towards Drumnadrochit). As road bends to L find gate into field on R and walk down to shore, bearing R down to wooded shoreline.

15 mins, 57.3264, -4.4431

371 INVERMORISTON, LOCH NESS

Waterfalls and two old highland bridges. Holy well and hexaganol stone summerhouse. Good tavern.

→ From main car park by Millennium Hall, head back to bridge and take path on L past Colomba Well and down to the river to find rocky pools, grassy banks and the summerhouse above. Glenmoriston Arms Hotel in the village is good traditional hotel and tavern (IV63 7YA, 01320 351206).

5 mins, 57.2114, -4.6160

372 LOCH TARIF, LOCH NESS

Serene and beautiful little roadside loch. Warmer and quieter than Loch Ness. Beach and offshore islets.

→ From Fort Augustus follow B862 (off General Wade's military road) NE to loch for 5 miles. Continue on to explore less visited SE shore of Loch Ness (B852) or Loch Mhor (B862). Good wild camping.

2 mins, 57.1500, -4.6062

373 DULSIE BRIDGE, R FINDHORN

Ancient bridge and gorge with rapids above and deep pools, waterfall and sandy cove below. Quiet.

→ Dulsie is signed off B9007 (via A939, S of Nairn). Park by bridge. Follow upstream path for view of gorge and paddling. Climb downstream from bridge on river's L bank to access deep river pools opposite waterfall. Submerged rocks downstream so take care. Just upstream of bridge (go under it) there is a very small sandy cove. Route here via Cawdor Castle (5 miles from Nairn) to visit inspiration for Macbeth (IV12 5RD, 01667 404401).

5 mins, 57.4507, -3.7814

374 RANDOLPH'S LEAP, R FINDHORN

Stunning wooded gorge on River Findhorn leading down to rocky headland with access to river beaches and very large river pool and islets. Some shallows for paddling.

→ Follow A940 S of Forres and bear L on B9007 following signs to Logie Steading. ½ mile beyond Logie find parking and gate down into Randolph's Leap woods. Bear down to L to see the Leap, shallows and head of gorge. Bear down to R to find headland and large river junction pool with islands. Look out for the flood marker stone. Warm up with tea afterwards at Logie Steading (café and craft centre, 01309 611378, IV36 2QN).

10 mins, 57.5272, -3.6708

375 LOWER FINDHORN GORGE

Great cliff jumping spot. Very steep access from remote forestry track.

→ Bring map or contact Ace Adventures in Relugas for guidance (IV36 2QL, 01309 611769, river bugging, canyoning etc).

20 mins, 57.5453, -3.6699

Cambus O'May

The Royal Dee and South Cairngorms

The Royal Dee is a regal place to swim. You'll find Queen Victoria's bridge over the Linn of Dee, the stately Balmoral Castle and some extraordinary ice-age geology. To the south west the Pass of Killiecrankie was one of Prince Albert's favourite places and there are many accessible waterfalls.

We don't know if the royal family like to wild-swim, but Royal Deeside is probably the best place to find out. The area has been the traditional summer holidaying ground for the royal family since Queen Victoria and Prince Albert bought the estate and built their Gothic castle there in 1852.

There are some beautiful swimming stretches along the Dee. Downstream of Balmoral is the Cambus o' May – literally, the 'bend in the valley' – with a quaint white suspension bridge donated by a gentleman from Kent in 1905. There is a deep section here and the sandy banks and flat rocks are popular in the summer for picnics and swimming. The Deeside railway line used to run this way and Cambus o' May station was regarded as one of the most picturesque in the Scotland, so much so that the directors of the Great North of Scotland Company had a special meeting wagon shunted out to it for their board meetings.

Just a mile up the valley is the Burn o' Vat in the Muir of Dinnet nature reserve. Children love to paddle in this spooky cave and climb up the little waterfall above into the secret ravine. The glacial meltwaters that carved out this great vat 10,000 years ago were ferocious – the rounded sides and arched roof show that this was once a churning whirlpool. Stumbling upon this curiosity when the woods are empty is an eerie experience.

377

376

382

Upstream of Balmoral and six miles west of Braemar – the home of the Royal Highland Games – you will find Victoria Bridge over the Linn of Dee, opened by Her Majesty in 1857, where the river passes through a furious and deep rocky gorge before slowing into shelving, sunny pools. From here you can also continue to the Linn of Quoich, a series of smaller waterfalls and rapids, popular with families. This is a fun but steep stretch of river with some plunge pools to dip in if you are cautious. If you look carefully at the river rocks you'll see the Earl of Mar's Punchbowl, a natural pothole, about a metre across, from which the Earl of Mar is reputed to have served hot whisky and honey punch to his Jacobite hunting colleagues in 1715. Three hundred years on, however, the bottom of the pothole has worn right through.

Referring to it as 'my paradise in the Highlands' it was to Deeside that Queen Victoria retreated when she was widowed. She suffered greatly after Albert's death and took refuge in her memories of their times together, of which their visit to the Pass of Killiecrankie, 25 miles to the south-west, was one of her favourites. Here, in a magnificent wooded gorge on the River Garry, a key battle of the Jacobite uprising was fought. The Soldier's Leap is the narrowest part of the gorge across which some soldiers are thought to have leaped as they tried to flee in 1689.

Further below, hidden from the visitor centre and car park, is the river that Queen Victoria and Prince Albert looked out over so excitedly in 1844. On a midsummer day, a warm breeze moving the leaves, I swam out into the blue of a wide pool reaching the white shingle bank on the far side. There I lay, my eyes closed, feeling my skin tingle and dry in the morning sun. Otters, pine martens, red squirrels and flycatchers inhabit this gorge, but all I spied that day were flecks of white cloud floating on a jetstream high above.

'We came to the Pass of Killiecrankie, which is quite magnificent; the road winds along it, and you look down a great height, all wooded on both sides, the Garry rolling below. I cannot describe how beautiful it is. Albert was in perfect ecstasies.' Queen Victoria's journal, 1844

380

376 LINN OF DEE, BRAEMAR

A dramatic slot canyon cutting under an elegant Victorian bridge leads to deep pool and river beach.

➔ From Braemar follow the road by church (signed Inverey) for 5 miles along the Dee to reach bridge and Linn of Dee parking. Walk downstream 100m for beach pool.
2 mins, 56.9884, -3.5435 🌊

377 LINN OF QUOICH, R DEE

Plunge pools set in woods and the Earl of Mar's Punchbowl - a round hole carved by th river from the rock.

➔ Continue along the road a further 3½ miles from Linn of Dee (past Mar Lodge) to road end in open meadow. Head upstream 300m to footbridge and pools (Punchbowl is above bridge) but for best pools continue another ½ mile to the upper falls.
15 mins, 57.0123, -3.4765 ⛰️ 🔺

378 CAMBUS O' MAY BRIDGE, DEE

Pretty gently shelving river beach above elegant white Victorian suspension footbridge. Deep sections and large flat rocks on the nearside.

➔ Heading E on A93 from Ballater, pass Cambus o' May Hotel (4 miles, AB35 5SE, 01339 755428) and find turn off opposite, signed. Follow old railway line footpath back up river 200m to bridge . Beach is on far side.
5 mins, 57.0659, -2.9568 🌊 🚻 🍴

379 BURN O' VAT / LOCH KINORD

A woodland stream with paddling only leads to a deep ravine, with caves. A fascinating relic from the ice age. Beautiful loch for swimming nearby.

➔ Continue 500m beyond Cambus o' May, turn L (B9119) and find Vat visitor centre car park after a mile with path up into woods. On opposite side of road is path to lovely Loch Kinord with standing stone (57.0857, -2.9273).
10 mins, 57.0839, -2.9499 🌊 🚻 🚻

380 SOLDIER'S LEAP, KILLIECRANKIE

A beautiful gorge opening out to a large, hidden river pool. Access is a scramble but peaceful and private once there. Railway line passes above L. White pebble beach on far side.

➔ Find Soldier's Leap visitor centre (National Trust for Scotland) well signed on old B8079 N of Pitlochry. Follow paths down to the Soldier's Leap, a narrow chasm, but bear down to the L, via an informal path through steep woodland, to reach flat rocks by large river pool, about 100m downstream of the Leap itself.
5 mins, 56.7420, -3.7740 🚻 🚻 🚻 🚻

381 LOWER FALLS OF BRUAR

Short walk to these popular falls and woodland gorge. Natural arch and caves.

➔ Signed Bruar / B8079 off A9 N of Pitlochry. Park at House of Bruar shopping and follow signed footpath 10 mins up through woods to first bridge and falls, with scramble down to pool.
10 mins, 56.7739, -3.9341 🚻 🚻 🚻

382 LINN OF TUMMEL

Impressive pools by these roadside falls. The lane continues along the wild shores of Tummel and Rannoch lochs (B846).

➔ Signed Clunie / Foss off A9 just N of Pitlochry S of Killiecrankie.
3 mins, 56.7185, -3.7827 🔺 🚻 🚻 🚻

North and West Cairngorms

The Cairngorms National Park is the wildest landscape in Britain. Containing four of Scotland's five highest mountains, the range is a rocky massif encrusted with snow and ice for most of the year. As one of the coldest plateaus in Britain it harbours wildlife normally found in the Arctic.

On the lower, warmer levels this granite geology has produced beautiful rivers and lakes. At Feshiebridge the river flows through smoothed strata of deep grey, layered with vanilla quartz and blueberry granite. There are narrow pools and rapids upstream and on a hot day the rocks act as solar heaters, absorbing the sun's rays and transmitting the heat to the water with their fins. Under the bridge the water falls in a tumbling helter-skelter that has cut deep circular eddies and a moonscape of fantastic shapes.

The pool beneath the bridge is large, clear and still. On the left bank stands a solitary Caledonian Scots pine, at least two hundred years old, its trunk furrowed, its long lichen-clad branches arching down to sip from the river. Its old roots provide perfect nooks and crannies in which to curl up and sleep among the soft litter of the pine needles. Opposite is a sandbank of pure white rounded pebbles, a delicious location to swim out to. As you dive through the water you are struck

383

386

387

by how clear everything is. Because of the granite the Feshie is not peaty like other Highland streams. Instead the water casts a golden yellow glow onto the riverbed and you can snorkel in between the rock shapes gazing at millions of years of time.

On the edge of the Rothiemurchus estate next door, the tree-lined Loch an Eilein also sits on the edge of the mountains, and at its centre is an island with a ruined, ivy-clad castle. Shrouded in the early morning mist this is the quintessential Scottish image. Estimated to be at least 600 years old, the castle fell into disuse several hundred years ago but its stones have lain protected by its island location ever since, though a small forest has grown up inside. The swim across to the island is probably not encouraged by the estate, but is serene nonetheless. The loch waters lie still beneath the gently shelving banks and although the castle is only a hundred yards from the shore the backdrop of the Cairngorms beyond rises thousands of feet high.

Where the castle wall meets the water there's a small doorway through which you can clamber. Inside the old hall is complete with tumbledown fireplace and trees growing through the roof. Wildflowers have sprouted in the kitchen range and a family of crossbills have nested under an old stone seat in the small garden.

A further twenty miles along the Cairngorm ridge, following the valley of the Spey, the Pattack tributary offers more pools and swimming. Strathmashie community forest is justifiably popular with wild campers who don't want to stray too far from their cars. Within a few metres of the car park you arrive at a large amphitheatre-like bathing pool, idyllically situated among cliffs and waterfalls, with lots of space to swim and even a small beach.

In Scotland it is now legal to wild-camp an appropriate distance from buildings but this means the most accessible beauty spots are now littered with fire pits and loo paper. The Cairngorms may be the wild home to endangered species such as twinflower, capercaillie, dotterel and mountain hare, but it seemed unlikely I would find them at Strathmashie.

384

383 LOCHINDORB CASTLE, GRANTOWN

An ruined castle set on an island on a quiet and little-known loch.

→ Signed L off A939, 7 miles N of Grantown-on-Spey.

5 mins, 57.4057, -3.7080 🏊 ⛰ 🖼

384 LOCH AN EILEIN, ROTHIEMURCHUS

Another tiny ruined castle on an enchanting lochan island. A busier place, but great fun to swim out to and explore. Or just paddle at the loch edge.

→ Signed Rothiemurchus / B970 from the roundabout at S end of Aviemore. After ¾ mile, turn R (Inshriach / B970), then L again after a mile (Loch an Eilein). Bear R 700m along loch edge to reach castle island.

10 mins, 57.1490, -3.8220 🏊 🚻 🖼

385 LOCH MOR (LILY LOCH)

Small quiet loch with lilies. Sometimes weedy.

→ Take path on L by Milton Cottage ½ mile before reaching Loch an Eilein.

15 mins, 57.1634, -3.8216 ⛰

386 FESHIEBRIDGE, KINCRAIG

Fabulous clear water flows down rapids into huge river pool with white shingle beach opposite. Interesting rock shapes and patterns. Rest under the large Scots pine on the bank. A great fun location and one of the few with clear, non-peaty water.

→ As for Loch an Eilein but continue on B970 to Feshiebridge. 3 miles beyond Eilein turn off. Park close to bridge to find pool downstream.

2 mins, 57.1156, -3.8982 🏊

387 EIDART FALLS, GLEN FESHIE

Deep large pools and waterfalls with clear water in this truly wild river valley.

→ Take the Aclean / Glen Feshie Hostel road, just before Feshiebridge, all the way to the road end. Then it's a beautiful 10 mile riverside trek on a good path to these impressive series of falls and pools. Look out for Allt na Leuma waterfall on creek to L too (56.9814, -3.8334).

240 mins, 56.9763, -3.7886 🏊 ⛰

388 STRATHMASHIE, R PATTACK

A large calm pool with beach beneath a waterfall on River Pattack in Strathmashie community forest. Right by road and popular with wild campers, so the site can be messy.

→ Between Fort William and Newtonmoe (A86, River Spey). 4½ miles W of Laggan on A86, look out for car park on R and find waterfall and pool opposite. Further narrow pools immediately upstream. Or continue a mile upstream to large waterfall (Falls of Pattack). Good food and warm welcome at nearby Monarch Hotel (PH20 1BT, 01528 544276).

2 mins, 56.9816, -4.3609 ℹ 🍴 ⛺

389 LOCH CAOLDAIR, LAGGAN

A hidden beautiful loch, surrounded by birch woods and interesting crags. Sandy beach at E end. Wild.

→ 3 ½ miles S of Lagan (A889, Dalwhinnie direction) and 50m before the white cottage (Halfway House bothie), find bridge, parking space and footpath to R, leading 1½ miles up to loch.

30 mins, 56.9791, -4.2677 ⛰ 🏊

Rob Roy's Bathtub

Trossachs and Perthshire

The national park of Loch Lomond and the Trossachs is home to several lochs and waterfalls imbued with Sir Walter Scott's legends and heroism, from Rob Roy's bathtub on the Falloch to the Lady of the Lake's island on Loch Katrine.

The Lady of the Lake has many incarnations in British folklore, but Scott's epic poem of 1810 is perhaps the best known. Set on Loch Katrine it features several young chief sons fighting for Ellen's love during the Jacobite uprisings a hundred years before. It's from Ellen's Isle (Eilean Molach) on Katrine that Malcolm Graeme, Ellen's true love, swims to shore in a fit of rage after his fight with Douglas.

There are several other islets nearby and it is quite possible, with boat support or in a group, to swim between them still. Access to these islands, and the entire loch, is only open to cyclists and walkers on a private, ten-mile road. The path does not quite loop around the whole shoreline but the cycleway does make a beautiful way to explore this remote and dramatic woodland with its countless places to swim and camp undisturbed.

Loch Lomond, to the west, was heavily associated with another of Scott's poems: 'Rob Roy'. Based on the real Rob Roy MacGregor, the poem, published on Hogmanay 1817, became so popular that a ship needed to be commissioned to take copies of the book from Leith to London, making Scott a rich man.

Rob Roy was painted as a colourful Scottish Robin Hood by Scott, though his adventures were heavily romanticised. He fought the upper classes, plundered cattle and joined the Jacobean rebellions with a dangerous band of 500 men. Many

397

396

391

of Rob Roy's adventures were set on Loch Lomond, also made famous through Robert Burn's love ballad 'Auld Lang Syne'. This is the largest freshwater lake in Britain, set beneath the high peaks of Ben Lomond, and is dotted with islands to the south.

From Loch Katrine and the Trossachs a ten-mile, single-track road through unspoilt country brings you to Inversnaid, the location of Rob Roy's lochside hideaway. This cave can be found among great fallen rocks, its entrance quite obscured, only feet above the waterline. You can step out of the cave almost into the loch to swim. A few miles north, at the head of the loch on the river Falloch is Rob Roy's 'bathtub'. This is a stunning setting for swimming and picnics with a great shiny black rock vat set beneath the Falls of Falloch. Almost 100 feet across, with steep sides, it is one of the largest plunge pools in Britain and certainly makes an impressive place to take a bath.

In 1715 Rob Roy became heavily involved in the first Jacobean uprising. His men seized every boat on the Loch and assembled them at Inversnaid. He then set off to fight at the great battle of Sheriffmuir near Dunblane, 30 miles away, where the Earl of Mar was attempting to take Stirling. The battle was fought across the Wharry Burn, now a more peaceful series of small falls known as the Paradise Pools by the families who visit them from nearby Stirling.

The shingle beach, plunge pools, rock slides and open meadows are set only a few miles from the motorway, making this an easy day out from Glasgow or Edinburgh. The famous Sheriffmuir Inn sits on the moor above and marks the site of the brutal and inconclusive battle. It was also once home to a famous wrestling bear. It now makes a pleasant après-swim location for a warming hot toddy.

'Then plunged he in the flashing tide. Bold o'er the flood his head he bore, And stoutly steered him from the shore… Fast as the cormorant could skim. The swimmer plied each active limb; Then landing in the moonlight dell, Loud shouted of his weal to tell.'

Malcolm Graeme swimming from Ellen's Isle, in *Lady of the Lake* by Sir Walter Scott, 1810

394

390 FALLS OF FALLOCH, CRIANLARICH

Huge plunge pot under a great waterfall, known as Rob Roy's Bathtub. Spectacular great lido provides a large area in which to swim and dive.

→ From Crianlarich A82 head S and find parking on R after 4 miles. Follow the woodland walk downstream for further pools. Historic Drover's Inn at Inverarnan (G83 7DX , 01301 704234).

3 mins, 56.3502, -4.6928 🏊 🍴 🔽

391 BRACKLINN FALLS, CALLANDER

Popular waterfall in Callander on the Keltie, with further pools upstream.

→ Signed off A84 in Callander. Continue ¾ mile to car park on R and follow signed path. For better pools continue on road, through gate 1½ miles to second gate and find track on R to footbridge with Scout Pool 200m downstream (56.2631, -4.1973) or continue through second gate another mile to pools at Braeleny farm.

15 mins, 56.2497, -4.1880 🏊

392 ROB ROY'S CAVE, LOCH LOMOND

Remote stretch of northern Loch Lomond on West Highland Way. Swim from Rob Roy's Cave.

→ From Inversnaid Hotel (FK8 3TU, 01877 386223) follow Highland Way ¾ mile N along lake to find cave signposted and marked with white letters on rock. Inversnaid can be reached from Aberfoyle or by ferry from Inveruglas A82.

15 mins, 56.2534, -4.6947 🏊 🍴 🖼 🏕 🏊

393 LOCH CHON, ABERFOYLE

Quiet roadside loch with good access.

→ On route to Inversnaid from Aberfolye (B829).

2 mins, 56.2090, -4.5384 🏊 🏕

394 ELLEN'S ISLE, LOCH KATRINE

Swim to the famous islet in this beautiful loch setting.

→ Follow signs for Trossachs Pier (A821 N of Aberfoyle). Then bear R and continue 1½ miles by foot or cycle along lake shore.

30 mins, 56.2437, -4.4365 🚴 🏊

395 THE HERMITAGE, DUNKELD

Beautiful woodland trail and pools along the Braan leading to Ossian's Hall overlooking Black Linn waterfall.

→ Well-signed National Trust for Scotland site, off A9, W of Dunkeld. Best pools are upstream of bridge and waterfall.

15 mins, 56.5557, -3.6179 🏊 🖼

396 RUMBLING BRIDGE, R BRAAN

Dramatic falls with many pools and ledges up and downstream.

→ Walk a mile up from the Hermitage or park at Rumbling Bridge, signed on R off the A822, 2 miles S of Dunkeld.

10 mins, 56.5517, -3.6338 🔽

397 SHERIFF MUIR PARADISE POOLS

Plunge pool with a fun rock slide.

→ Leaving the Sheriff Muir Inn, 3 E of Dunblane (FK15 0LN, 01786 823285) turn R and continue 1 mile (over weak bridge). Climb gate R down through open field into wooded gorge below pylons.

5 mins, 56.1872, -3.9046 ℹ️ 🏊

Games and Activities

To enjoy outdoor swimming in Britain it's important to be hot before you go in and to be able to warm up quickly after you come out, so why not have a few activities or games up your sleeve to keep everyone moving around?

A simple game of 'it' or 'tag' can be good with a small group but if there are more than four then some people will do less running than others. British Bulldog is better for getting the whole group moving. It's a traditional game in which everyone runs back and forth between bases, at least 20m apart, trying not to be caught by the 'bulldogs'. If you are caught you must join the bulldogs and help do the catching. The last person remaining wins.

To give this a watery feel, play it in a shallow river with people having to wade or swim across. To spice it up a bit turn it into kiss chase: the bulldogs have to catch and kiss someone to make them 'it'. We call this Nymphs and Satyrs and its good for adults too!

Basic running races are fun and excellent for getting warm quickly. If there's no room for a full-blown race, then staggered time-trials, sending people off at five second intervals, are good. Why not make an interesting route with obstacles and activity stations – such as star-jumps and tree climbing – along the way? Three-legged and wheelbarrow races are fun and active as are cartwheeling championships and hopscotch relays.

Don't forget to bring a ball to play football, even if it's only two-aside. A tennis ball or Frisbee can also make a very warming game of throw-and-catch, especially if your aim is very bad! If you are in a large pool then water polo, with ball or frisbee, will get everyone swimming wildly.

If you're not keen on swimming, a water fight is still fun. A supermarket plastic bag with holes in the bottom swirled around your head will send water spraying everywhere. Or buy everyone cheap water pistols and pretend you're in the Marines!

Ideas for other riverside activities

• Build river cairns or make rock arches

• Play Pooh Sticks with your own boats made from reeds and twigs

• Use hazel twigs to dowse for some penny coins thrown into the grass

• See who can skim a stone with the most bounces

• Do some yoga in the water or on the bank

• Practise a synchronised swimming routine

• Learn to play the grass whistle

• Make a feather-and-leaf headdress

• Create the longest daisy chain

• Collect flowers and press them under a book using river rocks

• Find a four-leafed clover

• Paint yourself in mud

• Bring string and make a mobile out of branches and natural things you find

• Make a pebble maze

• Buy a disposable underwater camera to take watery photos

Being Adventurous

Jumps Many places are well known for their jumps (p22 suggests some of the best) but do take great care. You must always check the depth on each visit, even if it was safe the day before. Underwater obstructions could have flowed down the river in the night. Start from a low place and work your way up as you gain confidence. Keep your legs together and your arms into your body, crossed over your chest, so your fist does not come up and hit you in the face on impact. And don't jump from more than 5 metres or you will hurt yourself. Above 20m you need special training and there is risk of severe injury from the impact of the water alone. Never dive from a height.

Tree swings The ubiquitous blue rope swing is always a good indication of a popular swimming spot (along with an old sock or two, it seems). In some locations you'll find small platforms in trees from which people leap (try Staverton 143 or Lacock 99). If you decide to build your own swing, use quick release knots so that you can dismantle the rope afterwards, unless you have permisson from the landowner.

Tubing the current In many places you'll find there's a current against which you can swim, like running on a treadmill. This is a good way to have a long swim in a small pool. Where there are small rapids try 'tubing' down them on rubber rings or inner tubes, though air mattresses are better at protecting your knees. This is quite popular on the Dart in Devon and the Wharfe in Yorkshire, though you should wear a wetsuit to protect yourself from bumps and knocks. Extreme versions of this sport are called 'hydrospeed' in France, 'river boarding' in the US and 'white-water sledging' in New Zealand. Take great care!

Snorkel safaris If there is less current, try a snorkel safari, through the reeds and underwater vegetation, following the course of the stream away from the footpaths and into the wild. Many moorland rivers are tainted tea colour from peat, but there are plenty of lowland chalk streams, spring-fed gravel pits and mountain pools that are crystal clear. With a snorkel and your head down your legs are brought up and you can swim in less depth, a metre is ample, so smaller streams become feasible.

Rafts and Boats

Whether you're more *Huckleberry Finn* or *Swallows and Amazons*, most people love building rafts and sailing them across to a deserted island. There are many ways to build a raft, some old, some new but don't expect any of them to be particularly fast or practical. And remember, just because you can swim it doesn't mean you will make it to the shore when your raft breaks up. Wear a lifejacket!

Reed Rafts The 'reed raft' is one of the earliest rafts known to man and was used for fishing and hunting on the Nile over 4,000 years ago. Similar craft were used by the Aztecs. You can still make them today from the common reed grass found along the banks of water, dried and bundled together.

Coracles The coracle is the oldest raft known in Europe, first used by the Romans. It has recently undergone a resurgence of popularity and there's now an annual Coracle Regatta in Leintwardine. Coracles are like bowls and are very manoeuvrable but also unstable; they tend to spin and tip but this makes them all the more fun. To make one collect strong bendy rods, poles or strips of wood – fresh hazel or willow saplings are the best. Lay out about five to six poles in each direction, tie the cross points with string, then pull two of the pole ends together to create a shallow curve, strung with cross-ropes, a bit like a bow. You'll need to weave more poles around the edge to construct a gunwale (rim), and to make the structure sturdy you might need a third cross-rope. Traditionally the vessel was covered in deer skin and tar but plastic sheeting is much easier. Throw some old carpet in as a base, then clamber in with an oar and pray!

Barrel Raft A more modern raft uses plastic barrels or polystyrene for flotation rather than wooden beer or wine barrels. Construct a frame into which the four barrels will comfortably nest, one on each corner, and tie them in. The longer the raft, the faster it will go but the more difficult it will be to steer. Try to ensure it is not over-buoyant or it will sit high in the water and be unstable.

Inner Tube Raft A similar craft can be constructed using several inner tubes from truck tyres tied to the bottom of a sheet of plywood. With over ten million inner tubes thrown into landfills every year in Britain your local scrapyard should be happy to provide you with some old

ones. Buy or assemble a large plywood floor structure, strengthened with cross struts if need be. Position the inflated rings underneath and strap them on tight using rope or old bicycle inner tubes passed through holes drilled in the plywood floor. This raft will float quite low and be fairly stable but you must hope you don't run aground on sharp objects. It's best for deep waters with sandy or shingle banks.

Raft Races All over the country each summer thousands of people turn their hand to raft-building for charity races. Why not get involved in your local one or set up one? Rotary Clubs tend to be the main organisers, though many races have taken on a life of their own. There are prizes for speed, but also for the novelty of the raft construction, the use of recycled materials and the fancy dress outfits worn by competitors. The River Dart (Totnes), River Wye (Monmouth), East Sussex River Rother (Rye) and West Sussex River Rother (Midhurst) are some of the better known races which have internet sites. It is also possible for children to learn raft-making with the Scouts, or for your workplace to organise a raft-making day out at an outdoor activity centre.

Canoe Camping

Nothing is more enjoyable than taking a few days to travel along a river by canoe, camping out overnight and swimming each morning and evening.

Canoes The most convenient are inflatable and cost about £300 from Sevylor, Stearns or Strait-Edge. With a cheap doubleaction hand pump they inflate in minutes and pack down to the size of a large tent. Or why not hire a canoe, complete with all the camping equipment, for a weekend on the Suffolk Stour or the Herefordshire Wye?

Camping If you need to wild camp with your canoe, arrive late in the day and leave early. Don't camp near property, do not damage crops and do not light fires. The River Thames Alliance produce a leaflet called 'go camping on the River Thames' (see www.visitthames.co.uk) and it's possible to camp on some of their remote lock islands if you book.

Paper Bag Lanterns Candle lanterns are good where fires are not allowed. Weigh down a small white paper bag, available from a baker, with sand or pebbles and place a tea-light inside.

Night Swims Don't miss the opportunity to swim at night. In calm, safe waters that you know well, it's magical. Choose a night with a full moon and no clouds and light some candle lanterns to act as homing signals. Try not to use torches so your eyes become accustomed to the dark. Know how and where you are going to get out before you start.

Hammocks and Sleeping Under the Stars If it is warm then try sleeping under the stars for at least some of the night. Just lie back, listen to the river flow and watch the slow passage of the Milky Way across the sky.

Riverside Sauna

The detoxifying and stimulating effects of cold water plunges are well documented but the pleasures are heightened by getting very hot in a riverside sauna first. Creating a temporary 'natural' sauna near your favourite swimming place is straightforward and involves filling an impromptu tent with the steam generated from hot rocks. It's highly effective.

1. The Steam-Pit Find a flat spot close to the water where you will cool off afterwards. Dig a small pit – about a foot wide and deep – at the centre of where you want your sauna tent. Ensure there is no vegetation in the hole otherwise it will create smoke when the hot rocks are placed inside.

2. The Sauna Frame Build a dome-shaped tent structure around the hole. If you can, use young green sapling 'rods' – ideally willow, hazel or sweet chestnut coppice, but bendy garden canes will also do. Stick about half of them into the ground like stakes marking out a five-foot circle. Bend them over to meet each other in the middle, as flat and low as possible, and tie them to create an igloo or 'bender'. The frame should be no more than four feet high in the middle otherwise it will be difficult to heat. Take the remaining saplings and weave them horizontally around the dome, leaving a gap for a small doorway. Cover the structure with old blankets, a tarpaulin and anything else that will help to insulate it and create a good seal, keeping the steam in, particularly around the base. If you can't find any of these natural materials, simply use an actual dome tent with the inner tent removed.

3. The Hot Rocks Build a substantial open fire a few yards from the sauna tent. Once it's going well load on four-to-five large stones. The trick is to ensure they don't crush the fire and that the flames can still lick up around them so they get hot. Don't use stones from the river as they can shatter on the fire as water trapped inside heats up.

4. The Sweat Lodge Once the stones are very hot after 20–30 minutes load them into the pit you dug using a spade or tongs. Then you and about seven guests (it's meant to be a squash!) are ready to undress and carefully crawl in and sit crouched around the hot stone-filled pit in the dark. One person should go in first with a torch to show

others the way. Watch your toes on the hot rocks! Close the door and once everyone is comfortable sprinkle some water with a few drops of essential oils (e.g. eucalyptus) on the stones. Phusshh! The small confined space rapidly fills with steam. Keep sprinkling. If you get too hot lower your head – it is hotter at the top of the tent. If you want you can sing, hum or tell stories. The American Indians believed the 'sweat lodge' was a sacred womb that could catalyse a transition in life. In the circle they would share what they wanted to let go of from their old lives and what they wanted to bring into their new lives.

5. The Plunge Once you are all hot enough, exit in a orderly fashion and make your way to the nearby river, lake or plunge pool. A string of candle lanterns is a beautiful way to mark the route and these might also illuminate the plunge pool. Coming out into the night air, with lanterns flickering and the scent of eucalyptus all around, is a primal and joyful experience that few people ever forget. Quickly, while you are still hot, plunge into the cool waters and swim in the night. This is the ceremonial 'rebirth'. You will never feel more alive!

Riverside Wildlife

Fresh water is an attractive habitat for many animals. The biodiversity of our wetlands is huge. Nosing through the water your size and scent are perfectly disguised, allowing you to get that little bit closer to wildlife. This is just a selection of some of the things you're most likely to see.

Kingfisher: the most famous. Once hunted for their beautiful feathers and the belief that their bodies could be used to predict the weather, the kingfisher population is now recovering, making the dazzling flash of blue in the corner of your eye a more common occurrence. As you swim upstream look for it perching motionless on branches above a sandy bank waiting to dive. Listen for the distinctive shrill 'ker-chee' call and you'll know when it's about to take off.

Dipper: the prettiest singer. The world's only aquatic songbird looks like it is wearing a tuxedo with its white front and dark brown back. Bobbing up and down on small rocks in the middle of shallow, fastflowing upland rivers it hunts for small insects by diving into the water and walking along the bottom of the river, an ability it shares with only the hippopotamus among warm-blooded animals. Highly territorial, they often fly around making a noise like a closing zip.

Grey Heron: the most Jurassic. Next time you are swimming along and see what looks like a grey and white pterodactyl launching itself from a branch above you, slowly flapping with a croaking call, you have seen a grey heron. Britain's largest fish-eating bird is almost as big as a golden eagle. If you see one in Scotland it is traditional to doff your hat and wish it good morning. Herons can often be seen standing motionless in shallow water or in fields waiting for a frog.

Mandarin Duck: the most colourful. The male Mandarin is often voted Britain's most beautiful bird. This duck originally escaped from exotic collections and has joined flocks of British ducks along the Thames, Severn and Virginia Water where it is more common than in its native Japan. The male's most distinctive feature are the two orange half-moon rear wings which project above its back. It has a red beak, brown and orange head, and black and white back with buff sides. It nests in tree holes up to 10 metres above the ground and can scare off any crows or squirrels it finds there.

Otter: the natural wild-swimmer. The name 'otter' comes from the Anglo-Saxon word for water. Superbly adapted for swimming, they have a long tail 'rudder' and very thick fur. Now recovering from their population crash in the 1960s caused by pesticides, they remain elusive, mostly emerging at dusk and dawn to feed. Their tracks – round pads with five digits – can be seen on mud along the river.

Water Vole: from *The Wind in the Willows*. It's clear from the descriptions in *The Wind in the Willows* that 'Ratty' is actually a water vole, once extremely common though now hunted by mink. They have stubby faces, little round ears and long furry tails which give them a much friendlier appearance than a rat. Often seen swimming across rivers carrying nesting materials in their mouths, water voles can most easily be seen in the Cairngorms, where they can be found at heights up to an astonishing 1,000 metres.

Dragonflies and Damselflies: the 200-million-year-old insects. These voracious carnivores, which have inhabited the earth for over 200 million years, are the most dramatic insects on the waterways, flying at up to 30mph. The dragonfly is larger than the damselfly and perches with its wings spread while the damselfly tucks its wings up against its body. Their young are called 'nymphs' and their species names reflect their colour and habits: Azure Hawker, Four-spotted Chaser, Red-veined Darter, Green Darner and Blue-eyed Skimmer. They are most active in the middle of hot sunny days and often fly close to the water surface.

Great Crested Newt: the most dragon-like. The Great Crested Newt is rare and protected. The male has a fabulous body-length crest that develops in the mating season from April–June. Females lack the crest but have a yellow–orange stripe along the lower edge of their tail. They live on land, under logs and vegetation, but are always close to water. Look in little pools, ponds, ditches or tributaries.

Wild Water Foraging

Waterways are home to a lush variety of herbs, plants and foods. These common and easily recognisable foods will have you pepping up your salads or even making punch!

Water Lily *(Nymphaea odorata)* This mythical plant, originally named after the water sprites and nymphs of Greek mythology, will add colour and appeal to any salad. Found in slow-moving rivers or lakes, the water lily's manner of rising pristine and beautiful from the murky waters has symbolised regeneration, purity and youth since the earliest times. Some species of water lily actually have mild aphrodisiac qualities. The pink, yellow or white petals of the water lily flower are fragrant and make a beautiful garnish to salads.

Water Mint *(Mentha aquatica)* This makes a fabulous minty punch and can be mixed with fruit juices, Pimms or used to make wild-swimmer's Mojitos. Instantly recognisable by its fresh mintysmelling leaves and frothy pink flowers, it is commonly found across Britain in the shallow margins of streams and pools, particularly in peaty or limestone areas. Its stem is squarish in cross-section, it grows to almost a metre high and its lilac or purple flowers are a little like a thistle flower with their bushy head, flowering from mid-to-late summer. To use, simply crush a few leaves and add to hot water, fruit juice, lemonade or punch.

Wild Garlic *(Allium ursinum)* With a characteristic odour that makes it easy to find, you will smell wild garlic (ramsons) long before you see it. The plants like damp wooded dells and carpet vast areas with white garlic-scented flowers between April and June. Related more to the chive, their taste is surprisingly mild. The leaves are long and elliptical and two or three rise from each bulb. The sweet flowers are beautiful sprinkled on a salad. Learn the difference from the similar-looking Lily-of-the-Valley. This is poisonous, doesn't have the distinctive smell, even when the leaves are bruised, and its white flowers are larger, bell-shaped and hang down, not point up.

Nettles *(Urtica doica)* Finally we can seek vengeance on these irritating riverside ankle stingers as cooking renders nettles harmless and edible. They help relieve rheumatism and sciatica, increase haemoglobin in the blood, improve circulation and help detoxification.

Young nettles are the best so take just the top two or three leaf pairs. Use scissors or a towel to stop yourself from being stung. Fry a chopped onion in a little butter, add about six handfuls of washed and finely chopped nettle tops, a couple of diced potatoes, water, a stock cube and plenty of seasoning. Cook for 20 minutes and serve with crème fraîche or wild garlic.

Reed Mace *(Typha latifolia)* This is one of the most versatile wild foods in Britain, though it should not be over-collected. It grows tall in marshy areas with large, long brown cylindrical seed-heads that are furry and shed large quantities of white down. In spring the young stalks can be pulled from the rootstocks, peeled to their tender white core and eaten raw (like cucumber) or boiled for 15 minutes and served like asparagus. In late spring the green immature flower spikes can be gathered just before they erupt from their papery sheaths of leaves. Boil them for a few minutes, serve with butter and eat like corn-on-the-cob.

Rowan Berries *(Sorbus aucuparia)* Rowan, also known as Mountain Ash, colonises upland streams as high as 1,000m. The berries are ripe from August to November. Squeezed fresh, the juice can be used like Angostura bitters. Add it to a Gin Martini, pep up some pasta or soup, or use it as a marinade for meat. The berries also make an excellent traditional jelly for venison or poultry. Boil plenty with diced apples and water and simmer to a pulp. Strain, add sugar, boil again skimming all the time, then pour into jars, cover and allow to set.

Bilberry *(Vaccinium myrtillus)* A sweet, superfood berry found in Scottish highland woods and streams, bilberries (or blaeberries as they are known in Scotland) are found in damp, acidic soils and form part of the ground flora of the old Caledonian Forests. If you come across the low bushes, often in clumps, pick some berries as an instant snack or collect enough to make fruit salads, fools or tartlets, such as the traditional Massif Central *tarte aux myrtilles*. Like all deep blue fruit, they contain pigments that lower the risk of heart disease and cancer.

Water safety

Like cycling, hill walking, canoeing and many other outdoor activities, wild-swimming has inherent risks and dangers. With the right preparation and information you can make wild-swimming very safe, without losing the sense of adventure.

Non-swimmers

Shallow water can deepen suddenly. If you, your children or your friends cannot swim make sure you scout out the extent of the shallows, set clear boundaries and keep constant supervision. Remember that even shallow sections of fast-flowing water can knock you off your feet. Be careful with inflatables, which can create a false sense of security and float off into deep sections or burst. Buy a good quality buoyancy aid for non-swimmers (about £40) and, best of all, learn to swim.

Life-saving

If you go swimming regularly why not learn how to save someone? Most of us know the basics of mouth-to-mouth resuscitation but rescuing someone is more difficult. The basic principle is to turn the person on their back, put your hand under their chin, grasp them to your front and backstroke to shore with breaststroke leg kick. Practise it on a friend for fun then be ready to save someone's life for real.

Slipping on rocks Rocks are very slippery when wet and you don't want to hit your head. Never run. Go barefoot to get a better grip or wear plimsolls with a rubber sole. If you enjoy more serious scrambling along rivers why not join a gorge-walking or canyoning (canyoneering) course?

Hypothermia and cold-shock
Swimming in cold water saps body heat. Shivering and teeth-chattering are the first stages of mild hypothermia, so get out of the water and warm up with a combination of warm, dry clothes and activity. Press-ups, star-jumps and running up a nearby hill are the quickest! Wear a wetsuit if you want to stay in for more than a quick dip. 'Cold-shock' is the involuntary gasp and rise in heart rate that occurs as the body enters very cold water. Test the temperature and wade in slowly unless you are already acclimatised to outdoor swimming.

Jumping and diving Always check the depth of the water, even if you visit the same spot regularly. Depths can vary and new underwater obstructions (sand, rocks, branches, rubbish) may have been brought downstream or tipped in. A broken neck from a diving accident could paralyse you for life.

Cramps and solo-swimming
Swimming cramp can occur in the calf or foot and tends to be caused by overexertion, over-stretching and tiredness. Cramp is not more likely after eating but dehydration, or a poor diet in general, can make you especially prone. If you get a leg cramp, shout for help, lie on your back and paddle back to shore with your arms. Swimming alone in deep water is foolish but, if you must, wear a life jacket or trail a float behind you on a cord.

Weeds Most common in slow, warm lowland rivers and lakes, weeds are quite easy to see and, while one or two aren't such a problem, a spaghetti-like forest can entangle a swimmer's legs. Try to avoid them. If you do encounter some, slow your swim speed right down, don't kick or thrash, and either float on through using your arms to paddle, or turn around slowly.

Blue–green algae and swimmer's itch In lowland lakes after warm, wet weather, usually in late summer, algae can multiply and a powdery, green scum (the blooms) can collect on the downwind side of a lake. It's obvious and unpleasant and can give you a skin rash or irritate your eyes if you bathe in it, and make you sick if you swallow it. Find a part of the lake without blooms or go somewhere else. 'Swimmer's itch' (cercarial dermatitis) can be caught from contact with little snails that live on the reeds around marshy lakes and stagnant ponds. It creates a temporary but sometimes intense itching sensation that can last for up to two days. It's not common, and requires no treatment, but it's best to avoid wallowing in the bogs!

Weil's disease In urban areas sewers and storm drains may harbour colonies of rats whose urine may carry the bacterial infection Leptospirosis. Never swim in urban rivers, particularly canals, and be particularly cautious after heavy rains. None of the locations in this book carry any significant risk but if you are concerned about water quality cover any open wound with a waterproof plaster and keep your head (eyes, nose and throat) out of the water as much as possible. If you get flu or jaundice-like symptoms three to fourteen days after swimming in high risk water ask your doctor for a Leptospirosis test. It is simply treated with antibiotics but if left it can develop into the more serious Weil's disease, which has been known to kill.

How dangerous is wild-swimming?
An analysis of recent annual accident data shows that of the 12 per cent of drownings related to swimming, 7 people drowned in swimming pools, 11 in the sea, tidal pools and estuaries, and 7 in rivers, lakes, reservoirs or canals. In addition there were 8 who died swimming drunk, 30 who died through 'jumping in' to water and 17 who died in 'jumping and diving accidents'. 95 per cent of all swimming drowning victims were male and many were teenagers. (Sources: *Royal Society for Protection of Accidents 2002 data; River and Lake Swimming Association; Jean Perraton in Swimming Against the Stream*)

Understanding currents and flow

Lots of our best water moves and swimming in and against a current can be fun, just like swimming in seaside surf. However, you generally want to avoid being taken downstream in an uncontrolled manner. Even shallow water, if it's moving fast enough, can knock you over and carry you away. Always consider: if I do lose my footing or get swept downstream, where will I get out? Identify your emergency exits before getting in and scout around for any downstream hazards (obstructions, waterfalls or weirs). When judging flow rates remember the basics: the shallower or narrower the river bed becomes, the faster the water must flow to pass through, and vice versa. That's why 'still waters run deep'. Throw a stick in the water to judge flow speed and avoid anything moving faster than you can swim. In tidal estuaries there can also be counter-flows, with seawater moving in and river water moving out. In deep rivers or gorges the water in the surface layer may be flowing more slowly than the water beneath. These confused waters aren't necessarily dangerous – you're not going to be sucked under – but they can be disorientating and may take you out into deeper water or close to an obstruction. You can generally feel what's happening under the water with your feet and body. Large eddies and surface 'simmering' also suggest something more powerful is happening beneath. Be particularly cautious in these unpredictable waters. Currents can be especially powerful directly under large waterfalls or weirs. As with breaking waves the water can be flowing in two directions, with some water exiting from the fall downstream while some creates a 'rip-tide' that is circulating to the back of the fall.

Semi-circular or 'box' weirs, which have three sides, create particularly dangerous re-circulating currents in the confined space within their walls. In a large plunge pool you'll generally feel the currents long before you are in danger of being pulled under the waterfall but if you are foolish enough to swim into the tumult, and are taken down, it's like being caught in a wave's undertow. Keep calm, hold your breath, hope you don't get dragged along a rocky bottom and wait a few seconds until you are spat out. If you live through this and want to know more about the extreme sport of riding river currents then search online for river boarding, hydrospeed or whitewater sledging. For more detailed information on water safety visit www.wildswimming.com

Water Quality and Ecology

Our rivers and lakes are cleaner today than at any time in living memory. Industrial and agricultural pollution almost succeeded in killing our rivers in the 1960s but the success of the 1974 Control of Pollution Act and subsequent European legislation has been remarkable.

The Environment Agency monitors rivers, streams and lakes regularly at over 7,000 locations in England and Wales. River quality targets are assigned based on biological, chemical and nutrient testing. Over 70 per cent of the rivers in England and Wales are very good (target 1 or A) or good (target 2 or B) on a five-tier water quality scale. Most people's first concern is usually sewage but with the new European Water Framework Directive in place all effluent now undergoes at least two treatments before entering a river and, increasingly, a third to make it completely sterile and pure. Any bacteria that do remain are quickly killed by the sun's UV rays, or eaten up in the micro-foodchain of the river so, the further downstream of the treatment works you are, the cleaner the water will become. Treatment sites are indicated on OS maps as a little cluster of four or six circles by rivers near towns. Although the water quality of almost every swim in this book is A or B there's still much to be done to make every river and lake in the UK clean enough to swim in. The World Wide Fund for Nature is taking action to improve water laws and policies, demonstrate better management of rivers and wetlands, develop sustainable land management practices and build capacity in community organisations to protect their own rivers. Why not get involved in supporting their work?
www.wwf.org.uk/freshwater

Finding your own swimming place

Any footpath, ford, footbridge or 'open-access' land bordering a river or lake is a good place to start looking. River bends often create shallow beaches on the inside and deeper pools on the outside. Small weirs and waterfalls create pools in rivers that would be otherwise too shallow. OS Landranger (purple) mapping is good but the larger scale Explorer (orange) mapping provides much more information. See this online at *www.bing.com*, *www.streetmap.co.uk*, or *www.getamap.ordnancesurveyleisure.co.uk/*.

It is also worth asking locally where people swim in the summer, or asking older people where they used to swim as children. Try looking at *wildswim.com*, *www.ukriversguidebook.com*, *www.uklakes.net* and *www.riverswimming.co.uk*. Find data on your local river at *www.environment-agency.gov.uk/maps*.

Links to all the above – together with Facebook groups and our online map – can be found at *www.wildswimming.com*

Staying Legal and Respecting Others

Unlike other European countries, including Scotland, there is only an explicit legal right to access water in some English and Welsh rivers and lakes. In other places swimming rights are customary and based on longstanding tradition or established use. These places are often found where public rights of way, such as footpaths or common land, meet lake shores, riverbanks, bridges or fords.

Give anglers a wide berth, especially in the mornings and evening when fishing is most popular. In salmon rivers try not to trample on spawning gravels, particularly in autumn when eggs are buried. Remember that fishermen pay for their sport and are an important ally in ensuring rivers are kept clean and pollution free.

You'll see an increasing number of no-swimming signs in popular bathing places. Some of these are posted by fishing clubs keen to scare swimmers away. Others are posted by local councils, the Environment Agency and other management bodies who, since the 1984 Occupiers, Liability Act, are at danger of litigation should you have an accident in their waters and decide to sue. Corporate lawyers now advise management agencies that, unless permanent lifeguards are provided at every river and lake in the country, they must forbid all swimming and fence off all waters. Thankfully a 2003 ruling by the Law Lords overruled this crazy decision but you'll still see plenty of No Swimming signs. Most landowners are primarily nervous of your legal actions and these signs are their first line of defence.

If you are asked to leave a private river by the river owner or their agent, do so politely. Despite misconception, trespassers cannot be prosecuted and the police can only be called in certain circumstances: when there are more than six vehicles on the land, when damage has been done or when abusive language has been used. If you have doubts as to who is confronting you it is permissible to ask for proof of identity or authority. If you are on a footpath you cannot be asked to move on. You can, however, be asked to leave the water, even if people have swum there for years.

Wild swimming and the law

In Scotland you can now access all inland waters if you uphold the Outdoor Access Code. In England and Wales – particularly in National Parks and on Forestry Commission, Wildlife Trust and National Trust land – there is extensive 'right to roam' (Countryside and Rights of Way Act 2000) that has opened up new lakes and river shores. However, there is no formal right to access the water. You are relying on customary rights and the owners' goodwill.

On about four per cent of our waterways special arrangements and laws exist to allow public 'navigation' (e.g. swimming and canoeing) such as on the Thames, Wye, Lugg, Suffolk Stour and Waveney (see www.bcu.org.uk and www.ukriversguidebook.co.uk for a full list). Statute laws also allow a legal right of passage along any river that is, or was once, physically navigable to small boats. The Rivers' Access Code and Campaign aims to bring English and Welsh access rights in line with Scotland www. riversaccess.org

Conversion chart

No	Grid ref (distance from nearest postcode)
1	SU205989 (0.137km from GL7 3EE)
2	SU353996 (1.275km from SN7 8SQ)
3	SU230980 (0.391km from SN7 8DA)
4	SU224983 (0.283km from SN7 8DQ)
5	SU256986 (0.417km from SN7 8BJ)
6	SP325112 (0.199km from OX29 0RR)
7	SP291115 (0.214km from OX18 4HL)
8	SP264114 (0.296km from OX18 4DT)
9	SP188158 (1.275km from GL54 3DL)
10	SP393164 (0.408km from OX29 8PN)
11	SP492081 (0.526km from OX2 0NG)
12	SP521071 (0.315km from OX3 0EY)
13	SU531938 (0.390km from OX14 4YA)
14	SU550956 (0.278km from OX14 3EF)
15	SU601854 (0.345km from OX10 6AX)
16	SU618791 (0.535km from RG8 9NH)
17	SU828843 (0.300km from SL7 2DX)
18	TL439568 (0.329km from CB3 9JP)
19	TL542696 (0.652km from CB7 5YQ)
20	TL284716 (0.451km from PE28 2BG)
21	TL220699 (0.612km from PE28 4UZ)
22	TL213669 (0.190km from PE19 5RX)
23	SP787396 (0.060km from MK11 1YT)
24	SP834428 (0.511km from MK19 7DX)
25	SP895515 (0.396km from MK46 4JH)
26	SP942141 (0.182km from HP23 5QJ)
27	TL010833 (0.145km from PE8 5ST)
28	TL061929 (0.358km from PE8 5JF)
29	SP887640 (0.361km from NN29 7TS)
30	TG318156 (0.532km from NR13 6HE)
31	TL826872 (0.305km from IP27 0TT)
32	TL831950 (0.171km from IP26 5JQ)
33	TG237228 (0.108km from NR10 5JF)
34	TG261201 (0.291km from NR12 7EX)
35	TG383156 (1.662km from NR12 8NJ)
36	TL801087 (0.199km from CM9 6QU)
37	TL487145 (0.055km from CM21 9LR)
38	TM067335 (0.363km from CO7 6UH)
39	TL950333 (0.368km from CO6 3AS)
40	TM332908 (0.362km from NR35 2JN)
41	TM339899 (0.082km from NR35 2JG)
42	TM286847 (0.515km from IP20 0NS)
43	TQ272862 (0.251km from NW3 2SN)
44	TQ271800 (0.329km from SW7 1LR)
45	TQ088889 (0.280km from HA4 7TX)
46	TQ041932 (0.059km from WD3 8UR)
47	TQ017727 (0.106km from TW19 6HE)
48	TQ009750 (0.582km from TW19 5NG)
49	TQ538655 (0.067km from DA4 0AE)
50	TQ057665 (0.214km from KT16 8LN)
51	TR197603 (0.529km from CT3 4AS)
52	TR109551 (0.160km from CT4 7JE)
53	TR229589 (0.411km from CT3 1SL)
54	TR232630 (0.220km from CT3 4DQ)
55	TQ533421 (0.475km from TN11 8AH)
56	TQ547452 (0.341km from TN11 8RZ)
57	TQ668334 (0.342km from TN5 6HJ)
58	TQ516013 (0.399km from BN25 4AH)
59	TV520990 (0.515km from BN25 4AD)
60	TQ384291 (0.639km from RH17 7AY)
61	TQ435148 (0.306km from BN8 5BT)
62	TQ442161 (0.560km from BN8 5BS)
63	TQ462217 (0.231km from TN22 2BX)
64	TQ333294 (0.535km from RH17 6UR)
65	SU890218 (0.227km from GU29 9AL)
66	TQ016127 (0.365km from RH20 1PB)
67	SU874432 (0.221km from GU10 2BN)
68	SU988453 (0.208km from GU7 3BT)
69	SU994481 (0.132km from GU2 4EF)
70	TQ128457 (0.074km from RH5 6JR)
71	SU845404 (0.663km from GU10 2QA)
72	SU830506 (0.927km from GU10 5BY)
73	SU961657 (0.305km from SL5 0HY)
74	TQ076582 (0.357km from KT11 1NR)
75	SU775524 (0.572km from RG27 8TB)
76	SU725518 (0.341km from RG29 1HQ)
77	SU568663 (0.428km from RG7 5SH)
78	SU626692 (0.018km from RG7 4BS)
79	SU683582 (0.096km from RG27 0DL)
80	SU477278 (0.204km from SO23 9SB)
81	SU476255 (0.372km from SO21 2BL)
82	SU440447 (0.035km from SP11 6QH)
83	SU389401 (0.070km from SO20 6BD)
84	SU342317 (0.234km from SO20 6LU)
85	SU151474 (0.176km from SP4 8JL)
86	ST987301 (0.341km from SP3 5RW)
87	SU037370 (0.214km from SP3 4NJ)
88	ST933316 (0.425km from SP3 5RZ)
89	SU304030 (0.093km from SO42 7TS)
90	SU167164 (0.435km from SP6 2LU)
91	SU146096 (0.352km from BH24 3PP)
92	SU147039 (0.498km from BH24 3AU)
93	ST805576 (0.293km from BA2 7RS)
94	ST805554 (0.318km from BA11 6QL)
95	ST615509 (0.127km from BA3 4RX)
96	ST791642 (0.145km from BA2 7BH)
97	ST806600 (0.096km from BA15 2HB)
98	ST681687 (0.341km from BS30 6LL)
99	ST920684 (0.340km from SN15 2LG)
100	ST953845 (0.550km from SN15 5JN)
101	ST564318 (0.082km from TA11 7DH)
102	ST547338 (0.329km from BA6 8PQ)
103	ST351377 (0.263km from TA7 8RW)
104	ST782143 (0.213km from DT10 1EG)
105	ST800135 (0.590km from DT10 2BU)
106	ST995000 (0.332km from BH21 4EE)
107	SY805894 (0.154km from DT2 8RJ)
108	SY923871 (0.058km from BH20 4LP)
109	SS793374 (0.801km from TA24 7LA)
110	SS816361 (0.619km from TA24 7SD)
111	SS859326 (0.925km from TA22 9QB)
112	SS872447 (0.426km from TA24 8JS)
113	SS723423 (1.175km from TA24 7LL)
114	SS943159 (0.304km from EX16 9PF)
115	ST097137 (0.253km from EX15 3JF)
116	SS986301 (0.759km from TA4 2JE)
117	SS750489 (0.634km from EX35 6NT)
118	SS752483 (0.705km from EX35 6LG)
119	SS793454 (2.032km from EX35 6NX)
120	SY040840 (0.680km from EX8 5EE)
121	SY087868 (0.503km from EX10 0LW)
122	SY091926 (0.454km from EX11 1RL)
123	SS487057 (0.092km from EX21 5NX)
124	SS545141 (0.428km from EX19 8AA)
125	SS582261 (0.289km from EX37 9EB)
126	SX428905 (0.636km from EX20 4QT)
127	SX605924 (1.104km from EX20 1QR)
128	SX564921 (0.457km from EX20 4LT)
129	SX722896 (0.300km from TQ13 8DP)
130	SX743899 (0.048km from EX6 6PW)
131	SX706883 (0.289km from TQ13 8DA)
132	SX652912 (0.524km from EX20 2QD)
133	SX759774 (0.840km from TQ13 9XS)
134	SX751785 (0.824km from TQ13 9UP)
135	SX662838 (1.047km from TQ13 8EA)
136	SX810828 (0.476km from TQ13 9PD)
137	SX697716 (0.935km from TQ13 7NY)
138	SX699713 (0.876km from TQ13 7SS)
139	SX710704 (0.383km from TQ13 7NT)
140	SX705701 (0.483km from TQ13 7RS)
141	SX715711 (0.473km from TQ13 7NT)
142	SX730685 (1.015km from TQ11 0HW)
143	SX790637 (0.178km from TQ9 6NZ)
144	SX643619 (2.533km from PL21 0JH)
145	SX645669 (4.240km from TQ11 0JQ)
146	SX532854 (0.923km from EX20 4AZ)
147	SX508845 (0.256km from EX20 4BH)
148	SX582704 (2.891km from PL20 6QH)
149	SX475699 (0.308km from PL20 7LP)
150	SX477677 (0.143km from PL20 7NS)
151	SX555647 (0.543km from PL7 5EH)
152	SX574630 (1.191km from PL7 5JA)
153	SX566735 (1.409km from PL20 6SS)
154	SX098633 (0.264km from PL30 4AH)
155	SX128652 (0.034km from PL30 4EQ)
156	SX222686 (0.522km from PL14 6RX)
157	SX030554 (0.470km from PL26 8YB)
158	SX249723 (1.327km from PL14 6ED)
159	SX255720 (1.000km from PL14 5LH)
160	SX080884 (0.249km from PL34 0HL)
161	SX072895 (0.206km from PL34 0BQ)
162	SX039793 (0.351km from PL30 3HZ)
163	SX163721 (1.226km from PL14 6PZ)
164	SX114759 (0.338km from PL30 4NL)
165	SW716408 (0.391km from TR16 5HG)
166	SW480355 (0.473km from TR20 8LP)
167	SH614492 (1.435km from LL55 4NH)
168	SH623516 (0.592km from LL55 4NQ)
169	SH649524 (1.304km from LL55 4NP)
170	SH601558 (2.250km from LL55 4UL)
171	SH618557 (2.115km from LL55 4UL)
172	SH618547 (3.055km from LL55 4NU)
173	SH581540 (0.989km from LL54 7YS)
174	SH798543 (0.324km from LL24 0SL)
175	SJ073294 (2.292km from SY10 0BZ)
176	SH666388 (0.952km from LL41 4EU)
177	SH608267 (0.468km from LL45 2LY)
178	SN729780 (1.060km from SY23 4QU)
179	SH735274 (0.556km from LL40 2LF)
180	SJ185477 (0.842km from LL20 8DR)
181	SJ211421 (0.100km from LL20 8RA)
182	SH621121 (0.304km from LL38 2TQ)
183	SH548495 (3.022km from LL55 4UU)
184	SN078300 (0.530km from SA66 7QX)
185	SH498533 (0.609km from LL54 7SF)
186	SH645344 (2.000km from LL47 6YU)
187	SH652412 (0.226km from LL41 3AQ)
188	SH659469 (2.944km from LL41 3ST)
189	SH901319 (0.343km from LL23 7BY)
190	SH717124 (1.714km from LL36 9AJ)
191	SO132262 (0.909km from LD3 7PJ)
192	SN842547 (1.050km from LD5 4TR)
193	SN859499 (0.307km from LD5 4TN)
194	SN809514 (3.086km from SY25 6NP)
195	SN777466 (0.806km from SA20 0PH)
196	SN633328 (0.185km from SA19 7YS)
197	SN585335 (0.118km from SA32 7SJ)
198	SN804219 (2.071km from SA19 9UN)
199	SN269415 (0.098km from SA38 9JL)
200	SH834061 (0.420km from SY20 9PS)
201	SO024226 (2.185km from LD3 8LL)
202	SO158202 (0.663km from NP8 1LT)
203	SO215181 (0.106km from NP8 1AR)

204 SO358092 (0.585km from NP7 9BA)	275 NY168068 (2.557km from CA20 1EX)	346 NT927202 (2.738km from NE71 6RG)
205 ST385948 (0.456km from NP15 1LY)	276 NY165009 (0.572km from CA19 1TF)	347 NU230114 (0.283km from NE66 3PT)
206 SO456203 (0.121km from NP7 8UG)	277 NY178001 (0.907km from CA19 1TG)	348 NN218519 (4.908km from PH49 4HY)
207 SO477172 (0.806km from NP25 5QG)	278 NY171003 (0.384km from CA19 1TF)	349 NN206512 (338.932km from PA40 4)
208 SN896092 (0.623km from SA11 5UD)	279 NY228037 (2.788km from LA20 6EQ)	350 NN179510 (4.671km from PH49 4AA)
209 SN891093 (0.824km from SA11 5UD)	280 NY217023 (2.457km from LA20 6EQ)	351 NM735171 (0.394km from PA34 4TB)
210 SN898084 (0.332km from SA11 5UD)	281 NY366077 (1.339km from LA22 9LT)	352 NM674692 (0.181km from PH36 4JY)
211 SN901095 (0.641km from SA11 5UR)	282 NY366072 (0.864km from LA22 9LT)	353 NN175888 (1.523km from PH34 4EJ)
212 SN905099 (0.668km from SA11 5UP)	283 NY346043 (0.268km from LA22 9HF)	354 NN000920 (1.064km from PH34 4EL)
213 SN918083 (0.746km from SA11 5NB)	284 NY336042 (0.442km from LA22 9HL)	355 NM444422 (1.296km from PA73 6LT)
214 SN923106 (0.806km from SA11 5US)	285 NY316017 (0.170km from LA21 8DJ)	356 NG434256 (4.917km from IV47 8TA)
215 SN922103 (0.915km from SA11 5US)	286 NY162183 (1.811km from CA13 9UZ)	357 NG416229 (1.677km from IV47 8TA)
216 SN928100 (1.422km from CF44 9JZ)	287 SD295918 (0.644km from LA21 8BL)	358 NG491294 (0.793km from IV47 8SW)
217 SN951715 (1.073km from LD6 5LE)	288 SD291910 (0.322km from LA12 8DW)	359 NG551214 (1.941km from IV49 9AU)
218 SN966656 (0.686km from LD1 6NW)	289 SD196930 (0.085km from LA20 6DT)	360 NG489197 (346.884km from IV49 9)
219 SO029523 (0.136km from LD2 3RD)	290 SD234993 (0.554km from LA20 6EF)	361 NG395643 (0.120km from IV51 9XP)
220 SO123403 (0.380km from LD3 0YU)	291 SD362887 (0.978km from LA12 8BL)	362 NG791039 (4.731km from PH41 4PL)
221 SO221425 (0.404km from HR3 5LA)	292 NY454032 (0.460km from LA8 9JJ)	363 NH287283 (2.230km from IV4 7LZ)
222 SN897683 (1.849km from LD6 5HS)	293 NY274129 (1.832km from CA12 5XG)	364 NH245264 (282.431km from PH32 4)
223 SN894886 (1.685km from SY18 6NX)	294 NY266110 (2.761km from CA12 5XQ)	365 NH276238 (3.072km from IV4 7LY)
224 SO587268 (0.541km from HR9 6QX)	295 NY228092 (3.003km from CA12 5XJ)	366 NG915239 (1.640km from IV40 8HA)
225 SO566279 (0.443km from HR1 4UB)	296 NY220084 (3.335km from CA20 1EX)	367 NG956417 (1.557km from IV54 8YR)
226 SO581188 (0.130km from HR9 5QT)	297 NY509114 (1.814km from CA10 2QT)	368 NG849537 (0.743km from IV54 8XP)
227 SO557167 (0.411km from HR9 6BJ)	298 NY400208 (1.064km from CA11 0JY)	369 NG929710 (1.475km from IV22 2HL)
228 SO549144 (0.207km from HR9 6DX)	299 NY436204 (0.673km from CA11 0JL)	370 NH530288 (0.391km from IV63 6XL)
229 SO536097 (0.043km from NP25 4AL)	300 SD786968 (1.031km from CA17 4JY)	371 NH421164 (0.318km from IV63 7YF)
230 SO336446 (0.116km from HR3 6BS)	301 NY781035 (0.645km from CA17 4JT)	372 NH424095 (3.567km from PH32 4BZ)
231 SO607102 (0.338km from GL15 4JS)	302 SD848920 (0.298km from DL8 3LR)	373 NH931414 (0.319km from IV12 5UR)
232 SO762380 (0.348km from HR8 1EU)	303 NY898009 (0.565km from DL11 6LJ)	374 NJ000497 (0.936km from IV36 2QN)
233 SO818250 (0.034km from GL19 4HZ)	304 NY888014 (0.244km from DL11 6LN)	375 NJ001518 (1.402km from IV36 2QN)
234 SO867298 (0.393km from GL19 4BX)	305 NY883015 (0.210km from DL11 6DZ)	376 NO063896 (3.224km from AB35 5YB)
235 SO827010 (0.845km from GL5 5PW)	306 SD999634 (0.072km from BD23 6BG)	377 NO104922 (2.289km from AB35 5YJ)
236 SP259573 (0.184km from CV35 8BB)	307 SD990645 (0.331km from BD23 5BS)	378 NO420976 (0.192km from AB35 5SE)
237 SP238563 (0.246km from CV37 7RD)	308 SE029617 (0.498km from BD23 6BN)	379 NO425996 (0.403km from AB34 5NB)
238 SP210556 (0.144km from CV37 7BD)	309 SE019867 (0.123km from DL8 4JP)	380 NN915625 (0.305km from PH16 5LF)
239 SP143522 (0.135km from CV37 8EW)	310 SE018888 (0.559km from DL8 3TH)	381 NN819663 (0.385km from PH18 5TW)
240 SP093505 (0.239km from B50 4NT)	311 NZ162009 (0.089km from DL10 4HW)	382 NN909599 (0.330km from PH16 5NF)
241 SO923422 (0.104km from WR10 3DD)	312 SE052596 (0.394km from BD23 6DD)	383 NH974363 (0.979km from PH26 3PY)
242 SO403738 (0.082km from SY7 0LA)	313 SE075542 (0.249km from BD23 6AL)	384 NH898079 (1.673km from PH22 1QP)
243 SO744603 (0.527km from WR6 6PG)	314 SE065562 (0.792km from BD23 6AN)	385 NH899095 (0.873km from PH22 1QT)
244 SO796532 (0.580km from WR6 5JA)	315 SD992314 (0.382km from HX7 8RG)	386 NH851043 (0.423km from PH21 1NG)
245 SO529508 (0.199km from HR1 3JU)	316 SD948225 (0.624km from OL14 6HT)	387 NN913886 (266.556km from PH21 1)
246 SO465613 (0.349km from HR6 0AQ)	317 SE077366 (0.140km from BD13 5BT)	388 NN566903 (1.711km from PH20 1BY)
247 SO530413 (0.434km from HR1 3NA)	318 SD818671 (0.261km from BD24 9QD)	389 NN622898 (1.684km from PH19 1AQ)
248 SO390584 (0.078km from HR6 9EY)	319 SD832670 (0.650km from BD24 9PZ)	390 NN336207 (2.748km from G83 7DZ)
249 SO631648 (0.751km from WR15 8RN)	320 SD803769 (0.360km from BD24 0JQ)	391 NN645085 (1.145km from FK17 8EU)
250 SJ554721 (0.107km from WA6 6NQ)	321 SD894662 (1.003km from BD24 9PU)	392 NN331100 (1.393km from G83 7DW)
251 SJ598656 (0.232km from CW6 9DB)	322 SD911633 (0.301km from BD23 4DL)	393 NN426047 (1.046km from FK8 3TS)
252 SJ435329 (0.396km from SY12 0QW)	323 SD694753 (0.720km from LA6 3JH)	394 NN491083 (2.265km from FK17 8HZ)
253 SJ453392 (0.349km from SY13 3DF)	324 SD726413 (0.214km from BB7 3LJ)	395 NO006415 (0.717km from PH8 0DX)
254 SK151514 (1.010km from DE6 2AY)	325 SD522647 (0.125km from LA2 9HU)	396 NN996411 (0.641km from PH8 0BP)
255 SK163481 (0.314km from DE6 2AB)	326 SE503832 (0.619km from YO7 2QD)	397 NN818010 (0.904km from FK15 0LN)
256 SK203293 (0.578km from DE13 9JL)	327 NZ762076 (0.101km from YO21 2AQ)	
257 SK121423 (0.183km from DE6 2ED)	328 NZ826021 (0.339km from YO22 5LB)	
258 SK009685 (0.845km from SK17 0TQ)	329 NZ888034 (0.396km from YO22 5JD)	
259 SK039612 (0.685km from ST13 8UL)	330 SE466991 (0.982km from DL6 3AL)	
260 SK181656 (0.440km from DE45 1JF)	331 NZ383107 (0.305km from TS16 0QS)	
261 SK205695 (0.331km from DE45 1FZ)	332 NY903279 (0.321km from DL12 0XF)	
262 SK177714 (0.661km from SK17 8SZ)	333 NY894380 (0.082km from DL13 1LU)	
263 SK172728 (0.096km from SK17 8SY)	334 NY909286 (0.494km from DL12 0UE)	
264 SK168953 (3.738km from S33 0BB)	335 NY640696 (1.538km from CA8 7EW)	
265 SK259692 (0.901km from DE45 1PP)	336 NY797613 (0.813km from NE47 5NT)	
266 SK244753 (0.117km from S32 3XT)	337 NY794697 (1.106km from NE47 6NL)	
267 SK014161 (0.538km from WS15 2UH)	338 NY927707 (0.227km from NE46 4HJ)	
268 SJ995225 (0.164km from ST18 0ST)	339 NT890072 (0.817km from NE65 7BN)	
269 SJ969186 (0.264km from ST17 0SS)	340 NU068015 (0.127km from NE65 7XH)	
270 SK332141 (0.678km from DE12 7RH)	341 NU241058 (0.271km from NE65 0UA)	
271 SK339272 (0.688km from DE73 7GL)	342 NT235404 (0.482km from EH45 8NH)	
272 SP837909 (0.797km from LE16 8XD)	343 NT933514 (1.042km from TD15 2XT)	
273 SK332229 (0.713km from DE73 7JP)	344 NZ233862 (0.122km from NE61 6SP)	
274 SK936080 (0.327km from LE15 8QL)	345 NT958170 (1.050km from NE66 4LZ)	

Converting to minutes and seconds

It is possible to convert decimal degrees (e.g. 50.1355°) to minutes and seconds (50°8'7.8"), should you need that format for paper maps, charts or satnavs. The whole units of degrees will remain the same (i.e. 50.1355° starts with 50°). Then multiply the whole decimal by 60 (i.e. 0.1355 x 60 = 8.13). The whole / first number becomes the minutes (8'). Take the remaining decimal digits and multiply by 60 again. (i.e. .13 x 60 = 7.8). The resulting number becomes the seconds (7.8"). Seconds can remain as decimals. Take your three sets of numbers and put them together, using the symbols for degrees (°), minutes ('), and seconds (") (i.e. 50°8'7.8").

Wild Swimming:
300 hidden dips in the rivers, lakes and waterfalls of Britain

Words:
Daniel Start

Photos:
Daniel Start, Petra Kjell and those credited

Editing:
Robin Gurdon

Design and layout:
Oliver Mann
Marcus Freeman

Fact checking:
Sarah Jones

Proofreading:
Michael Lee
Sarah Jones
Marijka Pascoe

Additional Research:
Petra Kjell
Luke Hudson
Lucy Tisserand
Michael Lee
Tania Pascoe

Distribution:
Central Books Ltd
99 Wallis Road
London, E9 5LN
Tel +44 (0)845 458 9911
orders@centralbooks.com

Published by:
Wild Things Publishing Ltd.
Freshford, Bath,
BA2 7WG, United Kingdom

hello@wildthingspublishing.com
hello@wildswimming.com

Acknowledgements With thanks, for inspiration and information, to the forefathers of wild swimming: Roger Deakin (Waterlog); Rob Fryer and Yacov Lev (River and Lake Swimming Association, riverswimming. co.uk); Jean Perraton (Swimming Against the Stream), Peter Irvine (Scotland the Best) and Kate Rew (outdoorswimmingsociety.com, wildswim.com).

Dedicated to my beautiful wife Tania Pascoe, and to the memory of Lucy Tisserand / Rouse. With heartfelt thanks to the friends and colleagues who helped find and test all these swimming holes, come rain or shine, and who supported us on the journey, particularly to: Petra Kjell, Ciaran and Izsy Mundy, Marijka and Tony Pascoe, Christina Ashworth and St John, Karen Wilcox, David, Dora, Lotta Cunningham, Owen Davis, Tom, Katie, Amelia and Rueben Alcott, Hannah Taylor, Martin Moore, Emily Walmsley, Julian Hodgson, Olivia Donnally, Annie Vanbeck, Fiona Smith, Anna Pemberton, Nick Hemley, Belinda Kirk, Biddy Hodson, Carl Reynolds, Tamara Giltsoff, Yvette, Matt, Kaspar and Minna Alt-Reuss, Emma Winterbottom, Vicky Moffat and Jules Peck, Jo and Xavier Keeling, Rosie Walford, Catherine Howarth, Roma Backhouse, Lucy Odling-Smee, Chloe Kinsman, Oliver Bullough, Nick Cobbing, Sam Coughlan and Daniel Aber. Also to: (South West) Joanna Johnston; Rosie Jones and Toby; Naomi and Suna Nightingale; Naomi Lumsdaine; Paul Miller and friends; Lucy Tisserand; Jon Rouse; Roderick, Tiggy and Wilbur Wiles; Lizzie Tom; Doodoo and Boy Tom-Baird; Aimee Tolhurst; Ruth Pratt; Toots Parkin; Stephen Clarke and friends; Brian, Mari and Florian Madigan; Douglas King-Smith; Luke and Amanda Hudson; (South) Alison de Braux; Natalie Start and Martin; Charlotte Macpherson and Pete, Rae and Flora Durgerian; Redge, Sophie and Anna Hurpy; Caroline Wilson; Maria Glauser; Ben Metz; Hendrik Tiesinga; Alan Wagenberg; Clover Stroud and family; Mari Plyons; Selena, Anthony and Christopher; John Start; Caroline, Ralph, Mishka and Jan Taylor; Lily and Thomas Moser; Ishbel Amyatt-Leir; Jack Thurston; Brian Madigan, Mari and Florian; Sarah, David and Robin Boyle; Deborah Doane, John and Myles Magidsohn; John Cullis and family; (Central and East) Sophie and Charlie Young; Tom Currie; Tor Udall; Katy Marks; Daisy and Daba Lees; Harry Cory Wright (with thanks to Roger Deakin and friends); Peter Strong and family; (Wales) Tom Parker; Leanda Thomas; Sophie Evitt; Harriet Stephens, Bob and family; Madelaine Mauwer; Cecilia Luttrell; Adrian Wells; Julia and Fernando; Sarah Cornell; Chloe Kinsman; Dela Foster; Tom, Charlie, Jenny and Willy Bullough; Mungo Amyatt-Leir and Clare Dundas; Ann Witheridge; Eliane Glaser; Eve Stebbing; Julija Duseviciute; (Lakes and Dales, North and Scotland) John Field; Kat Jones; Romilly Greenhill; Alison Penny; Jake and Isabel Willis; Marcus Freeman; Jessica Lack; Julian Hodgson. Special thanks to: Mark Lucas, Joanna Scott-Kerr, Emma Pruen, Sean Blair, Ed Halliwell, Melanie Gray, Nell Boase, Sophie Dawson, Thembi Mutch and Emma Critchley. With final thanks to all the local wild-swimmers we met who shared their knowledge so generously. Please swim nicely and respect their local countryside.

Photo credits All photographs © Daniel Start except the following, some reproduced by CC-BY-SA: p42 (middle) © Barbara Rogerson; p48 (bottom) © Jonathan Thacker; p58 (top) © Stephen Trussler; p116 © Peter from Geograph; p118 (bottom) © Steven House; p119 © Douglas Law; p123 (top) © John Lucas; p126 (top) © Rob Lowe; p130 (bottom) © Matt Buck4950; p134 (top) © Snappq2006; p135 © Nigel Davies; p162 (top) © Steve p2008; p163 © Yacov Lev; p166 (bottom) © Trevor Peach; p180 (top) © Andy Stephenson; p180 (middle) Colin Grice; p196 (middle) © George Tod; p200 (top) © Tim Green; p204 (top) © Martin Rankin; p204 (bottom) © Alan Green; p204 (bottom) © Ashley Dace; p208 (middle) © Alan Green; p212 (middle) © Jonathan Watts; p220 (middle) © Jim Barton; p224 (top) © 10 Corso Como; p224 (bottom) © Peter Bond; p228 (top) © Douglas Nelson; p232 (top) © Gerry Sharp; p236 (top) © Sarah McGuire; p240 (top) © Alan Findlay; p240 (bottom) © Ian Dela Cour; p244 (top) © James McNie; p244 (bottom) © Angus; p233 © Andy McGill; p248 (bottom) © Keithloaf1961; p250 (middle) Jesse Card; p254 (top) and p255 (middle, bottom) © Wes Modes; p260-263 © Kham Tran, Nottsexminer, Peregrine's Bird Photography, Gidzy, Mike Malz, Benimoto, Stephen Gunby, © iStockphoto.com/ AtWag, Witold Ryka, Gilles DeCruyenaere, VibrantLight, Robert Deal, Steve Byland, Andrew Howe, Christopher Wong, iStockphoto. com/ Dmitry Maslov, Josiah Garber, Viorika Prikhodko, Stefano Panzeri, Tom Allen, ra-photos.